20TH CENTURY

FRENCH DRAMA

By DAVID I. GROSSVOGEL

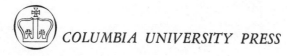 COLUMBIA UNIVERSITY PRESS

NEW YORK AND LONDON

To those A's, my first

20th Century French Drama was published originally
as *The Self-Conscious Stage in Modern French Drama*
Copyright © 1958 Columbia University Press, New York
Columbia Paperback Edition 1961
Fourth printing and third Paperback printing 1970
International Standard Book Number: 0-231-08522-2
Printed in the United States of America

Contents

Acknowledgments

THANKS ARE EXTENDED here to all who enriched a fleeting hour while unawares they influenced the form of this investigation.

The author owes particular appreciation to

Mr. Herman Liebaers, Conservateur en chef, Bibliothèque Royale de Belgique, in Brussels; to Mr. E. Clark Stillman, Secretary of the Belgian American Educational Foundation, Inc., and generally to all those connected with the C. R. B. Grant that made possible a part of this writing;

to two colleagues,

Professors Edward J. Geary and Edward P. Morris, both of Harvard University, for assistance beyond the call of pleasure in the hunt for those devils that subvert syllogisms, factual references, and the printed page;

and to two teachers,

Professor Justin O'Brien, of Columbia University, especially for his learned and patient work with the text; and

Professor Nathan Edelman, of the Johns Hopkins University, especially for his wise and patient work with the author.

Note

Mask: The false and usually colorful face that disguises something hollow.

Masque: The impersonal face of a timeless truth.

farce: Any manner of empty or gross comedy. Hence, "a farce. . . ."

Farce: A specific, significant, and ancient genre. Hence, "the Farce. . . ."

Unless a specific reference is given the author is responsible for each translation.

Some Implications of Laughter

IN THE SENSE that electrically charged wires are said to be "live," the live actor on stage establishes with the live spectator that unique contact which is the dramatic experience. In the living actor, the spectator finds the only extension of himself that will enable his reality to permeate the sham proposed by the actor for transmutation. Arts that imitate the drama, such as those of puppets or the motion pictures, demand auto-hypnosis by the spectator in order that he might credit them: he has to *imagine* a man who will become him. Arts that do not imitate drama, such as opera or the ballet, but that make use of the live presence on stage, intensify a part of that sensory presence for the gratification of a similarly sensory perceptor; these arts are called "pure" when the contact which they effect is direct, and they degenerate in proportion as their life is diverted for other ends.

Thus, it is incorrect to speak of a "spectator" (as distinct from the actor and his text) in a dramatic ritual. The term can be retained only for convenience but must be understood to mean "participant." The degree and the nature of this participation determines in effect the type and quality of the drama being "performed." Traditionally, the two general aspects of drama have been called comedy and tragedy: the comic play elicits laughter from the spectator whereas the tragic excites emotions that are responsive, such as Aristotle's pity and terror. That these apparently conflicting emotions are not as conveniently distinct from each other in the theater might be shown by analyzing the nature of the comic response, laughter.

When Freud asserts in his essay on *Wit and its Relation to the Unconscious* that laughter might be an escape for repressed aggression, he is in fact pointing to two essential aspects of laughter known to generations of theorists and disputed by as many who could not countenance so vexing an antinomy: the permissibility and the danger of mirth. Generally, laughter calls forth immediately the sunny side of experience, and although from Aristotle to Baudelaire concomitant "degradation" has been suggested for the act, laughter sounds too irresistibly like the crystal ring of all that is pure, joyful, young, and transparent for analysts not to attempt, recurrently, ingenious circumventions of evil. Freud himself proposed two types of wit, one of them "harmless"—directing attention to the sound rather than to the implication of words. Sully (*An Essay on Laughter*, 1902) formulated a "play" theory, according to which laughter is "a *sudden* accession of happy consciousness," resulting from "the sudden transformation of one's world, from the arrival of some good thing which is at once unexpected and big enough to lift us to a higher level of happiness." However, Freud failed to differentiate satisfactorily harmless wit from that which is not, and Sully merely resumed the automatic association generally made between mirth and pleasant occasions.

Another group of writers on the subject has assumed that laughter is somehow generated within the laugher. J. Y. T. Greig (*The Psychology of Laughter and Comedy*, 1923) and V. K. Krishna Menon (*A Theory of Laughter*, 1931) have formulated so-called "ambivalence" theories, which, in order to remove the lethal sting from mirth, find that "Laughter can result only from the action of two processes within ourselves: the impulse to activity or cognition and the check to that activity on re-cognition [. . .] the impulse to proceed and the impulse to draw back. [. . .] As a result of the collision there is, as it were, a bursting-out of the energy and hearty spontaneous laughter arises" (Krishna Menon). These theories only go over once again the ground already covered by Herbert Spencer in his physiological explanation of laughter (in his *Essays, The Physiology of Laughter,* 1863) as an overflow of nervous energy: the energy which has been stored up in view of meeting an event finds itself released in that muscular activity called "laughter" when the event has turned out to be smaller than expected.

But Spencer's "event," Krishna Menon's "impulse to activity," initially lie *outside* the laugher, and in establishing the relation between the two that will occasion the release, moral areas are suggested; these the analysts have been loath to tread on. Bergson (*Le Rire,* 1900), although he failed to remain faithful to his premises, did assert that man laughs only at the human, confirming two hundred and fifty years later Hobbes' very basic ideas: "The passion of laughter is nothing else but *sudden glory* arising from a sudden *conception* of some *eminency* in ourselves, by *comparison* with the infirmity of others, or with our own formerly" (*On Human Nature*).

Schopenhauer made the concept even more abstract in *The World As Will and Idea:* "The cause of laughter in every case is simply the sudden perception of the incongruity between a concept and the real objects which have been thought through it in some relation, and the laugh itself is just the expression of this incongruity." Half a century before him, Kant had already similarly disposed of the phenomenon in his *Critique of Judgement*. After these, Bergson, Freud, Munro and not a few others also variously intellectualized the process of mirth without ever successfully disposing of the human quality that gives its meaning to the exultation that mirth expresses. Whether the subject has perceived the inadequacy of Bergson's mechanical something "encrusted upon the living," or whether he has detected Schopenhauer's discrepancy between the illusory concept and the real object, he has done so as a human in a human context and his laughter is the mark of his particular being. There is no motivation for laughter without such a context—a man laughing perforce implies at least the suggestion of another man being laughed at.

In all theories of laughter, the words that designate spontaneity and force recur constantly: laughter is "sudden," it is "hearty," it is a "bursting-out"—even in its incipience it is maximal and whole. It is born at peak intensity and virulent or it is not laughter; otherwise it may be mask or mimicry, but not that "passion" of which Hobbes wrote. And if endless definers have attempted to mellow and subdue the quality of this brazen assault, one is tempted to surmise that they have done so because they could not accept this spontaneous residue of social mayhem in a generally ossified society.

Mask or mimicry laughter might become in that, admittedly, society exerts powerful strictures. No theory concerned with the psychological mechanism of man can afford to ignore these strictures; therefore speculation about laughter must account for that artificial form of mirth which expresses the more modest and less immediate triumph of man through reflection. However, even such subdued mirth ultimately fastens on a human being, though possibly through the bypass of a physical or mental symbol.

The mirth stimulus, which need not be a man, but which will remain dormant unless it suggests a man to a man, will likewise remain innocuous until it is recognized as mirth stimulus. The conjunction of the potentially funny with the potentially risible (that is, properly, "having the faculty of laughing") might be said to constitute the climate of laughter. The funny joke told at the convivial party fails when used as illustrative material for a theory of the comic: in the latter case its "solution" is lost in the quantity of psycho-physical energy mustered to "solve" the over-all theory; *climate,* established at the party, is lacking.

The ability of the subject to establish the relationship necessary for this climate depends on his degree of identification with the ultimately human stimulus. William McDougall has said that laughter is an antidote to sympathy. It is at any rate true that laughter does not occur when the stimulus is of too vital a nature and when the kinship between stimulus and subject is close enough for the subject to feel in him the reverberations of such a stimulus. There must be a *lack of identification* for laughter to take place—though to speak of complete detachment would be, of course, inane: laughter is that tenuous bond which aggression establishes this side of indifference. There will always be a minimum of identification between the laugher and his victim but there never can be more than that minimum.

This onset of man upon man finds a logical arena in the theater where an experience occurs whose singularity is derived from the fact that it is about man and performed by man. Henri Gouhier (*L'Essence du théâtre,* 1943) has convincingly shown how this human element sets the theater apart from literature and from all arts outwardly similar to it. The theater is never wholly abstract nor wholly unreal because of the living presence of the actor upon the stage.

But because of this modicum of truth and reality which the flesh of the actor will always insure, an equivalent modicum of fraternal cognition will always remain latent in the spectator and consequently the comic value of the clown on stage may suddenly cease to exist. And as the spectator can unaccountably assert these bonds, as he has done occasionally with, say, the former clowns Shylock and Alceste, the author cannot determine conclusively the fate of any of his characters.

This inevitable limitation upon the author has long rendered unsatisfactory his position as a writer of comedy. If he is to be reasonably sure that the spectator will not sanctify the comic symbol he is striving to create, he must so debase that symbol as conceivably to rob his entire drama of the human substance he might have wished to convey nevertheless. Indeed, the continued success of all forms of light commercial comedy shows that, granted a sufficiently eviscerated stage-type, the author can count on the responsive good will of his audience. Should the author, however, not be satisfied with such ephemeral success and should he seek more secure values in an analysis of the nature of plays, he will be confronted by a number of paradoxes.

The very name "play" suggests the first of these: the dramatic act is make-believe; it is a game although it is played with live pawns. Although, as previously noted, the very life of these pawns is an initial threat to the craft of the comic author, he might find brief solace in the insubstantiality of the game itself. However, laughter will occur only as the result of the aberrations of recognizably human inferiors. Therefore, not only will the figures of the protagonists remain alive, but they will evolve on stage in an atmosphere calculated to extend their own initial suggestion of reality. Thus, the whole comic performance will strive to imitate life.

In so doing it will fail, of course. The spectator will be reminded at all times by the footlights of the separation between the reality of his own world and the sham of the stage. The tragic author, aware of these limitations to reality, will not attempt to imitate a physical surface. He will instead call on the spectator to transfer the tragedy from the shallow dimensions of the stage into the full reality of his own being, relying for this absorption on the persuasive flesh of the actor, his presence and his reality as a human agent, and hence as a mesmeric one, but never relying on the credibility of his incarnation. The actor can convince only inasmuch as he is a human speaking to humans; as a character, his life and death depend solely on his acceptance or his rejection by the spectator.

The failure to make of the stage an essential continuum of life will be circumscribed at a certain point by the human reality of the actor on stage. In him the comic author finds not only his most pernicious foe, but also, if fortune wills it, his most effective ally. For should he succeed in sustaining the human credibility of the actor in his characterization, while preventing the integration of that living presence by the spectator for which the tragedian strives, the comic author will have succeeded in loosing a force—laughter—far more powerful in its assertion than any engendered tragic emotion. On stage no Iphigenia will ever really die under the sacrificial blade, and, knowing this, the tragedian merely requests of Iphigenia that she persuade some spectator to live Iphigenia's agony. The

most sensitive spectator in the theater will never feel agony to
the extent that he might should life this side of the footlights
suddenly claim an Iphigenia from among his beloved or single
him out for the part. But should the human on stage be recognized as a human by the spectator, and should the latter nevertheless find sufficient cause not to identify himself with that
human, there will be little about his laughter that is synthetic
and the artificial shell of the theater will have hatched the   ⊙
same explosion, as genuine, as violent, and as lethal as might
have life beyond the theater. In this sense, there is more *reality*
to the comic person on stage than to the tragic one.

Thus, whereas the tragedian will abandon the unreality of
the stage for the reality of the spectator and will use the physical being of the actor only as suasion, the comic playwright
will seek out the physical fact, the reality of the actor, and will
strive to make of the character and stage a world real enough
to feed anthropophagous laughter. But the mere desires of the
author and his skill will never be guarantees: his art waits
upon the whims of the vagrant spectator whose many areas of
jurisdiction over the fate of genres Pierre-Aimé Touchard has
shown in what he comprehends as a Dionysiac experience—
man reveling in man (*Dionysos: Apologie pour le théâtre,*
1949).

Conceivably, however, the comic playwright may not be as
interested in eliciting laughter as in conveying his own comic
view of life. This can be achieved of course without audible
mirth. Avowedly a tragedy, *Oedipus* may resume for some,
perhaps existentialists, the comic nature of man's disproportionate tussle with fate. Perhaps such a view was thought to be
universal by the poets who first conceived of tragic irony. Or
perhaps again such is merely the substance of all tragedy. How-

ever, if that particular irony is the aim of the comic author, the latter will find his control of the audience even more illusory, for a comic attitude is a philosophical stance, a reflective experience, in the same sense as that which the tragic drama attempts; it is not the immediate and vital participation of laughter. Only laughter is direct and audible speech in the audient part of the theater—and so might be a moan if tragedy could materialize truly—but *concepts,* of the tragic and of the comic alike, are inaudible soliloquy. And once the comic playwright abandons mere laughter, he abandons the game played on the stage with tangible, if erratic, quantities for that other removed from his realm and derived essentially from the spectator.

THE SPECTATOR's *stance,* his degree of identification which will deliver or doom the expectant puppets before him, is probably the essential aspect of that "communion" between playwright and audience over whose supposed loss many critics have brooded. However, in evaluating this unsatisfactory relationship, these critics (T. S. Eliot, Francis Fergusson, Gaëtan Picon, and others) have looked beyond the spectator to the author and the times. They have evoked as an ideal a Golden Age of the theater when actor, author, and spectator were united in a single religious weld. They have associated with the passing of the great myths the passing of great drama.

Such assertions cannot satisfy the theorist who believes that the spectator determines the ultimate fate of all things theatrical. Besides his conviction that every age coins and credits its own myths—though its deepest beliefs may not be formulated and though its formulated beliefs no longer be its myths—this theorist also believes that from century to century man's

wisdom remains as frail and his torment before the unanswer-
able as poignant, and that in this eternal quandary breathes
the essence of all drama and a language common to every age.

The brooding critic who mourns a Golden Age asserts by
his very sincerity that some of the golden seed endures. Nor
is his apprehension of ancient drama that of the audiences for
which it was written. The play he sees is in fact a far better
one, stripped of its frittering immediacy. Centuries later he
confirms the verdict of its immortality by viewing it as an embodiment of deathless truth in the masque of a bygone age
whose only significance for him is that of the oracular masque.
The masque is the mystagogic vestment of art. Because essential truth must perforce display a countenance unaffected by
temporal vagaries, the oracle cannot be too circumstantial:
realism belies reality, surface cannot render substance. But the
symbol yields an eternally repeated verity which the portrait
loses with its season.

The virtue of classical tragedy is essentially one of economy
—strict self-circumscription to a well-defined masque. Presumably, this economy shapes every aspect of such drama, the language that gives it voice being as bare as its action and as remote, essential, and telling as its masque. The definition of
classical tragedy is probably that of the genius that insures its
longevity. Essentially a mental exercise, its physical action remains rudimentary. The symbols of its conflict are drawn from
those stubbornly rooted areas of the human complex that defy
mores and solace. Equally distant at all times, such stylization
preserves for all spectators the noncontingency of the masque,
thereby enabling each in his generation to establish that contingency necessary for his own intimate communion.

Although such distance preserves the classical protagonist

and endows him with the dignity generally ascribed to tragedy, a sense of immediacy causes post-classical authors to view that dignity as dramatic effacement and to fear in the effected distance a further alienation by the spectator. An obvious solution therefore suggests itself: the enlargement or creation of temporal aspects in the protagonist which will grant him surface relief while developing for the audience areas of immediate recognition. Thus a Diderot calls for and achieves temporality through literal *embourgeoisement* of his characters, bringing them down from the supposed remoteness of regal loftiness to the familiar realm of the spectator—his language, his appearance, his perspective. The long view is traded for the short; the classical protagonist's short-comings are eliminated together with his excellences. The dramatic character now appeals to the audience for which he was created but remains, upon the demise of that audience, pointless and isolated. Even during the period of its lifetime, the queries that endure by reason of their refractoriness are relinquished for the immediate concerns of the times; the character tends towards didacticism and so anticipates death in the suicide which even his victories portend since they must at length render his battles obsolete— hence futile, or even ludicrous.

The romantic hero grows out of an awareness of these short-comings but is drawn from the very nature that has bred them. He assumes once more the loftiness of the classical hero but his detachment is no longer serene—he never loses sight of the audience for he no longer trusts it. His detachment is as self-conscious as it is artificial, replacing with enforced admiration based upon temporal attributes the trust which the classical hero placed in the spectator's power of intimate assimilation. As a result, the romantic hero's essential greatness is either a part of, or lost in, trappings meant to lure the spectator, and discrepancy grows between that essence and its frame—the hero's words, his acts, or the pattern of which he is a part.

The romantic hero so readily turns into a caricature of himself as to be a menace easily recognized. Not the least of his threats is that, thus contrived, his reality and his potentiality happen to be exactly those of the comic figure. He is now, because of his earthly attributes, a familiar presence on stage; and such attributes are dangerous ballast: should they fail to elicit the admiration for which they were designed, they will drag the hero down from his precarious heights to the sublevel of laughter—the contempt which such familiarity is ever in danger of breeding.

The persistence of this type must be imputed to a law of least resistance affecting the public's habits and the author's fear of them. The public apparently refuses protagonists who are not a priori captives of its own immediate reality. The author is understandably more unwilling to venture a character dependent for its life on the initial barrier it sets up.

By definition, the romantic hero initially courts the audience and *plaire* remains too fundamental a motto for the dramatist to give up such a happily endowed pawn. Conversely, the solidity, substance, and longevity of classical drama remain a constant taunt and aspiration. Curious efforts have been attempted to salvage both desirable principles of this antinomy. Cocteau and Anouilh, two of the modern dramatists who have expressed their views on the problem, have excerpted from the definition of tragedy that aspect of noncontingency which is its relentlessness. For Cocteau it became the infernal clockwork running down all through the lifespan of the fated victim. For Anouilh it was the same inexorability—in his words, no "good young man might have arrived in time with the gendarmes" *(Antigone)*. But since Anouilh (and Cocteau) did nothing about keeping the hero as rigorously purposeful as was to have been the clockwork, the author is beset by a multitude of such "young men"—contingencies—that eventually hamper even the uncoiling spring.

Such and other failures to reconcile incompatible elements led a very considerable number of writers (a more extended analysis would indicate this to be true of nearly every author writing serious drama today) to neutralize the romanticism of their protagonists by objectifying their relationship to these protagonists, detaching themselves from them in advance of others who might be tempted to do so, thereby removing some of the ground for such alienation.

The most effective and organic way of achieving this objectivity was to use the laughter latent in the character created. Not only is a hero mocked less likely to mock the author at some future date, but in electing laughter the author can now avail himself of the full resources of that medium. Through laughter he will anticipate the awkward response to any new forms he might select, since he knows that all factors alienating the theater world from that of the spectator are factors of psychological detachment and hence of potential laughter. Among these are uneasiness and strangeness, and closely allied to them is the social laughter of Bergson signifying intellectual awareness. Such laughter is reflective and secondhand, responding to an intellectual query rather than to a visceral impulse. It is, nevertheless, one of the two poles towards which the spectator must lean—and the one which will attract him if he does not select tragedy. Tragedy in alien form may likewise turn him in that direction.

BUT LAUGHTER, when it is not a self-conscious mask, may lead away from paths of negative choice and open broader areas of experimentation within which to preserve the hybrid hero sought by the author. The direction such new forms will take will be determined in part by the fundamental awareness that the comic author's world is built, in opposition to the mental one of the tragedian, around a living presence on stage. Indeed, the comic playwright finds himself the true heir of that domain which Touchard still calls Dionysiac. Alongside the record of laughter whose echoes have been muted in the solemnity of pantheons, runs the unrecorded laughter, deathless only in its continual rebirth, but too brassy, too spontaneous, and too brief for even the confinement of print or the blunting of repetition. It rings out with the unlearned buffoons of Greece who have preceded and outlived Herondas and who have seen Menander become but the effigy of the New Comedy. It breaks forth on Roman street corners where funambulists take up the gayer tatters that Terence has relinquished.

Without necessarily going back through time to ancestral fertility rites, most of the European dramatists could evoke the birth of integrated drama, their own national drama, erupting from the west doors of cathedrals as Farce striving to free itself from ritual. From its once again familiar streets, the crude spirit of Farce was still to assault the new houses of an art form whose contrasting sedateness was eventually to term itself "legitimate." Soon the drama demands the "stuffing" (Low Latin *farsa*) of laughter. Just as the French *Farce* relieved the *Mystère,* the nobility of the medieval Lowlands had the *abelespelen* that relate its own feats broken up by gross farces, the *boerden, sotternijen,* or *kluchten.* Renaissance spectators in Italy welcome the *intermezzi* between the acts of a drama whose life has been sapped by tedious considerations of dramatic theory. At the Hôtel de Bourgogne, that spirit endures in the verve of Gros-Guillaume, Gauthier-Garguille and Turlupin while the comic French stage waits, and bursts forth again in the earthy *Théâtres de la foire* when Molière is gone and the *Commedia dell'Arte* finds itself constrained by acquired credentials. Still later, it will find refuge in variety houses and music-halls, in the *Variétés Amusantes* and the *Vaudevilles,* when the sententious tone of bourgeois comedy has proven trying. It is unrecorded because it existed only for the moment, not for the enhancement of the stage.

While two segments of what had once been a single audience move further apart, writers of a "legitimate" drama that perpetually dies begin to take note of the ever regenerating popular forms. The meaning of the word Farce has long been lost—it still is lost for many—when modern dramatists turn to it once again, finding in this oldest of theaters the gusto and whiplash of a truly living form since, in fact, the Farce remains above all a lusty breath of brutal and pungent reality. Heedless of modes, it continues to draw sustaining power from the most elemental themes of physical passions: lust, gluttony, vanity, cruelty, cowardice, avarice. It relinquishes the heroic throes only to remain self-consonant in its exacting appraisal of man, though it never precludes the regeneration of the sinner through his pain. In the final analysis, it is drawn to the same founts as tragedy and therefore removes itself similarly from realism. If the original idea of the Farce is to be spectacle, to entertain, it too has come to seek timeless answers and the essential agencies of man. And thus, like tragedy, it now wears the masque. If it has retained of its traditional appurtenances a preponderant element of visual and auditory effects designed to provoke the most immediate kind of laughter—a coarse tone, mimicked buffoonery, etc., as well as incongruous situations which it imposes on otherwise recognizably real people—one should remember that these exaggerations are in reality litotes: speaking to more demanding audiences, the modern Farce sounds those depths most susceptible of yielding new significance and acquires overtones of the comedy of manners, of character portrayal, of the symbolistic phantasy. It now turns its crudest realism to symbols from which it will extract an essential gist: the original caricature which once sought only laughter now seeks, through abnormality, universal truths; it has become in its own right a valid masque, timeless and impersonal.

MUCH AS it has been throughout most of its history, French drama remains today the glass of fashion and the mold of form for a great part of the world's theater. Anouilh, Claudel, Cocteau, Giraudoux, as well as more recent converts to the stage, Sartre, Beckett, etc., furnish a dramatic leaven nearly as vital beyond the borders of France as it is within. Examination through the modern French stage of some of the problems suggested might thus provide insights into more than just the illustrative material.

I

*Intellectual Self-Consciousness: From
the Ridiculous to the Great Absurd*

1

Les Enfants Terribles

Jarry

SECURE AND UNQUESTIONED as Monsieur Prud-homme might have considered his world, its very existence was in jeopardy wherever it implicated art forms that brooked no concessions but to themselves. This confrontation of the "genuine" artist and the less dedicated cannot be isolated according to historical moments. Rather, it is a question of noting here the forces contending at this particular time and examining those which, by the end of the nineteenth century, were to upset the most solid edifices of conventional art. Because he had failed to solve, or even suggest, transcendental riddles, the bourgeois was now to suffer the advent of new values that accepted the riddle as an ultimate destined to supersede his numb and obsolescent oracles. Eventually, the new cult acquired historic tenure as the subconscious, surrealism, dada, non-objectivism, the absurd, etc., but not before the heyday of individual iconoclasts.

The individual experiments were not always sublime, but, collectively, they were of such dimensions as not to leave unchallenged any aspect of the times, including the theater. Here, the spurious surfaces on stage had been credited too long and now provided evident material for the image breakers who not infrequently focused their attention too exclusively upon only the exteriors of a generally superficial art. When they did so, they in fact substituted one shell for another, thus stifling their own efforts in the mask of intended victims.

Withal, *Ubu Roi*'s "Merdre!" which unexpectedly rang up the curtain at the Œuvre one evening in December 1896, was a brief but correct summation of a particular climate, and as such it echoed in time and space beyond the sensitive ears of first-nighters. Limiting the word's implications to the actual performance, it might be of more than sociological interest to speculate why it so affected the audience represented by its official critic, Francisque Sarcey, who walked out before the end of the performance.

This audience was willing to credit a stage world whose visible aspects, intensified by the living actor, allowed identification until the moment of comedy, that is to say, until one of its aspects was so demeaned or distorted as to be no longer a suitable projection of the spectator who then conveniently effected in laughter his withdrawal, signifying his understanding that the stage world was actually a fraud. As the curtain rose on *Ubu Roi,* the spectators may have had time to catch a preliminary glimpse of repellent masks disguising the human lure. Jarry himself, in a ten-minute allocution before the start of the play, had given fair warning:

It has pleased some actors to render themselves impersonal for two evenings and to play enclosed in a mask in order to be quite exactly the inner man and the soul of the huge puppets that you are going to see. [. . .] It was very important that we should have, to be altogether puppets, fair grounds music, and that the orchestrations be allotted to brass sections, gongs, and mock trumpets, which time did not allow us to assemble. [. . .] It must be added that we have perfectly accurate stage sets. [. . .] you will see doors opening on snow fields under a blue sky, mantlepieces decorated with clocks splitting open to serve as doors, and palm trees growing at the foot of beds so that little elephants perched on shelves might graze on them.

But the spectators took this warning to be part of a sham ritual acceptable only while it was not taken seriously. Jarry's little elephants perched on shelves encouraged such disbelief and strengthened the onlooker's refusal to acknowledge his own implication in the experiment.

However, it is doubtful whether the audience apprehended the masks in the short time allowed Gémier, who, as Ubu, immediately flung out the opening word. This word, though known to the spectators, was unacknowledged by the decorous part which they had lent temporarily to the ritual. Although it remains to be determined how much of its impact Jarry actually wished translated into laughter, laughter alone would have signified the successful absorption of the shock after the disturbance; in a comedy played according to the usual rules, this disturbance would have been wholly artificial. The fact that the audience could not re-establish its accustomed status through laughter shows that Ubu's initial intrusion did not conform to the standard contract. The spurious surface and the game were immediately forgotten: there was a genuine assailant on stage.

To overwhelm the fiction on stage is not the function of comedy since such overwhelming would have the effect of awakening the spectator upon whom the assault might have been effected harmlessly: the spectator's sensitive reality is now in question. In view of Jarry's procedure, one might ask whether he actually intended *Ubu Roi* to be funny. Jarry himself seems to have been one of the first victims of the Ubu myth, making his Catulle Mendès' opinions about the play by stating, in his "Questions de théâtre" (*Œuvres Complètes*):

"I wanted [. . .] this mirror [. . .] of man's eternal imbecility [. . .] Truly, there is nothing that might lead one to expect a funny play." Doubt might be entertained further when considering the tragic effects of the assumption of Ubu's personality by Jarry. Originally, however, the play *was* meant to be funny: it had started out, some ten years before its performance at the Œuvre, as a school boy's spoof against a certain physics and chemistry professor called Hébert, whose nickname, Le Père Hébé, was corrupted into the less perishable form vouchsafed to the hero. Satire cannot succeed if its victim is not shown in such a way as to enable the onlooker to assert by laughter his own superiority over the victim's simulacre. Whatever changes were made subsequently would hardly appear to encourage serious contemplation of a play that tells the story of an incredibly coarse, covetous, and cruel hero who, abetted by the ambitions of a wife whose moral ugliness is very much like his own, becomes king of Poland through a staccato series of improbable murders, battles, assaults, and diverse outrages, only to be routed with as little concern and ending his career on the open seas, headed back for France. As a matter of fact, Jarry's original intentions are confirmed by a letter which he wrote in 1894 to Lugné-Poë who entertained somewhat different ideas about the play. In regard to the staging of his farce, Jarry outlined a number of suggestions with the aid of which he hoped that "we would have something whose comic effect would be assured." The intent was certainly there.

In the same letter to Lugné-Poë, Jarry sets forth specific aspects of his dramatic vision. In summary form, his six main paragraphs call for a suggestive stage stripped down to a few essential symbols—masks, rudimentary sets, token individuals for crowds—as well as an "accent" or "special voice" for the protagonist and modern clothes as distant as possible from local color. These indications are early evidence of his concern to keep his stage world akin to that of puppets. The allocution introducing *Ubu Roi* (the play was indeed a puppet show in its original form, *Les Polonais*) merely repeats the idea. In an essay significantly called "De l'inutilité du théâtre au théâtre," Jarry suggests the replacement of the actor's fallible structure by masks: "The actor will have to substitute for his head, by means of a *mask* enclosing him, the effigy of the PERSONAGE which will not have, according to the tradition of antiquity, character traits represented by tears or laughter (which do not in themselves represent a character), but the very character of the personage: the Miser, the Waverer, the Covetous Man heaping up crimes. . . ." The play of artificial lighting *(la rampe)* upon planes of the skillfully moved mask would provide the mask with its own gamut of expressions. The author then refers again to that dramatic superman, *Guignol,* to show how, contrary to conventional, imitative pantomime, such masks could achieve "universal gestures." It is interesting to note that Jarry's indications never go beyond the plastic and that he seems not to have realized that all drama but superficial comedy relies on an essential stylization that demands more than just the token assistance of masks.

In none of this does the actor play a part except as skilled clockwork. It is curious to hear Jarry compare him at the end of his article to the "skeleton hidden under the animal flesh and whose tragicomic value has been recognized in every age." For, as a matter of fact, the skeleton can have tragicomic value only if it suggests a man, whereas Jarry wishes to invert this suggestion by having a man do no more than actuate a mask. Hollow surfaces are indeed the areas upon which laughter

assays the human want—but only *after* the delusion that had
given reality to those surfaces. And similarly, Bergson's suggestion of something mechanical grafted upon the human,
demands that the human allusion point up the humorous discrepancy. Jarry would appear to suggest a far greater depersonalization, one whereby puppets would not draw their life
from a suggestion of the human, but wherein puppets would
be true anti-people requiring the most precise machinery available—a man for the present. When the incongruous adven-
tures of Ubu and his crew are once again resumed in *Ubu sur
la Butte* (1901), Guignol himself introduces the action and
clearly defines the nature of its participants. However, in a
genuine *Guignol,* the dummy is granted evanescent life by the
naïve onlooker, while Jarry, by use of the mask, has not only
destroyed such evanescent realism but has also established,
through his brutal implication of the audience, the reality of the
human beneath the mask.

The failure of the dramatist Jarry, otherwise a perceptive
theorist of the stage, comes from overlooking the fact that the
stage is only half of the theater. The public, that important
other half, he ignored, or at best, regarded with the utmost contempt. "De l'inutilité du théâtre au théâtre" starts out in the
following manner:

I believe that the question of knowing whether the theater must
adapt itself to the crowd or the crowd to the theater is settled
once and for all. It is the same crowd which in olden days could
comprehend or pretend to comprehend the tragic and comic authors
only because their fables were universal and explained four times
over in a play, and because it was coached the greater part of the
time by a prologist; in the same way as the crowd goes today to
the Comédie-Française to hear Molière and Racine because they
are played nearly continuously. There is complete certainty, more-

over, that the substance of these authors utterly eludes it. Since the theater has not yet achieved freedom to eject forcibly the one who does not understand, or to clear the hall at each intermission before the clamor and damage, one might content oneself with this proven truth: that there will be a fight (if fight there is) in the hall for a work of vulgarization—thus not an original one and one therefore available previous to the original—and that the latter will benefit at least the first day from a public that has remained in ignorance and consequently dumb.

Still, in the pendant "Questions de théâtre," Jarry had written about *Ubu Roi:* "I wanted the stage to be before the public, once the curtain was up, like that mirror in the tales of Madame Leprince de Beaumont, where the one who is vice-ridden sees himself with the horns of a bull or the body of a dragon according to the exaggeration of his vices." The "one who is vice-ridden" here referred to *knew* that the reflected image was his because he was before a mirror and a mirror has only one reality, that of the one looking into it. In order for the stage to be "mirror" the spectator must first credit the figure on stage as his own projection. He obviously cannot afford the intromission of laughter which is merely a way of rejecting the reflection whenever it grows critical. And should even the spectator recognize in the reflection an existing aspect, he would operate the mechanism of comedy by recognizing *someone else.*

But even Jarry had to grant the existence of a public and its theatrical autonomy: "Art and the understanding of the crowd being so incompatible, we might have erred, we allow, in attacking the crowd directly in *Ubu Roi;* the crowd was angered because it understood only too well, no matter what it might say" ("Questions de théâtre"). That denial of comprehension had been made by Jarry, not by the spectator. In serious speculations, he is forced to acknowledge the autonomy of the audience, as when he refers to token sets that must be re-created by the viewer, the "character" who must be apprehended intellectually, etc.; but he limits his world audience to an aggregate of five hundred qualified participants. Whatever acknowledgment he makes, the terms of the acknowledgment are his.

In the chapter devoted to Ubu's creator, André Breton *(Anthologie de l'humour noir,* 1940) offers an insight into the nature of Jarry's dramatic contempt: "Literature, starting with Jarry, moves forward dangerously, upon ground that is mined. The author compels recognition of himself beyond his work." He then quotes from Freud to construe these writings as the author's instinctual projection. His surmising that there was no Ubu *creation* to which Jarry might have fallen sway, but that the character *was* Jarry, seems probable after the reminiscences of observers like Rachilde and Gide. In this light, the image of the hateful mirror can be understood to reflect especially Jarry's own aggressiveness. Even such symbolistic works as *César-Antéchrist* (1895), that apocalyptic projection of the Platonic soul in which Ubu again symbolizes the lowest order, or *Les Minutes de sable mémorial* (1894), bear the characteristic mark of Jarry's destructive satire though no hostile public could be aimed at here: the very esotericism of these works presumes the five hundred elect admitted by the author.

Furthermore, the image of Ubu upon which Jarry conferred moral utilitarianism after Ubu's fall from grace, making it the "mirror" of a degraded bourgeoisie, simply does not exist. Ubu exhibits gusto in mayhem and delight in slaughter; he constantly asserts his egocentricity, as in *Ubu sur la Butte* when surrounding Russian hordes cannot prevent him from eating and drinking heartily. In the same play he is superbly truculent and does not waste time in self-pity, even when led off at the end: "Good Lord, where will I hide? What will become of Mère Ubu? Adieu, Mère Ubu, you are ugly indeed today, is it because we are having people over?" Such traits hardly fit the description which Jarry himself gave of Ubu in his "Questions de théâtre" or his "Paralipomènes d'Ubu" *(La Revue Blanche,* 1896) when he characterized Ubu as a quintessence of all that is cowardly, vile and stupid. Rather, the character evinces healthy sadism and a general egocentrism reminiscent of that which the numerous anecdotes spun about and around Jarry himself suggest. It will be noted, moreover, that in *Ubu en-chaîné* (1899), the hero even becomes a moralizing voice after he has voluntarily chosen slavery in truculent avowal of his past misdeeds: his symbolically egocentric jail is a world of which the "free men" deliberately attempt to deprive him. This is the play wherein he has been sent as a galley slave to the Turkish sultan, only to be recognized as the sultan's dangerous and long lost brother who must be dispatched promptly, once again, upon the open seas.

It is hard to see Jarry's plays as anything beyond more or less felicitous formalizations of the author's personality—an effort at self-projection which he carried on throughout most of his life, according to the accounts of his intimates. Such self-projection into the drama invalidates another part of it, for it points to an exclusive concept of laughter—if laughter there is indeed—limited to the single device of shock. It has been noted that shock, within certain limits, might be a trigger of laughter. However, Jarry relied too exclusively on this single trick, jeopardizing the very mirth he appears to have sought and, incidentally, availing himself of only a handful of the many Farce modes. Contrasted with the contemporaneous *Champi-*

gnol and *Boubouroche, Ubu Roi* is striking especially by the paucity of means through which it sets about to achieve laughter. Debased but indestructible, his specialized creatures suffer the restrictions and the unwieldiness of automata. Little given to psychic motion, they and their world lack sensual appeal—that of color, physical suggestion, or spectacle—which characterizes those other worlds, the circus, the comic opera, etc., in which shells are not credited either, though their attributes never exclude a modicum of the senses. This is, instead, the world of Jarry, one in which sexual union is unavailing; it is that of his symbolistic *Haldernablou* (in *Les Minutes de sable mémorial,* 1894) whose title is interestingly derived from the juxtaposed names of the sadistic mysoginist, Duke Haldern, and that of his page Ablou. This is the stage world of the author who, in "De l'inutilité du théâtre au théâtre," strengthened his plea for puppets by drawing an image of women on stage, debased by "what is ridiculous in their profile and inesthetic in their walk, their contour stumped at every muscle by tissue —an odious thing because it is useful, productive of milk," and who concluded that no truly great author had ever entrusted roles to them, for "the majority of women are common."

Jarry's stage figures, from which all blood and all pain have been removed, walk their staccato course through a series of incidents owing little to their own psychic configuration and never truly affecting them. As the spectator notices quite soon that these personages are well-armored—that they are in fact only armor—his pleasure must be restricted to the Platonic contemplation of their blow-dealing. The fare is similar to that provided, in slightly different worlds, for Wilde's or Guitry's spectators. The puppets' aggressiveness is absorbed and enlarged by the thoroughly ill-tempered and abusive language that they hurl at each other. The exchange of vituperation has been carried out with such gusto in *Ubu Roi* that it frequently reveals the poet and has conferred upon Jarry distant kinship with Rabelais. Still, it is damning to hear Ubu come to life so clearly in anecdotes narrated about Jarry by Rachilde, Jacques-Henry Lévesque, and so many others, through the simple expedient of a clipped, incisive phrase using the regal plural and an occasional archaism. Gide remembers that members of Jarry's entourage were able to copy his manner "with varying degrees of success" (*Mercure de France*, 1946). Even the exceptionally gusty *Ubu Roi* long enjoyed contested paternity, supposedly having been written by a certain Charles Morin (see Charles Chassé, *Dans les coulisses de la gloire: D'Ubu Roi au Douanier Rousseau*, 1947).

How distant the Rabelais kinship actually is, can be readily ascertained by reading both men's *Pantagruel* (1903?). Jarry's homonymous play copies faithfully incidents such as Panurge's discussion with Pantagruel about the advisability of marriage, or Panurge's comportment aboard ship during and after the storm, but in so doing it robs them of their savour and life. *Ubu enchaîné* is similarly vapid, giving point to Mère Ubu's remark about her husband having seemingly "forgotten the word." Plays like *Le Moutardier du pape* (1905?) and *Par la taille* (1898?) remain equally listless even though the aggressive tone endures. It is not easy to understand Gide's estimate of the Ubu dialogue inserted in *Les Minutes de sable mémorial* as "an extraordinary, incomparable, and perfect masterpiece" (*Mercure de France*, 1946). The insistence on aggressive epithet and the remorseless egomania dull the sting which they were originally intended to deliver and require increasing indulgence to represent anything like laughter-laden revelations.

Idle criticism finds little difficulty in ascribing meaning to works already resplendent with the spotlight of notoriety and so *Ubu Roi* has come to be a "timeless, placeless" endeavor that "shamelessly displays what civilization tries hard to hide, and *that* is more than lavatory brushes and schoolboy swearing, it is an aspect of truth" (Barbara Wright in her introduction to the Gaberbocchus edition of *Ubu Roi,* 1951). But if this were an aspect of truth, as Jarry himself intimated—albeit belatedly —the audience would have turned its laughter to comprehension and assimilation. As it is, the truth apparently lay in the revelation of a rather pathetic figure, a Wizard of Oz amplifying his own fractious voice through the sound-box of what were to have been masks larger than life.

Apollinaire

Twenty years after *Ubu Roi,* Guillaume Apollinaire appended a foreword to a previously written play of his own, *Les Mamelles de Tirésias* (1917). Though couched amidst irrelevant remarks about Malthusianism, this preface attempted more than merely to raise some cheerful nonsense to the level of a pamphlet: it was in effect Apollinaire's *ars dramatica.*

The preface begins as a protest—and at first, the very protest seems anodine. Apollinaire wants to lift the theater out of the rut into which it has fallen because of vulgar naturalism. Reference is made to the successors of Victor Hugo and to the vacuity of subsequent "local color," the inevitable pendant of that skillful deception—naturalism—which Apollinaire wishes to supersede. In this phase of its development, the author's theory is too negatively circumscribed to afford much promise. Indeed, Jeanine Moulin (*Guillaume Apollinaire: Textes inédits,* 1952) reminds the modern reader that this *drame surréaliste* which today enjoys a cognomen that has gathered literary fame, was to have been labeled simply *surnaturaliste;* Pierre Albert-Birot, Apollinaire's publisher, suggested the more ambiguous term *surréaliste* whose implied extensions proved so felicitous.

But the suggestive word benefits even the theorist, and in calling for a return to "nature," though stipulating that this never be through servile imitation, Apollinaire finds his description adumbrating an esthetics: "When man wished to imitate walking, he fashioned the wheel that in no way resembles a leg. He thus achieved surrealism without knowing it." The theorist is now ready to turn from controversy to the development of his own concepts. He finds that a more viable drama will strive to concern itself with its own particular esthetics rather than with the usual surface imitations of life. If one ignores the occasional self-contradictions forced upon the theorist by the then soldier Apollinaire ("The subject will be sufficiently broad to [. . .] exert an influence upon the mind and mores in the sense of duty and honor") he is discovered demanding of the theater essentially what Antonin Artaud (*Le Théâtre et son double,* 1938) was to formulate: "The theater will be able to become itself again—that is to say, a means of providing true illusion—only by giving the spectator genuine dream precipitates."

Since the drama will be an essential and collective experience rather than a game made possible because of coincidentally valid facets (repeatedly, in preface and prologue, Apollinaire warns against *trompe-l'œil* shallowness), the audience will be drawn into the dramatic rite. He mentions as a hoped-for means of achieving this integration a double theater in the round, one that will bound the spectators from without as well, through an external, circular stage.

This theater, not about life but generating instead a life truly its own, will reject the strictures of any one genre. Such is anyway the author's cast: "It is impossible for me to decide whether or not this drama is serious. [. . .] I preferred to allow a free flow to that *fantaisie* which is my way of interpreting nature, *fantaisie,* which, according to the days, evidences varying degrees of melancholy, satire or lyricism." The word *fantaisie* is a felicitous one—the conscious author assumes the mantle which he and his public know to be his and suggests through the word those qualities of imaginativeness, conceptual freedom, spontaneity, and surprise found in his poetic opus. According to his biographers (Adéma, Pia, Billy, Moulin, etc.), this vein of Apollinaire waned after the poet's trepanation in 1916 following a head wound which he incurred during the war. That Apollinaire's artistic climate indeed required that *fantaisie* alluded to, is confirmed by the withering of subsequent drama which was not granted such a climate. In *Couleur du temps,* "Drama in Three Acts and in Verse" (1917), there remains little more than the author's war-inspired and maudlin sentiment.

Couleur du temps sends the prophetic poet Nyctor, a scientist, and a magnate in a plane-born quest for Peace. Protracted stopovers on a battlefield to rescue the mother of a dead soldier, and on a desert island to snatch away a repentant criminal, fail to prevent the discovery of Peace—a beautiful woman encased in a polar ice-block, "this peace so white and beautiful / So still and, in a word, so dead," over whom the four men fight and die. Many of the symbols are familiar: their neoteric had been the poet Apollinaire's for many years; the visionary Nyctor is the chanter of *La Chanson du mal-aimé* and "La Jolie Rousse"; the plane has already appeared in "Zone," etc. But those unredeemed symbols now remain solemnly pedestrian.

Nyctor is earthbound through partisan concerns; the plane, whose modernism no longer stuns nor uplifts, has become merely an unwieldy conveyance; the island from which "le solitaire" is removed, although it is hopefully anticipated as harboring "Serpents and also poetical monsters / Which we shall invent in order to please you" is a flat and moralizing landscape alongside that of "Onirocritique." Mavise, *la fiancée,* a momentary echo of the already saddened poet in "La Jolie Rousse," protests: "Though drunken with a will to fight / They would compel me to accept / The ignominious and sad peace / That blankets this deserted isle," but she is rapidly sacrificed as merely a woman to Nyctor and remains in the end a useless and passive commentator.

Apollinaire claims to have written all but the prologue and the last scene of *Les Mamelles de Tirésias* in 1903. The life and color which it evinces by comparison with *Couleur du temps* place it at any rate before the tragic spring of 1916. The title suggests the pertness and the ambiguity of the play: Thérèse's breasts fly out as toy balloons that she might shed her womanhood and become a "man"—Tirésias. Her husband, the moralizing force in this play concerned with repopulation, then takes over the duties of child-bearing, a task he prolifically accomplishes only to have a more subdued Thérèse return to him as the curtain falls.

Pascal Pia (*Apollinaire par lui-même,* 1954) notes that in chapter IV of Apollinaire's *Le Poète assassiné* (1916), the embryo of a similar plot had been sketched:

In the first act, a young woman rendered sterile through surgery was nursing her husband who was heavy with dropsy and very jealous. The doctor would leave, saying:
"Only a great miracle and great devotion can save him."

In the second act, the young woman said to the young doctor:

"I sacrifice myself for my husband. I want to become hydropic in his stead."

"Let us love each other, Madam. If you are not unfit for motherhood, your wish will be granted. And what sweet glory shall be mine!"

"Alas!" whispered the lady, "I no longer have ovaries."

"Love," the doctor would then exclaim, "Love, Madam, is capable of working many miracles."

In the third act, the husband as slender as a rod and the lady eight months pregnant congratulated each other upon the exchange they had effected. The doctor read to the Academy of Medicine the result of his research on the impregnation of women who had become sterile as the result of surgical operations.

The same novel, in which a Lacouff first appears (he does so later in *Les Mamelles*), also contains a number of other burlesque outlines whose purpose is to ridicule the then prevalent forms of drama. In these outlines, the author is merely spoofing, albeit with verve reminiscent of Jarry—a literary figure whom Apollinaire not only knew and admired (see references to Ubu's creator in *Il y a* and *L'Esprit nouveau et les poètes*) but one whose influence on Apollinaire probably accounts for the intellectual fringes of the author's Rimbaldian *fantaisie* (see Jeanine Moulin, *Textes inédits*). However, in transferring such a satirical outline to the full dimensions of the stage, Apollinaire has had to shift his sights. What had been a simply destructive protest will now attempt to be construction as well: the protest gives way to the exemplar. Whereas the spurious plot outline merely pretends to be a play in order to mock real plays, the real play now created by Apollinaire will seek substance, in conformity with the ideals of the preface—from within itself rather than through parody. It might not be amiss to note here that Apollinaire's third and last dramatic attempt extant, *Casanova* (1918), which is called *comédie parodique,* fails, betraying in its very title the substance of those ideals. *Casanova* was to have been the libretto for a comic opera, an episode drawn from the Italian adventurer's life, and as such, the pastiche of an Italianate genre which Apollinaire might have remembered from the pre-war days when he had written *Le Théâtre italien* (1910). Perhaps the subdued author of *Vitam Impendere Amori* (1917) was consciously seeking elsewhere an effervescence no longer in him. Whether or not such speculation be valid, the contrived and glossy fun of *Casanova* remains bookish and static even in its sallies: the promise of the stage has not been fulfilled.

In *Les Mamelles de Tirésias,* Apollinaire has chosen laughter from the start, the indecision of his preface notwithstanding. Pascal Pia, who believes that *Les Mamelles* was written in 1916, bases a part of his evidence on a tone which he finds reminiscent of the first poems of *Calligrammes.* Availing himself of a fun-seeking device at least as old as Aucassin's visit to Torelore, Apollinaire has retained, as in his comic sketch, the inversion of sexual functions. In line with this facetious mood, the play favors puns, elementary figures of intellectual laughter, which it occasionally strings out at length, such as in II, vi, where topical allusions beg the audience's connivance:

THE GENDARME: But the population of Zanzibar
       Famished because of these new mouths to feed
       Is in a fair way of starving to death
THE HUSBAND: Give them [ration] cards—they replace everything
THE GENDARME: Where does one get them?
THE HUSBAND: At the Cartomancer's
THE GENDARME: That's divining
THE HUSBAND: Sure! Since it's a question of foresight

Apollinaire acknowledges in his preface that he would have no objections to formulate were even the comic elements to gain the upper hand: "Rest assured, the reputation which would be justly conferred upon the author of *La Farce de Maistre Pierre Pathelin,* were his name known, keeps me from sleeping." He takes note of accusations according to which he has availed himself of means used in revues and defends himself against these accusations, but only casually, as he has no fundamental objection to them either.

However, whether Apollinaire's comic ambivalence be genuine or simply retrospective, his humor eventually acquires other dimensions; the play is quite obviously not simply a revue. The puns, while still at the intellectual level, partake of multiple extensions: in II, iv, for example, the *scène*-Seine play on words indicates universality as well as dramatic essence and condensation. In so doing, it echoes the fundamental equivoque of the entire play which is laid in Zanzibar (frequently identified with Paris by participants), a city that derives its name from a homonymous dice game whose attribute is the megaphone shaped like a huge dice box and used by various actors at intervals throughout the play. The pun upon which the physical locus of the play is established has moved, like that of its hero, beyond mere intellectual oscillations—it truly partakes of two inherencies.

Such devices, if they merely seek to extend the fun-making into new dimensions, and properly scenic ones, are innocuous enough. However, Apollinaire's preface speaks of "sufficient newness to shock and rouse to indignation." The word "striking" is used to designate the new esthetics that aim at a spectator "struck." Shock is indeed a mechanism of laughter—just as newness is concomitant with artistic transmutation. But neither requires outrage to the beholder. Artistic newness is a re-creation in which the spectator participates, and the shock that leads to mirth is sufficiently mild to be overcome through laughter. Thus the implications of Apollinaire's troubled awareness are not that the experiment might fail, making its author merely another writer of farces, but rather that the farce might prove unable to disguise the perpetration of new modes. At this level the mirth shields a revolutionary, someone who wishes to upset, whose voice, when it sought no protective mask, had pleaded in "La Jolie Rousse": "Pity on us forever struggling at the brink / Of the unbounded and of what is yet to come."

This is the voice that had elevated all things surprising, the new and the unknown, to the level of an esthetics and whose literary testament, *L'Esprit nouveau,* was read by Apollinaire in 1917: "The new spirit is also to be found in the astounding. The astounding is that which is most alive and most fresh in that spirit." Few of Apollinaire's commentators have failed to note his motto "I astonish"—one spoken evidently in full cognizance of its etymon.

The theater is quite properly a place of wonderment and, therefore, developing a genuinely theatrical esthetics might indeed have been for Apollinaire not only a congenial but a fruitful issue. Thérèse's breasts flying out to the audience (and later, as the curtain comes down, being tossed out as plentiful rubber balls to that audience) gave evidence of the author's concerns. Whereas Jarry's initial shock had suddenly severed stage and audience, this action allows Apollinaire a mechanism of surprise while at the same time it facilitates psychological communication across the footlights (all this quite apart from the cumulative effect of the sexual note which must certainly

have been hoped for by the author of *Ombre de mon amour*).
The audience thus intimately participant was the one for
whom the theater in the round had been planned. And so was
of course the spectatress who in II, vii, spontaneously picks up
a stage cue.

But Thérèse's peregrinating protuberances also indicate another aspect of Apollinaire's theater, one hinted at in II, iv
during a topical exchange between the fecund husband and a
newly created son:

THE SON (*he rocks a cradle*):	We hear from Montrouge
	That Monsieur Picasso
	Is painting a canvas
	That moves like this cradle
THE HUSBAND:	And long live the paintbrush
	Of our friend Picasso

Avowedly, the play is a cubist experiment, one that came
to life under the sponsorship of the cubist publication *Sic*. Marcel Adéma (*Guillaume Apollinaire le mal-aimé*, 1952) quotes
an article in *Paris-Midi* (June 26, 1917) by Paul Souday, en-
titled "A Cubist Play," though Souday was certainly not linked
in any way with the movement. Adéma also recalls how a certain number of cubist painters disavowed Apollinaire after the
performance, accusing him of having ridiculed them. This particular protest is curious in view of the close contact Apollinaire had enjoyed with so many of the group and its sym-
pathizers, like Picasso, Braque, Chirico, Picabia, and the many
articles he had written for *Les Soirées de Paris* on behalf of the
new school. These articles, gathered in 1913 and published as
Les Peintres cubistes (originally titled *Méditations esthétiques*)
contain some of the first and more perceptive definitions of
cubism attempted hitherto.

Apollinaire first defines the new movement's program—
methods and aims:

Wishing to attain dimensions of the ideal, no longer limiting
themselves to humanity, the young painters offer us works that
are more cerebral than sensual.

What makes cubism different from the old style of painting is the
fact that it is not an imitative art but a conceptual art striving to
achieve creation.

He sees four tendencies of this new art, or better, two paths
of what he calls the *art pur* and two others of a trend that fails
to merit that denomination. Among the genuine art forms are
scientific cubism and orphic cubism. Scientific cubism strives
to create new artistic entities with elements derived not from
the "reality" of vision but from the reality of a true knowledge.
Orphic cubism substitutes, for the essentially factual components of scientific cubism, components entirely created by the
artist though endowed by him with vital "reality." To further
delineate these two art forms, their anti-forms are also described. Corresponding to a debasement of scientific cubism is
physical cubism built with elements merely understood by the
eye, while orphic cubism gives way, at an inferior level, to instinctive cubism, which is the compound of shapes created by
an artist lacking either fundamental artistic perception or
belief.

How close the positive aspects of this program are to the
dramatic ideals set forth in the preface of *Les Mamelles* need
hardly be emphasized. Picasso is naturally cited as an exponent of both scientific and orphic cubism and the reference to
Picasso in Apollinaire's play as the author of "a canvas that
moves" calls to mind the fact that, in turning to the stage,
Apollinaire had tried to create a play "that moves." Properly

speaking, *Les Mamelles de Tirésias* is an attempted cubist drama, one that will, in conformity with the cubist esthetics, reject imitation for creation and hope to achieve thereby an artistic truth derived from the medium itself. To understand what aspect of cubism Apollinaire's experiment will espouse, it is necessary to keep in mind the demands of the stage as well as another aspect of the dynamics of cubism. Writing in *Les Soirées de Paris* (June 15, 1914), Apollinaire devotes an article to *Simultanéisme—Librettisme,* in which he says:

For some time already, the idea of simultaneity has been a concern of artists; as early as 1907, it was the concern of a Picasso, a Braque, who were attempting to show figures and objects through many planes at the same time. It became thereafter the concern of every cubist, and you can ask Léger what pleasure he feels in capturing upon canvas a face seen at once from the front and in profile.

This attempt to give an additional dimension to the reality of the canvas, one already evident in Cézanne, undoubtedly accounts for the meaning of "a canvas that moves." And in this way, the puns alluded to (*scène*-Seine, Zanzibar, etc.) attempt first an intellectual and then an artistic oscillation between the idea and the stage reality. However, in reference to the visual demands of the stage, these intellectual or semi-intellectual transmutations give way to wholly physical ones. Thus it is that Thérèse undergoes sexual changes on stage; that her husband creates a baby reporter by mixing in his crib scraps of things associated with the journalistic trade; that various participants die and are resurrected according to the demands of the action; that the kiosk, an inanimate object, dances and sports a living appendage, an arm, that is mechanical.

As ambiguous as the ambivalent hero whose oscillations are

to harmonize color areas and lines. The "surprise" that a painter causes may be artistically valid, and even validly challenging, but it can never exist independently of the elements of its creation. These determine the artistic worth and fate of any canvas regardless of whatever nonplastic values that canvas might also exhibit. In the case of Chirico, it is doubtful whether the surprise which his paintings first produced had anything to do with their longevity—if for no other reason than that the terms of surprise and duration contradict each other.

In the theater, however, the surprise will be derived not from a flat and inanimate surface but from all those dimensions that extend from the living performers on stage (whose life is dependent on the living re-creator for whom they perform): hence its "mainspring of surprise" will be at once a more legitimate and a more dangerous one to use. No matter how integrated are both parts of the theater, the footlights mark the limits of two distinct worlds. The fictitious life on stage can render itself meaningful only if the spectator assimilates it as his own real world. An attempt to invert this process by making the spectator physically participant in the stage life can only result in destroying an element of the spectator's reality—truly making some part of the spectator "play." Furthermore, it is questionable whether this reverse process can operate unless the spectator is rehearsed and becomes simply a performer, abdicating his former being entirely. And yet, barring this change, will he be prepared to enter any strange or alien realms? The assimilative act is at best a slow, incomplete, and tenuous one. In the prologue to *Les Mamelles,* Apollinaire speaks of the unbounded materia which are the dramatist's to transmute: "His universe is his play / Inside of which he is the creating God." But this claim gives him a dominion whose vassalage has not been considered: at its confines reside the spectators without whose reality it has none of its own. These are the omnipotent judges for whom the scheme to "shock and rouse to indignation" is planned. As with Jarry, the vital half of the theater has been, ultimately, slighted.

In his articles on cubism, Apollinaire had described that art as being more cerebral than sensual. Although color and line may well be perceived sensually, their sensual effect will be generally less direct and less telling than that which the human being itself can achieve. Creating on stage an art more cerebral than sensual removes from the actor one of his fundamental assets and from the spectator one of his legitimate anticipations: in effect, the most essential lure of the stage is lost to a genre that depends upon recognition and acceptance.

When, in "Onirocritique," the dream wanderer comes upon the sacrificial augur who has desired that his own stomach be opened and discovers "four I's, four O's, four D's," the poetic rhythm of the event merely continues the dream journey that had proceeded on a multitude of nonintellective levels. When, in *Les Mamelles,* the journalist appears with only a mouth, he may be an ideational symbol which is not difficult to comprehend. However, when he laughs through the megaphone upon the four vowels A, E, I, O, he breaks the human thread implicit in laughter and replaces it with no alternative suggestion even though his contrivance vaguely recalls that of "Onirocritique." In parallel fashion, when Picasso, during his "blue period," diversifies that one color so as to modulate with various effects its play throughout the canvas, he builds his composition and the totality of his creation; but when Thérèse appears on stage with a blue face, etc., she simply creates a shock achieved at the expense of the woman who had been antici-

pated and whose human presence would have been necessary
to entice the human presence upon whom the experiment depends. And similarly, the disappearance of Thérèse's breasts
becomes more than a superficial loss of feminine being and
appeal.

In the realm of deliberate fantasy, these experiments might
have given dramatic dimension to what must otherwise remain, as in *Casanova,* the simple transference to readers of
nondramatic writing. But in the dramatic form which he has
chosen, Apollinaire's initial shift to laughter would appear to
be the expression of a fundamentally bad conscience. He
claimed in *L'Esprit nouveau,* for example, that Jarry's laughter
gave the poet a new lyric mode, and having asked "What happened to the days when Desdemona's handkerchief appeared
to be inadmissibly ridiculous?" he claims for "even the ridiculous" a place in poetry. Desdemona's handkerchief shocked
only susceptibilities that had grown to consider tragedy far
more exalted than life and handkerchiefs far less. But to make
the innocuous handkerchief a central element to be capitalized
on would necessitate first recapturing such Victorian susceptibilities solely in order that they might be inverted—an obviously senseless contradiction.

Jarry's verve did indeed rise on occasion to lyric heights, but
such lyricism was not in itself—any more than that of the
aforementioned *Casanova*—capable of any dramatic materialization. It failed him before the footlights because it failed to
create stage people. Similarly, Apollinaire's own laughter
serves only to alienate (properly the function of laughter) his
people from the audience. His experiment was fated, in common with all experiments, to elicit first the laughter of the uninitiated before being able to induce response. Such awkward

laughter, born of uneasiness rather than of assimilative triumph, must be imputed to Apollinaire himself if his sincerity (confirmed by his cubist ethics and the dramatic esthetics of Jarry which *Les Mamelles* so frequently illustrates) is to be credited. The intimate experience which the theater in the round would have anticipated, demanded first human presence and second, total dedication. The costumes designed by Serge Férat for the first performance might have made their wearers form interesting patterns in an over-all design of the same nature. (Were Férat's intentions conforming to an artistic totality or to a comic one? The successful combination of both could have been achieved only through luck more extraordinary than is usually deemed to be artistically safe.) On stage, these disguises rendered the living performers barbaric and abstract, for, contrary to Jarry's ideal masks, these could not enjoy artistic autonomy in a framework concerned with effects of its own. Healthy laughter, already frustrated by the absence of realistic surfaces, becomes spiritless or hostile through such accumulative alienation.

In fact, the mechanical aspect of its performers slowly mires the action of these two acts whose dynamism seldom appears to stem from true spontaneity: the experimenter repeatedly betrays the comic author and the latter finds himself betrayed in turn. Harbingers of laughter must offer an initial threat to the intimate familiarity of spectator and actor: the figures of Apollinaire elicit at best mild admiration.

In *Les Mamelles,* the quest for laughter not infrequently dominates the experiment and the play loses form. It is no longer easy to understand readily why the husband speaks with a distinctly Belgian accent off stage and loses it after he has appeared (it is even doubtful whether that off-stage person is clearly recognizable). It is hard thereafter to tell whether the original performance had the gendarme and the journalist played by women for any particular purpose or merely because of nonchalance towards the over-all validity of the performance. One inclines to the latter belief after having failed to find any essential reason for their existence and noting the episodic form of the play as it moves fitfully to its ineffectual conclusion.

One will likewise impugn the entire cubist experiment when its devices are viewed as stage actions rather than illustrative material for that experiment. *Casanova,* an undramatic stage materialization of an aspect of the author's earlier romanticism (albeit presented as a pastiche) and *Couleur du temps,* the ponderous restatement of a number of conceits, point to the primary failure of *Les Mamelles*: the failure of a drama to draw substance from its own soil. The failure is the more noticeable in that, as a truly perceptive theorist, Apollinaire had understood this dramatic necessity. The form of *Les Mamelles de Tirésias* as it now exists would appear to be the instance of an initial betrayal of the dramatist by the experimenter and thereafter betrayal of the experimenter by the uneasy dramatist seeking to disguise the experimenter's excesses.

Upon such grounds, the dramatic experiment could not fructify: the experimental is awkwardly obvious, surprise frustrates the communion, mechanical artifacts inhibit the human. Even the farce is seldom funny, for unlike Jarry, whom Apollinaire admired for his genuine truculence, the author himself seems to have remained outside the circle of his synthetic creation. And so the cubist drama remains an odd assemblage of disjointed parts out of whose hermaphroditism the dream world was to have soared.

Cocteau

Apollinaire's concern to establish 1903 as the date at which *Les Mamelles de Tirésias* was written may have been due in part to the advent of another play, *Parade,* performed in Paris in May 1917, a month before his own. If one considers as standard the works of François de Curel and Henry Bataille, of Georges Courteline and Georges Feydeau, that were ruling the Parisian stage at the time, Jean Cocteau's *Parade* can be viewed as an experiment not unlike that of Apollinaire. However, the experiment bears closer scrutiny. *Parade,* termed a *Ballet réaliste,* is in fact merely a ballet with the addition of a few music-hall turns: the brief appearances of fair barkers, acrobats, a Chinese conjurer, and a little American girl. Its choreography was devised by Léonide Massine working with Cocteau; Picasso was called on for costumes and *décor;* and Diaghilev's troupe performed. One might assume that it was *Parade,* (1916) and as well as Cocteau's immediately subsequent theater, *Le Bœuf sur le toit* (1920) and *Les Mariés de la Tour Eiffel* (1921), that led Clouard to call the author "that child born to Anna de Noailles by the Ballet russe." Cocteau's social connections earned him access to Diaghilev's world from the very moment when Parisian literati (amongst whom Madame de Noailles) enthusiastically "discovered" the Ballet russe. These were the years before the First World War when Jean Cocteau was in his early twenties, and had published only three books of small verse: *La Lampe d'Aladin* (1909), *Le Prince frivole* (1910), *La Danse de Sophocle* (1912)—he was to renounce all three subsequently. But a part of his early life which he did not renounce was his love for the circus and for the theater whose dramatic rite his family and family friends

nurtured. It was predictable that Cocteau's poetry would ultimately find a theatrical projection such as *Parade.*

Jean Cocteau has consigned to the pages of *Le Théâtre et la
danse* (July 1939) what he considers to be an important occurrence: Diaghilev's withholding praise and telling him, in 1912,
"Surprise me." Cocteau thus found himself challenged by an
esthetics whose scope and whose limitations Apollinaire had
already experienced. In *Parade,* Cocteau's use of cubist back-
drops and costumes was supposed to implement this bias. As
in *Les Mamelles de Tirésias,* the fusion of artistic entities
could not be effected satisfactorily and as a result the viability
of the play was jeopardized in the same fashion as was that of
Apollinaire. Margaret Crosland (*Jean Cocteau,* 1955) says that
the fair barkers, "Who were practically built into their square
costumes and must have looked more like walking pieces of
machinery or robots than anything else, merely made people
laugh." The public remained detached from the unfamiliar experience, laughed—evidently uncomprehendingly—and *Parade*
flopped.

And yet, his dictum of "surprise" notwithstanding, Cocteau
had attempted to cajole the public. The man who was defining
himself at the time in the words "Je suis Parisien, je parle
parisien, je prononce parisien" (*Le Potomak,* 1919), had given
his very public the combination of entertainments that had
most pleased him and that had met with most favor in that
same Paris: the circus (or music-hall) and the ballet—entertainment whose fun, color, and rhythm contributed to make
it a generally joyful experience. Moreover, this joy was the
essence of the poetry he conceived. In 1919, speaking of Max
Jacob in whose footsteps he found himself at the time, he had
written in his *Paris-Midi* column:

Inventors have fun. Often, a game, a prank [*une farce*] might be the source of the Attractive New. The public gets angry. [. . .] Poetry is one huge pun. The poet associates, dissociates, turns the syllables of the world inside out. But few people know it. Few people are supple enough to hop from one plane to another and to follow the lightning-swift game of connections.

The metaphysical implications of the "world" were hardly apparent in *Parade,* though a hint of these, and Cocteau's first "writing" for the theater, is seen in the little American girl and in the nostalgic aura she drew with her. The character was supposed to "vibrate" in imitation of the early movies, and distant echoes—the call of ships' sirens, planes, typewriters, Morse code—backed up Erik Satie's score. Cocteau regarded these inserts as cubist *collage* upon the canvas of his experiment, and to that extent, the innovation might have been translatable as "surprise." But if this was the case, the surprise was not to imply more than the grateful acknowledgment by the audience of familiar elements within the customarily specialized and hence detached figures of the dance. This was still a bribing of the audience—Molière's *plaire* in an idiom peculiar to this moment of the twentieth century. However, all such "gestures of life" failed to entice the public just as had the esthetic attempt. Whatever revolution Cocteau had operated went not so much against the substance of any genre as against aspects of form. And he erred in not realizing that the genres upon which he chose to experiment were essentially arts of form, so that the public could only be dismayed at not recognizing them in their habitual shape.

Three years later *Le Bœuf sur le toit* confirmed the close juxtaposition that existed in the author's mind between art and fun. Darius Milhaud had written a fantasia named after

a folk song and based on rhythms he had heard in Brazil during the war years. Much to Milhaud's dismay, Cocteau, after
he had borrowed the name, set his ballet in the Nothing-Doing
bar during United States prohibition days and turned it into
a "Farce." However, this had the effect of bringing the ballet
down to earth and increased its appeal, as did the sets by Raoul
Dufy and the performances of the Fratellini clowns; this time
the form was made more easily assimilable and the play enjoyed a fair success.

This measure of achievement encouraged Cocteau and his
following endeavor, *Les Mariés de la Tour Eiffel,* though its
score was written by Le Groupe des Six[1], added for the first
time a non-musical voice to its performers—that of two phono-
graphs at the sides of the stage. This device is reminiscent of
the megaphone in *Les Mamelles de Tirésias* and may have
served an intent similar to Apollinaire's; Cocteau was once
again attempting an experiment and his preface to the play
defines it:

With men like Serge de Diaghilev, Rolf de Maré, we see appearing little by little in France a theatrical genre that is not properly
speaking the ballet, and that does not fit the Opera, the Comic
Opera, or any of our *boulevard* stages. It is there, upon that border-
land, that the future is coming into shape.

The "Attractive New" was more sensed than defined. The
author was merely hopeful that from conventional worlds
he might free the wonderful potential: somewhere, Gide's "part
of God" must lurk; certainly it must within the flies over yet
unlit prosceniums. "That part, that escapes even the poet, has

[1] Six young French composers (Auric, Durey, Honegger, Poulenc,
Germaine Taillefer, Milhaud) for whom the equally young Cocteau
acted as a public relations man.

surprises in store for him [. . .]. The true symbol is never fore-seen. It comes into being by itself." And like Gordon Craig, "I am trying to substitute a 'poetry of the theater' for 'poetry in the theater'."

It is interesting to note that, once again, the genres from which this one departs do not credit the reality of the stage ac-tion but are all aspects of a surface variously fashioned for spe-cific ends: the ballet, the opera, the comic opera, the *boulevard* play do not claim to represent on stage a human being as such. Cocteau's experiment still consisted of working on appearances and his "poetry of the theater" was still a wholly visual projec-tion of poetry, a game for the eyes, in the manner of his first two attempts.

Pierre Dubourg (*Dramaturgie de Jean Cocteau,* 1954) com-plains that the public failed to understand the experiment and appreciated only the superficial farce. One can hardly blame the spectator who, when the curtain rose, found himself on the first landing of the Eiffel Tower, hearing the play's very first line spoken by a phonograph and seeing as the very first actor on stage an ostrich. Thereafter the action flowed with the speed of a series of free associations derived from inter-linking puns. The ostrich emerging from the camera of a photographer who had cautioned too long "Watch the birdie!" brought in its wake the photographer, a crazy wedding party, a hunter; in the ensuing confusion, every inane cliché of which the play was woven attained meaning by the incongruity of the situation ("Three o'clock! And that ostrich that won't come in"). Cocteau had merely achieved a successful rejuvena-tion of Labiche's *Chapeau de paille d'Italie:* there was little more to "understand" because little more had been said. The voice of the dramatist (and of the poet) remains in part sound and in part sense. The form had been successful to the point of discretion (Cocteau himself seems to have understood this in the commentaries he has consigned to *Le Secret professionel,* 1922); the spectator so appreciated the experiment that he failed even to notice it. As for content, Cocteau had not yet concerned himself with that.

Cocteau's *Roméo et Juliette* is further evidence of his concern to express only the scenic aspects of drama. Since 1918, he had in his files a rough, fairly idiomatic translation of Shakespeare's play which he had sketched as one might "Copy quickly, standing, in the museum, on a sketchpad, a well-known painting." The Count Etienne de Beaumont, at one of his *Soirées de Paris,* was going to enable Cocteau to make of that summary sketch, in 1924, a "Prétexte à mise en scène." From the flying prologue to the mobile forms of the sets whose stage machinery was concealed by blinding red footlights and a black velvet drop, the play was used to exploit scenic resources: these were the depositaries of its poetry. The actors—in black but for white plastrons, white gloves, and pale make-up—were actually figures in a choreography devised by the author. Cocteau also played Mercutio, and Roger Lannes (*Jean Cocteau,* 1948) says of the duel that it was "regulated like a Chinese staging." In a reflective dedicatory note to the Beaumonts, Cocteau recalls of the *décors,* costumes, etc., that "the slightest error would conceal the action and make it turn awry." If one considers the original text—Shakespeare's—Cocteau's words shed considerable light on his stage concepts at the time.

The curious gymnastics of the *précieux* are evoked by the artist who, in an effort at renewal, is determined to elicit admiration through surprise, thus using a mechanism of shock and detachment to attach, and who nevertheless depends on a me-

dium whose success demands the response (the identification)
of the subject attacked (*frappé*). The type of shock that cul-
minates in *Roméo et Juliette* is more of the sort that Louis
XIV's entertainers attempted for their patron than that which
causes riots in the theater (though Margaret Crosland recalls
a fight when *Roméo et Juliette* opened, "with a noisy interrup-
tion by the surrealists"). But even if shock is not more than
spice for jaded appetites, the mechanism used to integrate the
spectator with the rite is still admiration rather than self-projection, distance rather than identification. The thought may
have given Cocteau pause. In 1922, with an adaptation of *Antigone,* and in 1925, with that of *Œdipe-roi,* he appears to be
seeking in the works of Sophocles a drama less dependent on
surfaces.

The script of these two dramas is once again one of "condensation" in the author's words, the original text has been
"flown over." There is little effort indicated beyond telling the
tale in few words. Gide was left feeling that this *Antigone*
had been dressed up with ultra-modern sauce and that it suffered as a result. The relatively unpretentious text would seem
to indicate that Gide's criticism bears upon the "tone" of the
play and the tone, even here, becomes more a function of the
stage than of the text. In 1927, the *décor,* that had been Picasso's
in the original production, featured what was eventually to be a
Cocteau hallmark: five huge plaster heads masking the chorus
pit. In addition, Cocteau notes that the participants wore semi-
transparent masks and that the costumes were slipped on over
black tights—"The over-all effect calling to mind a sordid and
regal carnival, a family of insects."

As for *Œdipe-roi,* Cocteau asked of the *décor* that its center
piece be a reclining statue, gilded and draped in red, to house

the chorus. The acting cast was not to be slighted, however: "Gaudy costumes, in gypsy style. Dark faces. Long hair." Ismène, it was suggested, might carry with her a little toy horse. Cocteau had not trusted Sophocles too far within his own realm.

Considering Cocteau's belief in the privileged insight of the poet and the dramatist's responsibility, his own drama was singularly airy, free from any but scenic conjuring, up to this point: the ambitious and clear-sighted statements of the theorist easily outdistanced the craftsman who did not give them full expression in practice. Already in 1924, the preface of *Les Mariés de la Tour Eiffel* notes the poet's gift of perception and urges the implementation of these rejuvenating powers:

The poet must remove objects and feelings from their veils and their haze; he must show them suddenly so naked, and with such speed, that man has scarcely time enough to recognize them. They strike him then with their youth, as if they had never become official oldsters.

Le Secret professionnel repeats the idea and this time extends its scope, claiming for the poet "occult power" and including, among the areas of the medium's perception, death: "The poet does not dream: he counts. But he walks upon quicksands and sometimes his leg sinks into death." That same year, Cocteau wrote *Orphée* (1926) which Henry Bidou was to call "a meditation on death."

At first glance, the plot, loosely that of the Greek myth, confirms Bidou's appreciation. Set in a present-day version of classic Thrace, it tells of the discovery by the renowned poet Orphée of a mysterious horse who taps out poetic messages from the beyond. One day, enthralled by the horse and its otherworldly transmissions, Orphée gives up his lofty and comfortable status. Eurydice, who fails to understand him, confides her woes to a mysterious glazier, Heurtebise, recognizable to readers of *Le Grand Ecart* (1923) and of *Opéra* (1925-27) as Cocteau's familiar angel. Eurydice is eventually slain by the leader of the Bacchantes whose club she had forsaken for the love of Orphée, who now sets out to find her in Hades with the aid of Heurtebise. Orphée is allowed to bring her back on the terms of the myth but a family squabble sends Eurydice back to hell for good. Meanwhile, the enraged Bacchantes descend upon Orphée and he accepts death at their hands to be reunited with his wife. The arrival of the police on the scene of the crime affords an amusing contrast between the prosaic seekers of evidence and the agencies of the unknown attended by Heurtebise. The latter, after diverting himself awhile, ascends to other spheres to rejoin the now inseparable Orphée and Eurydice.

The play is obviously jerky in spots: the killing of Eurydice, the squabble with Orphée that seals her doom, Orphée's subsequent change of heart, are the acts of people conforming more to a myth than to their own configuration. Orphée's final explanation to Heurtebise about why he must find Eurydice in death leaves his character muddled. "Life is hammering me, Heurtebise! It is accomplishing a masterpiece. I must endure its blows without understanding them." This either makes Eurydice a rather sinister character or it leaves Orphée in the concluding moments of the drama quite far from any sort of tragic realization: the fact is that neither had previously exhibited a character that might have lent credence to the epic gestures of the myth. The 1950 movie version sought to correct a number of those defects. It made the figure of Death fall in love with Orphée while, less plausibly, Heurtebise fell for Eurydice. But here, a more coherent Eurydice voluntarily returned to hell after her second chance, having understood that she can never regain the love of Orphée. The seeming point of the play is spoken by the princess—Orphée's Death—when Orphée is killed by the *avant-garde* faction of the poet Cégeste. Realizing that her love is in vain, she sacrifices it to the living: "A poet's Death must sacrifice itself to render him immortal"—since properly speaking, the great poet must remain death-less. The characters being what they are, it is, however, more easy to understand Heurtebise's final commentary upon the couple, "It was necessary to put them back into their dirty water," than to understand how such pedestrian promiscuity will yield the sublime immortality that had been promised.

Still, it was the film that enabled Cocteau to say: "I wanted to touch the gravest problems with a light hand and without philosophizing in a vacuum." How much of this turns to leger-demain and to what extent these delicate hands waft away the tragic is matter for analysis. Death is an elegant young lady in evening dress. She is kind enough to explain why: "But, my poor boy, if I were as people wish to see me, they would see me. And I must enter their world without being seen." More-over, her doors upon the living are mirrors: "Mirrors are the doors through which Death comes and goes [. . .] look at yourself throughout your lifetime in a mirror and you will see Death at work like bees in a glass hive." If this play is a medi-tation upon death, one wonders whether these witticisms and Death's effortless materialization do not elicit admiration over their cleverness more than they stir up anxiety over the mys-tery of the unfathomable: are not Cocteau's so-called "meta-physics" foiled by his general use of the pun? Moreover, was not the film a temptation because it yielded greater scope to the non-metaphysical, the scenic parts of the experiment? This temptation might indeed account for the whole segment of Cocteau's opus which he has called "writing of shadows and light" and which is properly his "cinematographic poetry." In the case of *Orphée* the transition seems especially indicated as, in addition to the instances already cited, the play demanded walking through mirrors, Heurtebise (named after an elevator trademark) and his feats of levitation, the severance of Orphée's head, and its speech when it is transformed into a piece of statuary—all tricks so much more reminiscent of the conjurer's craft and of stage machines than of a drama that must communicate its own inexorable necessity. Cocteau's stage tricks would have been as admirable with any text, but *Orphée*, even with these and its wit, does not offer people sufficiently real to receive the spectator's truth.

The first in a long list of plays that use the same device, *Orphée* raises the problem of modern dress in re-creations of classical drama. The author can plead a fairly obvious intention: the modern dress that clothes the old myth merely extends physically what the poet attempts spiritually—the rejuvenation of an immanent truth. Moreover, by contrast, the archaic vestment in a tale written by and for moderns would be burdensomely awkward. However, the virtue of truth is endurance while modernism can woo but for a period of time which it is the first to delimit. Apollinaire's notion of modernism as that of an eternally repeated attempt upon the unknown is quite different from the symbols of modernism which he is forced to use and which remain static markers of eternally receding ages: spiritual excitement may endure but its material correlatives are only temporal. The insistence on the modern prop thus becomes as burdensome as would be that upon the archaic; only the noncontingent will escape the passing of

modes. In a nonrealistic play such as *Orphée,* insistence upon
modern dress becomes the more suspect, especially in that it
opens upon Orphée's living room that "looks not a little like a
conjurer's parlor [. . .]. Even familiar objects have a curious air
about them" with, "squarely in the middle" (as usual), a kennel
housing a white horse (ever a toy symbol in Cocteau) whose
legs "very much resemble a man's legs." Here, the modern dress
is reminiscent of the little girl in *Parade* and of her new-world
sounds—just as it anticipates even greater efforts to deliberately
wrench the framework of the myth with *L'Eternel Retour*
(1944), Cocteau's motion-picture that brings Tristram and
Isolde down, not only to earth, but to a bar.

Still, a mirror that physically leads into the beyond or a
young girl that is Death redeem mirrors and young girls as
objects: their only sin is their now overwhelming presence as
objects which prevents their suggestion of either the beyond or
death. The virtues of *Orphée* send the critic back to Cocteau's
credos for closer reading to discover that the poet has in a sense
played fair. Has he ever claimed to do more than evoke a po-
ètry of objects? One of Cocteau's 1933 articles in the *Nouvelles
Littéraires* had said: "Those whom we follow hid the object
within the poetry. [. . .] Our role will be henceforth to hide the
poetry within the object." And when, in *Le Secret professionnel,* he had noted, "This is the function of poetry. It unveils in
the full sense of the word. It shows us, naked, in a light that
shakes off drowsiness, the surprising things around us that our
senses record mechanically," were not those "surprising things"
simply "a dog, a hackney, a house" which the naïve vision of
the poet had transmuted? Even thoughts acquired the non-
extensible attributes of objects: "Give a commonplace its proper
setting, clean it, scrub it, light it in such a way that its

youth will strike with the same freshness, the same gush that it had at its source and you will behave as a poet." The very notion of death into which "sometimes his leg sinks" is the sensuous evocation of a physical image. Objects, the material part of the stage, are indeed endowed with a life which Cocteau's people, attendants of the wonderwork, are denied.

But occasionally, an inspired form of stage expression pales words and transcends its own mechanics. Such is the one in *Orphée* that justifies its subtitle, *Tragédie en un acte et un intervalle*. Just before the first curtain, Orphée takes his leave from Heurtebise and departs for Hades. When he is gone, the mailman slips a letter under the door warning Orphée of the Bacchantes' ire. The curtain slowly falls. It rises immediately thereafter upon the same scene in which the postman is introducing the letter under the door and Orphée returns from Hades with Eurydice, astonished to find Heurtebise still there. Time thus rendered meaningless by otherworldly forces wafts a chill breath of the hereafter on the stage: an intangible concept has benefited from the poet's expression. The part of the game that is played with colored and insubstantial shells looks the more hollow by contrast.

A number of the random thoughts in *Le Mystère laïc* (1928) continues the call for "miracles." Cocteau was to spend the end of that year and the first part of the next in the clinic of Saint-Cloud for a cure: he had been taking dope. Claude Mauriac (*Jean Cocteau, ou La Vérité du mensonge,* 1945) cruelly stresses that even the poet's hallucinations were mechanically (or chemically) derived, thus breeding the experiment on sterile, intellectual ground: "He paints the supernatural with all his genius."

Cocteau's next full-sized play, *La Machine infernale* (written in 1932) takes up for the third time the Oedipus myth. From his first use of Sophocles' material in 1925, through the opera-oratorio *Oedipus-rex* (1927), interpretations of the myth have undergone a number of scenic elaborations, the most noteworthy of which is probably the figure of the sphinx that halts Oedipus before the Theban walls. Conceived as a young girl, the sphinx is first seen lost in a dream of love, pensively holding the jackal head of Anubis in her lap. Oedipus is a fatuous youngster whose only dream is the glory awaiting him beyond the walls. But the sphinx loves Oedipus and attempts to detain him, and to that end plays a veritable scenic ballet of transformations with the aid of Anubis. The effort breaks down because of the naïve conceit of Oedipus; he will carry off her useless effigy to his doom, over which the veiled figures of Nemesis and the leader of the dead now rise to preside. Two gods have been vouchsafed the magic of objects.

Machine infernale the play was to have been in that it illustrates the relentless working of the gods, but in fact the gods here descend from the stage machine that functions throughout, from the introductory ghost of Laius visible only to the spectators, to the reincarnation of Jocasta in death. Cocteau notes (*Maalesh,* 1949), that when he took the play on the road after the war, he spent the night adjusting lights—recalling his statement in the preface of *Les Mariés*: "The chief electrician, with his reflections, has often illuminated the play for me." The mystery of fate appears to have fascinated Cocteau especially because of the stage sleights that its dramatic representation allows. If these terms are accepted, *The Comedy of Errors* is likewise a commentary on fatality. Where the Greek audience relived a familiar myth through an inner view of Oedipus, Cocteau's public is similarly informed through the prefatory voice so that, in Anubis' words: "From his birth to his death, the life of Oedipus is spread flat." But this is only so that Cocteau's public might fully savor the magical way in which the stage will proceed to implement fate.

Like *Orphée,* the play is idiomatic and puns on the signifi-cance of the myth. Anubis warns the sphinx about Oedipus: "Many men are born blind and they do not notice it until the day when a whopping truth knocks their eyes out." The pun had been taken up early in the play to give a central property its meaning: Jocasta's brooch "that sticks in everyone's eye" makes rather light of Oedipus' final revelation. "Poetry" re-mains "one huge pun" but its flippancy does not always facili-tate Cocteau's interpretation, recalling instead the questionable puns of *Opéra* or the significance which he attributed to "L'ami Zamore de Madame du Barry" (*Opium,* 1930).

Jocasta's brooch is but a single item in her evil world of hos-tile and insidiously lithesome objects so very reminiscent of the surrealists: "The stairs hate me. The stairs, the clasps, the scarves. Yes! Yes! They hate me! They wish my death." An Isadora Duncan in more than one respect, this coquettish young queen with a foreign accent dies, with the literalness of Cocteau's vision, at the hands of a scarf that had long since left threatening imprints of fingers on her throat. In this theater of magical objects, fatality becomes their refusal to remain inani-mate, but in so doing, their very autonomy robs the living of their own gestures before the unknown: Jocasta's scarf and brooch mute the shepherd's message. Denied his own figures on stage, the spectator would credit these remarkably endowed objects if he could. As it is, he can only admire; in concealing poetry beneath the object, Cocteau again neglects the casings wherein the spectator was to have hidden.

This baroque drama, whose truth resides in its decorations, had little use for the sober vestments of the classical Greek myth: romance and fairy tales were more appropriate vehicles. *Les Chevaliers de la Table Ronde* (1937) and *Renaud et Armide* (1941) sought new expression for the magic, the first in the Arthurian legend, the second in Perrault's *contes*. The tricks remained, however, recognizable. The ghosts and the changing figures of *La Machine infernale* were tailor-made for Merlin's demoniacal helper Ginifer who reigns invisible on the stage of *Les Chevaliers de la Table Ronde* or becomes, in turn, every other member of the cast. In the same play, the figments of King Arthur's madness acquire visible proportions as had once the dream of Oedipus. When Dubourg says of *Les Chevaliers* that "It is the struggle between truth and lies, between what is real and what is false," his words are more acceptable in a scenic connotation than in an ontological one. In *Renaud et Armide*, Cocteau attempted still another poetical grafting— that of a seventeenth century mode of speech. The poetry of objects that so effortlessly dispossesses the immanent substance of beings could less easily dismiss this new insertion that was meant to give it a voice—confirmation anew that Cocteau's "poetry of the theater" was supposed to be seen, not heard.

Between the performance of *Les Chevaliers de la Table Ronde* and that of *Renaud et Armide,* three three-act plays of Cocteau were produced: *Les Parents terribles* (1938), *Les Monstres sacrés* (1940), *La Machine à écrire* (1941). Each offers a parenthetical comment on the author. *Les Monstres sacrés* marks the logical completion of a circle. The theatrical climate that had graced so many different worlds was now examined for its own sake. *Les Monstres sacrés* is a *Portrait d'une pièce,* a stage interlude about the stage: the rabbit has been replaced within the hat. *La Machine à écrire* was to have been a realistic slice of provincial life—an extravagant undertaking for the stage magician who had so often proclaimed his Parisian essence. He himself was to admit in *La Difficulté d'être* (1947): "*La Machine à écrire* is a disaster."

Dubourg does not appear to notice that when he says about *Les Parents terribles,* "It is the utter absence of wonders to which the public was growing accustomed," he is underlining an irreducible trait in Cocteau instead of pointing to an emancipation. Jarry's friends recall how, after his extravagant ways had once procured him an invitation to dinner, he appeared in neat dress and acted the subdued part of a proper guest during the entire evening: the withholding of an expected surprise is yet another way of surprising. *Les Parents terribles* can establish more valid claims to fame, especially in that, the objects having nearly vanished, the stage has been returned to its people. These people are the members of a family such as might have tenanted a Greek tragedy—or a *boulevard* comedy: heaped one upon the other are the weak father Georges, the possessive mother Yvonne, Aunt Léo whom the father did not marry, the son Michel who breaks away from the mother for the love of Madeleine who had long been Georges's mistress. The given names convey some of the stifling intimacy whose visual translation becomes the familiar untidy bedroom (which appeared in *La Machine infernale, Les Enfants terribles,* etc.). Here, for there are still some affinities to Cocteau's habitual style, the visual notions of order and disorder help establish the difference between worlds of which the people (Léo, Madeleine vs. Georges, Yvonne, Michel) are only excrescences. However, though these people remain mute before their fate, as had remained all their predecessors in Cocteau's dramas, their fate appears more plausible since there are fewer material properties to actuate it. Some critics, like Gabriel Marcel who believes the play to be a "bewildering exception" in Cocteau, have found *Les Parents terribles* to be the author's best: if it is, it has achieved that distinction by disguising its author's hallmark.

L'Aigle à deux têtes (1946) and *Bacchus* (1951) add elements to the picture without changing it. From its melodramatic complexity to its complacently decorative deaths on stage, *L'Aigle à deux têtes* is a Romantic drama. Critics were prompt to mention Victor Hugo upon its first performance, and, indeed, the play serves as a reminder that Cocteau's dramatic creed is not so very distant from that set forth in the preface to *Cromwell*. The climate of *L'Aigle à deux têtes* gives a particular saliency to the transposition of physical features, the lightning storm, the spectacular deaths, the monologue, whose Romanticism might have been less subject to detection in *La Machine infernale,* in *Les Parents terribles,* or in *La Voix humaine* (1930). Somewhat as in *Les Monstres sacrés,* fate is largely an agency of the stage. With an ingenuousness that is nearly a stepping out of character, the actress who is the queen demands a tragic or dramatic (the terms are not distinct) destiny. After an expectation of ten years, Cocteau furnishes that destiny in the person of Stanislas, the living replica of the dead king. The meanders of court intrigue and of the principals' love are jointly observed until the time when the queen, still manipulating destiny, angers Stanislas into taking a fatal dose of poison and stabbing her before he dies. It is unfortunate that protagonists who question their destiny for the very first time on Cocteau's boards should do so when that destiny has been, according to their own admission, so artificially elaborated—and in a genre known for self-searching, if overlong and somewhat superficial, speeches. The *décor* mutes the cry of its protagonists: their call is deprived of its anguish. In these surroundings, their apostrophes to fate sound like the lament of people hoping to acquire the glamor of Cocteau objects.

Bacchus, set in Germany during the Reformation, gets its name from the title given the individual who, in vintage time, was granted unchallenged rule during seven days of license. Hans, who has been biding his time, feigning madness, becomes, as Bacchus, the revolutionary force of goodness undisciplined. In this role he is pitted against the force of orderly good represented by the Church's envoy, the cardinal—a clever man with a tongue as nimble as Cocteau's very own. As his term expires, Hans has made sufficient enemies to dig his grave: the cardinal will speak of a spurious recantation to reclaim for the Church a dead body. Here, as in *Les Parents terribles,* are once again confronted the forces of order and disorder, of calculating good and of innocent good. No fundamental conflict opposes them: ironically, in this theater of surfaces, their difference too is one of surfaces. Cocteau, whatever the appearance of his people, has created only fundamentally "good" ones, even though like Madeleine in *Les Parents terribles,* they may have been able to say, "I am very amoral" (note the curious modifier of what is supposedly an absolute attribute). Cocteau's reminder contained in his *Journal* of *La Belle et la Bête* (1946), "This ferocious beast is not a bad creature," might well be placed as a commentary upon his entire opus for he has never allowed an internally disturbing presence to interfere with the interplay of his surfaces. The latter could thus assume freely any shape since, at worst, they only disguised a conventional and reassuring good. One is mindful of Cocteau's voice on the soundtrack alongside the tiresome and juvenile pranks of Paul and Elisabeth in *Les Enfants terribles* (1950) giving repeated assurance of their fundamental innocence though their insignificant acts result in death. This moral concern of Cocteau's, just like his continued experiment upon the aspect of things, is a peripheral concern that makes him lose sight of man whose essence must develop regardless of such considerations.

Cocteau's skillful shapes, that so well take the form of life, can imitate even tragedy—but in so doing, and to use his own expression, they can only become "sketches." Tragedy in Cocteau is literally an object lesson, never a live vortex into which the spectator might be drawn. The author, like his play, is too clever, too all-comprehending for genuine mystery to subsist. He therefore creates mystery synthetically, transferring the drama from the depth of the spectator's being to that of the stage. As he himself wished to be, Cocteau is a poet of objects, but when he talks of metaphysics he refers only to propositions whose tangible shape fascinates him at the expense of their substance. His luring of the spectator assumes that the spectator can be attracted only through externals—he ignores identification: thus his stage poetry or his morality.

Claude Mauriac notes (*La Vérité du mensonge*) that throughout his critical writing, Jean Cocteau "forestalls a necessary judgment by discrediting it." This is the whole strategy of comic self-consciousness. Similarly, Cocteau's plays discount the fallible human and focus upon the admirable object, a strategy that eliminates criticism of his drama by eliminating drama. Dubourg, Lannes, Maulnier have defended him against accusations of facetiousness but have insisted upon his right to laughter. Laughter may indeed afford the most legitimate drama, but the right that these critics defend for Cocteau is the right to build upon a single aspect of the theater, upon the show, which is also the aspect of other worlds (such as Cocteau's own beloved circuses, music-halls, etc.), while neglecting what is properly germane to only the theater—the dilemma of man. Heads that live, statues that kill, hands that create, ideas that acquire material shape, are masks more important than what they conceal. Properly, they belong to that domain of fantasy which the cinema might be if it, in its own way, were not likewise intent on imitating surfaces of life. *Le Sang d'un poète* (1932) is able to take the forms of simple thoughts and play with them visually through the hypnotic effect of the light and shade provided by the running film. Where Jarry had wished for only Madame Leprince de Beaumont's mirror, the cinema, in *La Belle et la Bête* (1945), allows entrance into that very mirror and can follow effortlessly, thereafter, the world of distorted shapes that it discovers. Throughout all of this, as before Cocteau's stage, the eye listens—the author has little need for the rest of the spectator. With Cocteau, the stage has been handsomely decorated but not as yet lived in.

2

Perils of Debate: Giraudoux

VICES ATTRIBUTED TO Cocteau—pliancy, cleverness, childishness, the love of mystification, egocentricity—are natural attributes of a born creature of the stage. Accusation on these counts might impugn the poet, the essayist, or the writer of novels; it falls more lightly on the man within the theater whose concerns are not what is moral or intellectual. If the spectator should be successfully drawn into the dramatic act, criticism is left with only secondary considerations, none of which can affect the act itself. Drama lives or dies in action—analysis remains external, retrospective, and confronts a mere memory. This is presumably what Jean Giraudoux means in *L'Impromptu de Paris* (1937)—that one-act play about the meaning of theater—when those who speak for him with most authority, Renoir and Jouvet, deny vigorously that theater can ever be "understood." Not the least irony about Giraudoux is that his own theater illustrates this belief in the manner that so frequently illuminated his metaphor: through absolute contrast.

Giraudoux came to the theater through the novel: *Siegfried et le Limousin* became *Siegfried* before the lights in 1928. The author was over forty-five and had been writing for better than twenty years: something of the novelist inevitably remained in the newborn dramatist—the more so in that the novelist had long been distinguished by a singular style. In all these years, the Giraudoux novel had been an article admitting of only restricted patronage, a flawless item, neoteric and elegant. Where the younger Cocteau and the older Apollinaire had composed hymns to new and tangible objects, the Giraudoux novel distilled the essence of newness. All in its vision was, by the very selection of that vision, by its definition, pristine and archetypal. The too assertive objects of Apollinaire were non-existent in Giraudoux's world, though deceptive emanations usually assumed conventional shapes and names for more subtle trickery.

The elemental parts of these novels were new not only because they were sunrise, youth, and springtime—the harshly jealous first loves, the young girls, the virgin islands—but because even the seeming likeness of what is commonly symbol of the new was here the projection of a private and exclusive image. This godlike vision is a part of the poetic mechanism referred to by Cocteau when he suggested that the poet's gift rejuvenate the hackneyed—or, more precisely, that his gift make the hackney, the dog and the house suddenly become themselves. But Giraudoux's newness is of another sort and the hackney, the dog or the house which he produces will be "themselves" not because a gifted poet has removed them for a brilliant moment from a habit-dulled world, but because they are the unique furniture of another world—Giraudoux's. The hackney, dog and house of that world might fleetingly suggest earthly counterparts, but at a closer glance they will appear quite alien to and utterly unfit for any but the world to which they belong.

Giraudoux's is an assimilative genius. He refused Cocteau's definition according to which the poet is the one who illuminates the object; he believes instead that the object is to be absorbed so that, transformed, it might illuminate the poet. The poet's gift to objects thus becomes an autocratic gesture: in choosing an object, he grants it its first birth and its single meaning and these in turn deny the birth and meaning of replicas that might have made the poet's world accessible. In this inversion of the Platonic hierarchy, false copies as the world knows them are forever made to vanish before the insolent original.

The object, that living and glamorous inhabitant of Cocteau's stage, assumes human shape in Giraudoux's novels. Since archetypes are removed by definition from contingencies and conflicts that might impair their essence, they must participate for better or for worse of the object's permanence. The life in the Cocteau object was its human frailty; the object that stifles the life in the Giraudoux human is that human's impassive perfection. Where Crusoe discovers Friday, that necessary externalization of a life too long pent up, the heroine of *Suzanne et le Pacifique* (1921) discovers a corpse. And that corpse is to be "exhausted like a newspaper": the heroine-object extends her being intellectually; no sense of death allows that this might be anything more than the exhausting of a newspaper.

Such intellectual extension is typically a function of the object: it is the object's way of growing. It does not mean that the object will become symbol, that it will give way to an immanent idea. In *Siegfried et le Limousin* (1922), the absence of Germany creates the same feeling as might the absence of bristles on the right side of a dog's nose: the simile offends neither dogs nor Germany, since all have equal value in this world of incomparable archetypes. Eglantine, in the novel to which she gives her name, must choose between Moïse and

Fontranges. This has been taken to mean that East and West are being contrasted. Commentators have inferred from Eglantine's choice of Fontranges that Giraudoux espouses Western ideals. It will be recalled that Eglantine's decision is determined by the differences inherent in two ways of tossing salad. Elementary gestures of this kind might indeed convey a difference to the imaginative beholder. The reader, however, is hard put to make these trivial instances sustain the significance with which he must constantly bolster them if he is not to believe that they have been deliberately selected to mock significance; he must exercise equal parts of gullibility, good will, and nimbleness to keep the tenuous texture from disintegrating. In the author's *Amphitryon 38,* the trumpeter has but a single note, but he assures whoever will hear him that he plays entire and varied gamuts before this perennial conclusion: it is only the good will of his listeners that can bring to life these silent symphonies.

The psychology of archetypes derives from the skill with which a clever author can intermix them while preserving their unaffected identity even as he preserves an illusion of life. Giraudoux is a game and witty gambler: any datum is acceptable to him. Chance or the consequence of an unconsidered fillip proposes one arrangement out of an infinite number of possibilities through which Giraudoux proceeds to maneuver his characters, seeing to it that each emerges unscathed. Alcmène says of Amphitryon, "My husband can be Jupiter for me. Jupiter cannot be my husband" and the evidence that contradicts her words gives point to what she is saying—while it also proves how utterly reversible such propositions are. One situation is as good as another: the elegance of preserving unchanging and flawless performers in every sort of pattern is all. This game might well be a very pure art: at least one commentator (Maurice Bourdet: *Jean Giraudoux, son œuvre,* 1928) saw it as classicism.

Withal, the elegance of the dextrous performer is matched by the elegance of the language. Giraudoux had said of the French novel that it remains epic poetry (F. Lefèvre, in *Les Nouvelles Littéraires,* 1926). At times, an insidious thought suggests that just as a clever mind is tampering with what appears to be a pattern of life, the clever word is likewise assuming what looked like flesh and blood. Actions and words more than occasionally seem to exist especially because of their musical or rhythmic value. When this suspicion is verified, the author is discovered contributing to the postulated detachment of his creatures through his own. This ultimate posture follows logically from the nature of objects whose substance remains so constantly in danger of alteration through contact, but it renders even more difficult the apprehension of the singular object. Eventually, mere sound must be granted meaning if a purely verbal game is to be avoided, if the reader is to confront more than a poetic rhythm or a series of empty puns. Claude-Edmonde Magny (*Précieux Giraudoux,* 1945) recalls the episode in *Bella* (1926) when the prosaic "café-filtre," ordered by the narrator in imitation of a gesture by the woman he loves, must acquire the full extension proposed by its homonymy: "We were moving out of the realm of food to enter into that of philters." Such strain imperils these word-created figments ever in danger of reverting to mere words. Victor-Henry Debidour (*Jean Giraudoux,* 1955) comments: "It often happens that Giraudoux starts by tossing a surprisingly accurate ball, and ends up, without anyone quite understanding how, by juggling with soap bubbles." At those moments, language engulfs not only the illusion of the flesh but even the construct that had simulated life. It is then that the author is heard laughing, and that laughter will be the only one to ring out in this world whose creatures have no laughter, lacking as they are in the faculties that might commit them or in any way alloy their substance. It will remain to be shown why frowns, which for identical reasons cannot exist here, are likewise the author's.

In Giraudoux's *précieux* existentialism, the expectation of a god is constantly frustrated by the appearance of a man— though none of this is ever about a man. The archetype executes serenely immutable gestures that deny as they recall them the gestures of men. The central figure in *Juliette au pays des hommes* (1924) knifes the one assaulting her; but this man meant to give her up and Juliette does not kill him: the incident has preluded their friendship. There is no blood in the knifing; there had been little of the flesh in the assault. These first ideas of things act out only pantomimes of life. Suzanne remembers that as a girl she burned holly over a candle in order to get the exact smell of opium: this is a world in which every savor of life is only imitated. Landscapes are functional, for they are merely dotted with the exotic notations that will give form to a young girl's concept of exoticism (*Suzanne et le Pacifique*), or with French provincial traits that must redefine a victim of amnesia whose memory will become French (*Siefried et le Limousin*). Such landscapes are quintessences of the tropics or of the Limousin but have no single trait of their own by which they might be distinguished elsewhere than in the circular mechanism that creates them even as they create their specialized indweller. And likewise, the ideas bred on such ground exist only inasmuch as they are informed by it and reflect nearly tangibly their speaker and his province. Countryside accepted as French bespeaks France, and, as its topography and that of the one raised on it allow, nationalism and war. But even if war and nationalism should be suggested, it is evident that in this world, neither can ever be more than a question of landscape.

THE NOVEL, as conceived by Giraudoux, coincided in more than one aspect with that other play form, *the* play—while also containing many of the congenital weaknesses from which plays die.

Among the more striking affinities was the author's inability to create a character that could be termed "common." The archetype is by nature a dramatic creation in the word's every sense. The stage character lives too brief and too specialized a life to be anything less than utter purpose in the area for which he is created. Giraudoux's objects, from his people to his landscapes, were strongly committed to this kind of artistic dedication. Their constant concern to be the original model of all things approximated the design of the stage figure that must achieve, though for utterly dissimilar reasons, a similar uniqueness. Giraudoux appears to have realized to a certain extent that the life of the theater derives from an assimilative act by which a universal masque on stage allows the re-creation of an original model according to the individual's vision. In *L'Impromptu de Paris,* the critics had been chided as a race for refusing the gift of themselves to these symbols:

In brief, it [the public] loves. But it does not love selfishly, narrowly. Motionless, relaxed, it loves as God can love when it falls to his lot to observe through a hole suddenly opened in the clouds, the play of some wretched or magnificent creatures. [. . .] But they [the critics], on the contrary, have stiffened themselves once the curtain is up, have isolated themselves out of conscience, out of a mistrust of themselves that has become a mistrust of the play.

But if Giraudoux intended his creatures to be reborn in this godlike love, it follows that some change must have been effected in the distant and merely admirable objects of his novels. The archetype must undergo debasement—humanizing —if it is to change from detached exemplar to universal mold. Although both are alike in form, the first is created immutably unique; the second becomes so only after contamination. Although both are conceived as lifeless prototypes, the first exists as such, preserved from the contact from which the second will draw life. The test of Giraudoux's ability to create a play thus becomes largely that of his ability to make of universals that endure through isolation universals that will endure through intimate association.

The first of Giraudoux's plays proposes a man, Siegfried. The physical shape of the play, when contrasted with the novel gives evidence of an initial trimming. Automatically lost in the stage transference is the discursive presence of the author as such. This is noteworthy only to the extent that analysis will be left to participants in the action. It does not follow necessarily that delineation of these participants will be affected otherwise.

Contrast of the novel's first pages with the first scenes of the play shows a more significant difference. Set in Siegfried's home, the action is evidently to be his, rather than that of the narrator Robineau for whom the novel's Siegfried had remained pretty much of an object. The audience is to learn only gradually that Robineau and Geneviève, who was Jacques Forestier's fiancée before he became Siegfried, are here in response to the call of Zelten, Siegfried's romantic enemy and anti-type. The play opens upon the world of Siegfried, a powerful man in the affairs of Germany, but one who had been discovered naked and amnesic upon a World War I battlefield seven years before and who is still seeking his identity—visually conceived in these first scenes as a handful of prospective parents.

From these premises, the play is free to develop along either of two distinct lines. What follows will be the story of a man grappling with the definition of his being in order that either a man or a problem might be elaborated. The ultimate symbolism of Siegfried is important because it must determine what part of the audience will be encouraged; whether that audience will be made up of critics or of spectators as defined by Giraudoux. If the man Siegfried is eclipsed by the problem —a discussion of nationalisms—the debate is best judged or entered into by the critic, the one who contributes only his intelligence to the play. If, on the other hand, the problem is that of a man, and also, since Geneviève is present as well, that of lovers, the godlike love invoked by Giraudoux will be needed to inform this love, as it must inform this man if he will be the magnificent or wretched creature of whom the author has spoken.

Certainly, Giraudoux, the witty author, has not removed himself completely from these scenes. The place is Gotha, and Gotha is a familiar absolute, a point on an eleven hundred and fifty kilometer radius from Paris, not to be confused with another point upon that same circumference, Nice. This tells very little about Gotha and scarcely more about the play. But it does not jeopardize the play as yet inasmuch as it does not jeopardize its people.

The prospective parents are, however, people, and of these, Jacques Houlet (*Le Théâtre de Jean Giraudoux,* 1945) has said: "Pity for those who are of humble stature—who would believe it—that feeling so seldom noted in our author, here casts a glimmer." Pity, since before Aristotle, has been recognized among the principal forces that might help in effecting the necessary contamination that shapes the dramatic experience; a dramatist is ill-advised to give it up lightly. Houlet bases his evidence on a line spoken by one of the prospective parents, a Mrs. Patchkoffer (how much attention should be paid to the name, that will be woven into the dialogue?):

> The mother of a soldier who has disappeared, and who will attempt to recognize her child in Siegfried, tells the valet who has pointed out to her that the picture of her son does not resemble Siegfried:
> "If he had not changed, he would have been found already. . . ."
> A few words, and the invincible hope of a poor old mother is brought forth.

Even without Houlet's pathos, Mrs. Patchkoffer's line might indeed have conveyed the feelings that he mentions: those of human beings. However, here is the scene in which that particular line is the climax:

MUCK: I wrote to you, Mrs. Patchkoffer! It appeared to me that there was not too much sense in your journey here. You said in your letter that your son is short and dark. Mr. Siegfried is tall and blond.

MRS. PATCHKOFFER: We have already seen dark ones in Berlin, at the re-education clinic.

MR. KELLER: But the size, Madam?

MRS. PATCHKOFFER: We've seen all the short ones too, haven't we, Patchkoffer?

MUCK: All right, all right.

MRS. PATCHKOFFER: If he had not changed, he would have been
found already. . . .

Mrs. Patchkoffer's obstinacy appears to be more the blindness
of a comic character than that of an invincibly hopeful mother.
The parents are being mocked: they are still prototypes,
but because the events about them have been allowed a superior
validity, their stubborn refusal to comprehend these events
makes them ridiculous.

The laughter at Siegfried's parents establishes an initial detachment from Siegfried the human being. And when the
romantic Zelten, who represents the Niebelungen side of Germany; when General de Fontgelois, who represents the prot-
estant and militaristic aspect of Germany; when half a dozen
accessory characters have been presented, from prototypical
Schupos to prototypical generals, each of whom defines himself and Germany as glibly, as wittily, as arbitrarily, and as
superficially as Suzanne had defined in a sprinkling of sentences a sprinkling of countries from around the world, it
becomes evident that Siegfried himself—he who wrests the
name of Niebelung by right of might—will be, at best, a character thrown into an intellectual game.

Before Siegfried stands Geneviève, the first of those who are
to become the celebrated *jeunes filles* of Giraudoux's stage.
She has not been told why she was coming to Germany and
her dramatic sin derives from the difficulty which the spectator
will have deciding, after the fullest knowledge that the play
allows of her, whether or not she would have undertaken the
journey had she been told of its object. Debidour (*Jean Giraudoux*) has noted about Giraudoux's *jeunes filles*: "Sensuality
in Giraudoux is not sexual: it is made of a readiness for, and
a surrender to, all the caresses and embraces of the world,

amongst which, for a woman, that of the male is but one amidst the rest, the most wished for, the most feared—the most superficial too, perhaps." The sexuality of the woman on stage defines the many shades of her being; lacking that sexuality, she becomes an object of intellectual apprehension. Her own apprehension of the world, and the spectator's through her, must be similarly the embrace of her particular sexuality. That sexuality is lacking in Geneviève. Her tenderness for Siegfried—"Siegfried, I love you!" are her very last words, but *only* her very last—must be inferred rather than heard, assumed rather than felt. The words of this girl, of this fiancée, of this lover, combine their clever play with those conveying, in parallel fashion and without discrimination, epigrammatic thoughts about fatherland, French verbs, and war. Her words are part of the monotone—words such as issue indifferently from the tipstaff Muck, from the generals (Waldorf and Ledinger serve no purpose in this play but to debate), or from Zelten, in veritable tirades. Giraudoux's language, as fluent and light as it is precise, spins images that are philosophical propositions or skillful representations of emotions, without ever distinguishing characters that speak them with a common voice. These images of feelings, of philosophy, become a poetry about the notion of such terms, but they are never better than a semi-transcendency, for no more than the people who utter them are the feelings or the thoughts themselves ever implicated. Amidst these, Geneviève's voice and sentiments are scarcely distinguishable. If something is noted about her, it will be that she is rather too cold for a woman who has long lost the man she loved and who now recognizes him while he fails to recognize her; conceived as a fiancée who will have to lead herself and her lover to the discovery of their former selves, this young woman is rather too self-possessed for being able to conform so well to the general game.

Siegfried's dramatic failing is the same. The man who for seven years has continued alone the search for himself, will give of amnesia and of his regrets only witty definitions ("East and West will, I imagine, permute about me"), free from even an echo of anxiety—as once Cocteau, with death. Siegfried will be sad truly (Giraudoux's men are ever less perfect than his women) but only a single time and only briefly, and it will not deface his dramatic epitaph, the lesson which he is given to speak about the coexistence of nations in what remains a speculative and moral play.

FOR ALL his gifts and experience as a novelist, the author of *Siegfried* is a man still new to the theater. Never again will Giraudoux allow so explicit a moral to edge a play out of its dramatic bounds. *Siegfried* might thus be viewed more as an indication of biases which the novelist carries with him onto the stage than as a fair example of his ability to give substance to what will be dramatic theories nearly ten years later—all ten of these years having been spent in active theater work.

Two years after *L'Impromptu,* Jouvet's troupe gave *Ondine,* the last original performance in Paris of a Giraudoux play during the author's lifetime. The theme of flesh and fantasy, one not new to Giraudoux, was especially fitted to that which *L'Impromptu* had hoped the theater might achieve for the spectator:

We give this worn-out slave [the spectator] all-powerful rule over colors, sounds, and airs. We give this automaton a heart of flesh with all of its compartments properly inspected, with generosity, with tenderness, with hope. We turn him into someone responsive, handsome, omnipotent.

In the person of Ondine, a delicate figure was attempted, one free from the coarse and mortal bulk of man: a figure meant to replenish in the worn-out spectator (not in the critic, certainly) what he was lacking in spiritual and poetic values. Ondine was given a duet to act out with the knight Hans von Wittenstein zu Wittenstein (Giraudoux's own coinage), the pathetically earthbound man who stumbles momentarily and hopelessly into Ondine's realm. At the death of Hans, at the airy departure of Ondine, the spectator was to be left with the regret that those privileged moments are not for man, though he will be elevated by having been drawn into them awhile and comforted in the knowledge that somewhere, such transcendental worlds endure unsullied.

Ondine has been designed as a functional figure of candor. Not only does she speak her mind from the moment of her very first appearance, and on every occasion thereafter (such occasions as will cause, for example, her unpleasant words at court), but she can also read other people's minds: spiritually and physically, little in her allows the play of nuances. She is not a simply decorative or simply suggestive figure: she has a definite use. And so has Hans, called "stupid" a sufficient number of times to afford clear understanding of his spiritual nature; Hans who is drawn in physical conformity to this spiritual portrait, plodding, heavily weighed down by armor: "it takes me ten minutes to unscrew the shoulders alone." In a play whose poetic structure is so clearly defined, the characters will have to exert great care not to burden its texture. Rather than upon Ondine and Hans, it is upon the exquisiteness of the first and the defeat of the second that must be spun the web within which will be caught the spectator's dream and his mourning. And yet, it is on this delicate structure that Giraudoux allows his intelligent and facetious demon to begin his work of destruction.

The water image, which together with that of nakedness so often adumbrates the virginal symbols in Giraudoux, becomes the occasion for a number of puns with little more justification than the immediate laughter which they elicit and the superficial nature of the heroine. Such fun hampers the play, calling attention to its surfaces rather than to its substance: if Ondine is merely amphibious, her accomplishments are limited indeed. The meaningful image, as once before the obliterating snow about the amnesic Siegfried, has been willfully lost. When the illusionist causes time to fly, he serves a dramatic purpose; when he fails in his tricks (as he does in II. ii), he achieves laughter at the expense of a thought that was to have been credited for the progress of the play. Such stepping out of character removes a character from the play and leaves instead a shell.

The flippancy of its form slowly infects the substance of the play. Quirks that once marked the novels are still apparent. Characteristics become as effortlessly malleable as the images themselves: undines are deathless when such a definition is needed (as befits especially the heroine: "I am fifteen years old. And I was born centuries ago. And I shall never die") but there are skulls of dead undines a moment later (II. xi) to suit a different image (quite inverting the legend that renders mortal only the watersprite who marries a mortal). And as in the novels, the witty author is ready to juggle with any combination of facts, no matter from what direction they might be tossed at him: when the notion of faithlessness is detected by Yseult in a tribe of undines who utterly ignore the concept, a slip that could have been eliminated without loss to the action is allowed to remain so that, detected by the author and played with in the usual way, it might evidence an additional, gratuitous sleight of mind.

Ondine herself is the ultimate negation of the play. The spiritual figure meant as a symbolic contrast to the earthbound knight, the young girl of whom the author's spokesman, Yseult, says that she is "transparency," that elfin spirit too often disappears because of leaden attributes meant to signify her etherealness. Any material representation of transparency would seem like an exercise perilous enough under optimum conditions, and the image of childhood chosen by Giraudoux is hardly auspicious, for though it is one of candor, naïveté, frankness, and virginity, its opaque areas are easily revealed and in those moments, Ondine sounds rude rather than outspoken, self-willed rather than straightforward, querulous rather than perceptive, spoiled rather than tragic.

Ondine also represents the frowning side of Giraudoux, an instance of his failure to draw the pristine young creatures that have been said to be his hallmark. Geneviève, who was created merely a woman, might have been diminished by human flaws, diminished especially by an inherent harshness more typical of humans than of their ideal image. But Ondine was not created human precisely in order that she might not suffer from any such impairment. And yet, there is a disturbing resemblance between these two women. The harshness of Geneviève was, in fact, not due to human traits but rather to defects that can be found in Ondine as well. It is their nonhuman birth that conditions these creatures, for Geneviève and Ondine alike achieve their being through preservation from the contact of humans and of their emotions. The last words of Geneviève have been noted for their curious ring. The last words of Ondine, whose memories of Hans disappear with his death—"What a pity! How I would have loved him!"—do not suggest the oppressiveness of regret as much as they reflect an airiness that corresponds to the underlying indifference of the woman throughout the play.

Because they are prototypes, these creatures are twice fashioned by the dramatist's irritation. The indifference to the world that gives them their inner shape reveals by contrast the unpleasantness of the less perfect world from which they are set apart. But the outer shape which they take—that of women in this case—shapes in turn the physical immediacy of that world and it is they, in their present disguise, who suffer the author's resentment. Figures of revolt, Giraudoux's women are marked by the author's resentment at least as much as they mark it.

The image of revolt squares poorly with that of transparency, since the first effects a demonstration which must be an immanence in the second. It squares even less if one considers that the figure of revolt demands a commitment which the author's economy of human emotions does not allow these personages; their ironic fate will be to die from the contact of the author who had designed them to live only while free from every contact. In *Intermezzo* (1933), an earlier incarnation of Ondine had fared better for having been less of a physical presence and so withdrawing more successfully from the author, while allowing, by the same token, that a more obtrusive outer world absorb what shafts the author still intended. A ghost provided the symbol of aspiration and the note of contrasting purity: the symbol was maintained in satisfactory transparency at the physical as well as at the spiritual level. Moreover, Isabelle's affair with the specter was rendered evident especially through its effect on the small town. In this manner, the principals remained nearly wholly spiritual, the action concerning itself mainly with their tangible shadow. Even when Isabelle was forcibly removed from the specter's embrace and fell into a deep swoon as a result, her smelling salts were again the small town gathered about her, in essence this time, through the sounds of its municipal band, of its card-playing café patrons, its squabbling old maids, its mildly pompous officials. Whatever this symbolic recovery of her senses made of Isabelle, her return to pedestrian realms was not a tragedy: the author had not created characters sufficiently earthy or important to draw his ire. The spokesman for the callous side, the inspector, was allowed to speak the mildly optimistic conclusion: "The Isabelle incident is closed. The Luce incident will not occur for another three or four years."

In *Intermezzo,* the body of the protagonists is the small town: the town can safely die, for as a masque, it allows the idea of the protagonists to live on. If Isabelle had not been so easily brought back to life, Giraudoux might have written a tragedy. In three plays, *Judith* (1931), the only drama of his that is called "tragedy," *Electre* (1937), and *Sodome et Gomorrhe* (1943), Giraudoux gives evidence of having wished to preserve the viability and the significance of his protagonists.

IN EPIGRAPH to a demonstration of Giraudoux's tragic vein, Bert M-P. Leefmans (*The Kenyon Review,* 1954), quotes the following from Giraudoux's *Visitations,* written in 1942:

Epochs are in good order only if, in those radiant confessionals which are its theatres and arenas, the crowd comes, and in so far as possible in its most dazzling confessional dress, in order to augment their solemnity, to listen to its own avowals of cowardice and sacrifice, of hate and of adoration. And if it cries also, "Bring on the Prophet!" For there is no theatre without divination. Not that factitious divination which gives names and dates, but the real, which reveals to men these surprising truths: that the living must live, that the living must die, that autumn follows after summer, spring after winter, that there are the four elements, and happiness, and billions of catastrophes, that life is a reality, that it is a dream, that man lives by peace, that man lives by blood, in brief, what they will never know. . .

Cocteau had shown long since that divination can be a shallow word and that only the extent and nature of the divination are of any consequence. The poet's truths will always be, to a degree, "surprising"—even if they are merely semantic—but the adjective is apt to define the poet more than his vision unless that vision indeed transcends the commoner sort. Until the writing of his tragedy, Giraudoux had shown especially that the living must die, a proposition more airy than the proposition that states that they must live; that life is a dream, and far less that life is a reality; "what they will never know" and never "*that* they will never know." *L'Impromptu de Paris* spoke about what might be *given* to the spectator to make him more complete—little was ever said about what might be removed from him to make him greater. Heretofore, the highest aspirations suggested by Giraudoux derived their charm from a foreknowledge of the failure to which they were doomed. Within these delicate spheres lit by ideal objects and darkened only by the implication of the shadow which they cast upon the real world, the terms of life and death were emptied of that weight without which aspirations lost cannot truly define the loser. The stubborness of tragedy derives from the fact that it postulates only the irresoluble. That is why its stage figures demand from the spectator that part of him that cannot be solaced. Short of such despair, the loss can be contemplated and that very contemplation, as Giraudoux had proved, might not be unpleasant. The dramatic transposition of these terms is a theater of poetic states: its most sublime and lingering queries last two and a half hours. Such drama is self-contained; it answers all its own questions. It evokes not despair, but despondency; its cast is not one of people but of dreams.

To make a tragedy of *Judith,* Giraudoux had to transform the usual elements of his cast no less than the original material itself. The aprocryphal Book of Judith is a song of triumph: the heroine slays Nebuchadrezzar's general Holophernes and gives the embattled Jews of Bethulia victory over the Assyrian troops. The episode ends on Judith's song of praise and the promise of rejoicing.

Giraudoux's Judith will not be a virtuous widow. Juxtaposing the notion of his own world and the notion of tragedy that demands contamination of its figures such as will render them accessible to the spectator, Giraudoux allows a *jeune fille* of his to become a human being. However, since this act of contamination must also become the upward movement of the tragedy, certain of the usual data have been modified. The *jeune fille* Judith is deliberately shown in her beauty and pride to be an unaccomplished quantity. Her flirtation with life has not preserved, as it would have formerly, a unique splendor: nearly the opposite is suggested by the contrasting figure of the soldier Jean, who might have loved her. Her virginity is an emptiness: no more than a vague longing. The angel of God will tell her eventually, "Love has indeed been drawn across this drama. But not by you. By Suzanne." And though at that moment the words are tragically ironic, they serve to distinguish the young girl before her ultimate glory from another young girl who very nearly resembles Judith.

It is not Holophernes who will be Judith's antagonist but the high priest Joachim, and the one whom he serves. She is warned early enough by joseph, the usual mouthpiece who circulates through Giraudoux's plays:

JOSEPH: Beware of Joachim, my little Judith, I beg of you. . .
JOACHIM: There is no Joachim here. There is God. . .
JOSEPH: Beware of God, Judith. . .

Judith accepts the mission out of pride, but from the moment she enters the enemy camp, the contamination by that which is human will begin. In its fullness, the figure of Holophernes reveals to Judith for the first time the immensity of the desert which has been her life: he gives shape and consistence to all of her most tenuous cravings, the germs of her salvation. Echoing the original legend and the undertone of the drama, Holophernes can rightly identify himself as the "enemy of God":

Within these thirty square feet. It is one of those uncommon areas of mankind that are truly free. The gods infest our poor universe, Judith. From Greece to the Indies, from the North to the South, there is not a country upon which they do not swarm, each with his vices, with his odors. . . . The air of the world for the one who likes to breathe is that of a barracksful of gods' bunkbeds. . . But there are still some places that are out of bounds to them; I alone can see them. They subsist upon the plain or mountainside like spots of earthly paradise. The insects that inhabit them are not tainted by the original sin of insects: I pitch my tent upon them. . .

The love of Judith for Holophernes is the first stage in the transformation of Judith, *la jeune fille à la mode,* into the woman Judith. Her life henceforth—the triumph in the legend—will become the mechanism of the tragedy. The magnificence of the moment, Judith's archetypal love, cannot endure by virtue of its mere statement: Judith is no longer a *jeune fille* living as these once did in a world that was the creation of their irradiance. Only death can prevent the decay of what is fleetingly sublime. Judith kills Holophernes, but according to the terms of the fable, does not kill herself. This will enable the angel of God, in the body of a drunken soldier, to impart the lesson to Judith: the entire action was performed within the palm of God. Even this love had been a simple instrument fitted to His own purpose. The vindication to which Judith aspired is nothing: a human being has been canceled.

This is black tragedy, for whereas death in classical tragedy affords the apprehension of latent though unachieved values, Judith lives to see her significance eradicated. The author will thus allow her, that the play might not be pointless in its finality, to "hide away" within the drunken guard the assertion of her truth that makes a liar out of God. And the voice of the angel within that soldier will also allow Judith to know, "if your sorrow can be lightened thereby," that in the eyes of a spirit now fallen for having so believed, the name of Judith will remain one of tenderness.

In that Judith does become a human being, Giraudoux has succeeded in writing a tragedy. When in *Amphitryon 38* (1929), the same adventure had befallen a *jeune fille* that could not be affected by such an experience, the drama had been simply a comedy. Alcmène, upon whom Jupiter imposed his will, even as Jehovah imposed his upon Judith, was the surface of a figure beyond which the very gods could not reach. Jupiter was forced to conclude, "there is [. . .] in her something unassailable and closed that must be the human infinite." A god might be forgiven for failing to recognize in the outward figure of a mortal one of his betters, especially when as here, the stubbornness of the creature turned Jupiter himself into a mortal, forcing him to become, in what he had hoped would be only the disguise of Amphitryon, Alcmène's husband—the only symbol she was willing to acknowledge. But neither Alcmène nor the play had any significance beyond that of intransigence, whereas Judith, in terms of human values lost, could invalidate a city's rebirth and shame even the victory of God.

Even though the stage in *Judith* is taken up by people, the author still asserts his presence. This might have been more trivial in *Amphitryon 38,* whose Alcmène defined herself as "a simple and straightforward soul," and where an occasional fit of Giraudoux's ill temper at the simplicity of Jupiter, or of men, turned the young woman's badinage into the virtuous tones of a housewife that confirmed her own definition. But the blows which fall on Judith, and through her reach the entire race, are less easily dismissed for they impose unrelated concerns upon the central action of the tragedy. When Judith tells Holophernes that she is not a virgin—"Do you believe that I would have gone as a virgin towards an unknown horror?"—Holophernes' answer destroys the fuller implication of the word to lash out at merely those whom it now improperly designates: "Towards what then would virgins go?" The gratuitousness of such wit narrows and demeans the significance of the action: the universal characters of tragedy become merely irritating archetypes.

oncile some of these conflicting demands of form and content whose balance allows tragedy. The god who descends *ex
machina* in *Judith*, dooming too suddenly the people of the
drama, is here allowed to hover in sight throughout the action.
At every moment, except in the ironic title, it is known that
Argives and Trojans must fight. The materialization of fate
stands from the start in the midst of the participants in the
detached person of Hélène: "My obstinacy? There isn't a
thing I can do about it: it isn't mine." Clustered about this
symbol are the people of the drama who frequently mistake that
symbol for one of their own kind, pleading with it, hating it,
attempting to remove it: the sane and balanced, mother and
wife, Andromaque, the clear-sighted and somewhat cross-
grained Cassandre, the ironical and shrewd Ulysse, the ear-
nestly well-intentioned Hector. But the play remains relatively
static because whatever their individual gestures, its characters
do not really call fate in question. At the level of tragedy, the
characters have all a common impress; in the words of Ulysse,
"Fate has gone over everything of yours with a particular
color of storm. [. . .] There is nothing to be done about it.
You stand in the light of the Grecian war." At a physical
level that is belied by their symbolic uniformity, these people
are witty commentators upon the tangential aspects of the
drama as the perspective of each allows, and with consequences already noted in *Judith*. The play becomes an annotation on the processes of an inevitable doom rather than a
revelation of these processes, and because the annotation is
urbane, yet another step is taken away from tragedy.

Gestures that are made without disturbing a uniform and
passive acceptance of the myth cannot be a commentary upon
its substance. The dynamics of the myth derive from the indi-

vidual interpretations that its significance allows and from the clash of two sensitivities that renders its drama meaningful once again. *Electre* was to attempt a genuine commentary by blending the significance of its people with that of their doom.

Electre is never a *jeune fille à la mode*—she is from the very first "the sort of woman that makes trouble." She is not a performer in a particular action, she is not the Sophoclean heroine who knows what is going on and who laments her fate. She is a symbol: she does not know what this tale will be about but she knows what her role will be in any event ("I hate them with a hatred that is not mine"). She is the Hélène of this play, but an active one.

Across her path stands Egisthe. He is a privileged character in a company of specialized forces: he understands. At first, he understands a part of Electre, that which is a menace to the state, to his state: "There is at present in Argos only one creature who can make a sign to the gods, and that is Electre. . . ." So she must be married off to the gardener—Euripides' method for getting rid of troublesome young girls.

Electre, because she is a symbol, and Egisthe, because he will be various symbols, know just what they are doing in this play and will speak about it constantly. But there are also a number of non-participants who analyze it from a multiplicity of vantage points. There is the gardener who will never marry Electre but who wished to because there is only one woman who has Electre's significance; this gardener conveys the views of a human being: he is a man loosed in this conflict of symbols and as such, the link between these and the ones whose perception is needed to turn the symbols to flesh. There are three little girls who keep on growing, the Eumenides. They play the actual roles of the principals but without the concealing robes that these principals still wear: they keep on growing because they are the development of the action itself. There is a beggar who defines himself to Egisthe, both physically and spiritually, in this fashion: "As for me, I have one quality. I do not understand the words that people speak. I have no education. I understand people. . . You want to kill Electre." This is not the play of people; it is the play of an interrelated series of constructs deriving from the axiom of the myth.

Like Egisthe, the beggar knows that sooner or later Electre is going to make that sign to the gods—in his words, "she is going to declare herself." The miracle of Electre is that when she does "declare herself," all those worth saving will likewise declare themselves, including Agathe, a *jeune fille* left in for decoration, who will blurt out to the figure of convention—her husband—the admission of her years of betrayal, not only with Egisthe, but that which began with the very "wood of the bed, my first adultery."

Such is the strength of the symbol Electre—that miracle of purity of which the gardener speaks, utterly unable not to see, not to hear, not to understand—that in her light Egisthe too will declare himself. Having first sensed the danger that Electre represented to the part of him that was a moral symbol, the dissolute lover as well as the conscientious statesman, he now senses the full danger of Electre in her own totality and in the total scheme of things. And so it is that in the second of these two acts, "Egisthe appears. He is infinitely more majestic and serene than in the first act. High in the air, a bird hovers over him." He has turned away from Clytemnestre even as Electre is now moving away from Oreste, out of sheer dramatic incompatibility: like the Eumenides, these two are

growing while the others recede. Egisthe is even endangering
the role of Electre:

EGISTHE: What is the matter with all of you, that you should look
at me in this way?

THE BEGGAR: The matter is that the queen is waiting for a perjurer,
Electre for one who is impious, Agathe for one guilty of infidelity. That one there is more modest, he is waiting for the one
who caresses his wife. . . In a word, it is you who are expected! And it is not you who appears!

EGISTHE: They really have no luck, have they, beggar?

THE BEGGAR: No, they have no luck. To expect so many good-for-
nothings and to have a king enter! I don't care about the others.
But for little Electre, it is going to complicate matters.

EGISTHE: Do you think so? I think not.

And of course, Egisthe is right, for the growth of each antagonist is of a different nature. Egisthe's is a change in kind,
Electre's is a growth in strength—she cannot be deflected. As
later Anouilh's Créon to Antigone, Egisthe attempts the hopeless explanation on behalf of those who assume responsibility
for any segment of the world and for whom the notion of
moral absolutes breaks down because of the awareness of details. But Electre's virtue is that her vision is nothing short of
total and absolute. So Egisthe's bird comes down. It turns out
to be a vulture: the myth can now proceed to its conclusion.
Orestes, an ill-equipped redresser, accomplishes his time-ap-
pointed gesture, but off stage and through the eyes of the beggar. The city of Egisthe will thus be destroyed, for contrary
to that of *Judith,* this one is not to be the site of a tragedy. The
symbol Electre triumphs; the people lost are a small price to
pay for such a victory.

But do such people, the Egisthes, the Clytemnestres, the

Orestes, disappear with as little consequence from the drama? As in *La Guerre de Troie,* they hamper the symbols in nearly every case, and most conspicuously, in Electre's. For her to say that she hates those about her with a hatred that is not hers can be acceptable as a statement of purpose. But when in her relentless harshness she comes up against someone who is not a symbol, but merely her mother, the rigor of her symbolic words may not be sufficient to disguise the fact that she is also an extremely unpleasant daughter. And daughters are more readily understandable than moral symbols. Nor is the fact that she is created impervious to reason sufficient to dismiss the reasons that a mature Egisthe puts forth to disculpate himself. Whereas the enemies of Electre can turn into people from one moment to the next and incline the audience toward them, Electre remains ever uncompromisingly distant from that audience. It is not Electre who is at fault but an author who has allowed lesser people to assume more enticing parts.

The dramatic flaw appears when Electre achieves her victory, that of utter purity, at the expense of people, the effortless dismissal of whom is not compatible with purity: the symbol, at such times, is prevented from performing its act because of the intrusion of those who do not conform to that symbolism. Intrusions of this kind define the figure of Electre as a reader's irritation might once have defined the prototypes of Giraudoux's novels: Electre is a *jeune fille*—but with a vengeance, one in whom residual charm has been eliminated to make room for her full part of unpleasantness.

The temporal that inhibits the absolute in Electre does so even in those who are most clearly symbols—as once did Giraudoux's Jews inhibit the absolute in humanity, or the virgin inhibit that in Judith. The gardener, whose figures of speech degenerate into trivia (the "bitterness" of orange sirup which he drinks alone on what was to have been his wedding night; "Joy and Love" that should be inscribed "on a silken kerchief, it's so much better, or with dwarf begonias"), drowns much of his wisdom in words. The Eumenides, for all their penetratingly bitter role, act and talk like little girls, and little girls are more easily recognizable than Eumenides. The beggar, prophetic nearly by inadvertence, is obtuse and absent-minded—a true figure of comedy—and a clown is more easily apprehended than a spokesman for destiny.

Even in this play of intellectual syntheses, Giraudoux still favors tangible attributes and what is prolix, baroque, and external—the letter—contends, often too successfully, with the inner designation—the spirit. A stripped drama such as focuses on merely the tragic mechanism within its performers has not been achieved. *Sodome et Gomorrhe* proposed this type of drama.

The sin of which the two cities stand accused is as terrible as can be only that which is measured by an absolute. It is a sin beyond sin, and calls for damnation such as has never been fathomed by man: "an end of the world was hitherto a sound thrashing or a serious hip-bath," says the archangel, "but it was never handed out with real resentment. Tonight, if none of the spies tracking Sodom has found what he is after, it will be retribution in all its fire and death, it will be the hatred of God. . . ."

What God is after is the expression of the absolute whose form is love. He is looking for a genuine couple and the word "genuine" is going to be plumbed to its utmost depth. One after the other, the couples of Sodom have been eliminated until there remains between the city and the rain of fire only the team of Lia and Jean. Samson and Dalila are briefly consid-

ered to be candidates because they are happy together, but very
soon it becomes apparent, even to those in imminent danger of
God's wrath, that their happiness is the felicitous balance of the
wife's deceit and the husband's stupidity. There is no question
of love between them. And there is no one else: gone are even
the beggars, the gardeners, the Eumenides. Jacques and Ruth,
another couple, are introduced, like Samson and Dalila, for
analysis but in fact, there remain only Lia and Jean. And until
this morning, according to the archangel's report, all was still
going well:

They smiled while speaking to each other, they were reciprocally
buttering their bread, they slept in each other's arms. In Jean's
office, there was a bird and roses. In Lia's room, a dog and gar-
denias. Creation is still undivided between them. . . But already,
it would seem as if each were secreting his own light—that is bad,
it means that each is secreting his own truth. Each is irritated with
himself—that is bad, it means that each will be irritated with the
other. If in her case, it is because she is with child, if in his, because he is absorbed in his work and imagines things, all the sins
of the world can still wait. But if it is that each is taken by the
plague of Sodom, by the awareness of his sex, God himself will
not be able to do anything about it. . .

Quite clearly, there are to be no nuances—and it is just as
clear that the plague of Sodom is already on the principals. As
so often in Giraudoux, this absolute statement is essentially a
matter of the dramatic stuff of which the people are made. Lia
and Jean belong to different species. Like glimpses of Siegfried,
like Hans, like perhaps the Holophernes that life might have
revealed, Jean is a man. The word means, morally, that he is
simple, somewhat shallow, and unable, perhaps through lack
of desire, to penetrate things beyond their surface. Dramatically, it means that he is not a symbol, that his humble flesh

and blood are not of the sort that tamper with myths. He would be like one of the audience if it were not for the fact that he remains too supine not to be eclipsed by the sheer strength of the symbol Lia.

Lia is of another kind; she is the archetype once again, that can be variously symbolic of aspiration or of the naked strength of an idea—Ondine or Electre. Here, she is an Electre, and her match with Jean is revealed in the full light of its pathetic ridiculousness: these two represent an antinomy at least as blatant as that of the ironclad knight and the watersprite. Lia explains:

My soul is tired unto death. Five years I tried to have this man. I threw myself full face upon him, with all of my strength, completely open. He was sewn up on every side. I then contented myself with living against him, sleeping against him; I would have found contentment within myself from only his impress. Nothing left a mark.

The obverse face of the impossibility to achieve a total communion is presented by Jean:

Angel, I married this woman so as to have my light. I was kindled on my wedding day even as a lamp. My work, my rest had their flame, and she was it. I was only the oil and the wick; and being only that sufficed me for as long as her radiance was born of it. But a day came when she no longer fed on me. She burns, she scintillates, but not through me and not for me. I do not know what wind has carried her away, her satiety or her pride. I am the lamp, and my flame is burning all alone somewhere upon the lip of a well or in a tree. And it flutters or burns straight up according to unknown moods. And I live in the night.

This, however, is but the limited sadness of a man, not the loss of a symbolic force, and no sooner has Jean finished speaking than Lia will be pointing it out:

LIA: That does not prevent him from finding today's weather splendid.

THE ANGEL: As a matter of fact, you too must answer the question. Is the day fair or foul in Sodom?

JEAN: Doesn't it go without saying? The sun shines. The sky is without a cloud.

LIA: It is awful.

JEAN: The swallows are flying high. The insects are at their highest in the sky.

LIA: We are in a raging storm. The shutters are rattling.

JEAN: Everything is calm. There is not a ripple on the wheat. Isn't that so, Ruth?

The question addressed to Ruth represents another part of the attempt to square the circle. Jacques and Jean, because they are men, are approximately the same man. But Ruth is no Lia —she is a mere woman. Cannot the terms be re-arranged? Lia will fail with Jacques, that is a foregone certainty. But cannot Jean and Ruth succeed on the common terms of their weakness? It is the achievement of this new match that gives Jean for the first time an inkling of Lia's truth and projects him into the debate: "I loved you and these days with Ruth have been successful and triumphant. That is why I left her. I wanted to keep within me the memory of my first happiness." That which his love for Lia has become is valueless—it can be found anywhere: thereby will he achieve awareness of the validity of Lia's intransigence. There are now two lucid minds facing each other, separated forever by the nature of love itself, and even after God has destroyed them, their debate will not end:

THE ARCHANGEL: Won't they finally keep quiet! Won't they finally die!

THE ANGEL: They are dead.
THE ARCHANGEL: Who then is speaking?
THE ANGEL: They are. Death was not enough. The scene continues.

Quite properly, beyond the life of humans, the value of symbols endures. The world may be destroyed; it will be a gesture as empty of significance as Argos' destruction: the essential part of the drama did not have human form. That part escapes death, it evades tragedy, it confronts the mind with the impersonal terms of the equation: the prototypes have acquired metaphysical significance. Within even the author's very last play, *Pour Lucrèce,* the idea will displace the person. Lucile, again a physical representation of absolute purity, is able to accept the moral implications of a rape until she finds out that the rape was in fact a hoax. She will then die for having been forced to lose faith in herself: a symbol will be physically deleted because it did not remain itself symbolically. But the woman Lucile has never existed (the other characters in the play make this adequately clear), no more than did the little girl Ondine, the little girl Electre or the woman Lia. These are the *jeunes filles* of the novels, projected into a metaphysical role—that is to say, prototypes whose sole statement is no longer sufficient and who thus have been given the vestment of myth. However, true to their own nature, they have assumed the role of the gods, of destiny itself, rather than assume the role of the ones upon whom gods or destiny work and whose names these prototypes wrongly go by.

IF THE vitals of an essential theater are those of the spectator, then Giraudoux has sought a critic as spectator no matter how roundly that critic has been denounced by him. His very myths are myths for critics—the struggles of ideas, not of people. When looked at a little more closely, the god whose love he called on to replace the critic's detachment may yield a clue as to just what sort of spectator this theater has been designed for. *L'Impromptu de Paris* defines that god thus:

A god who is paralyzed, powerless—further areas of resemblance to the real one perhaps—but who feels like the latter, full of pity and gratitude for those fraternal or filial beings who have agreed this evening to suffer, live, and die in his stead.

Although Giraudoux does not want a critic who will be utterly removed, the type of spectator here defined is nevertheless kin to the critic. He is paralyzed and powerless, not all-powerful as is the spectator. He agrees to have someone suffer, live and die in his stead—he does not undertake to suffer, live or die himself. This is going to be a spectacle performed *in front of* him; this is going to be a theater *before* the public. That much detachment *is* countenanced, and detachment is what distinguishes the critics from the spectators.

Not only does this notion of the spectator's relation to the drama render comprehensible the archetype that will be substituted for the human, it also helps elucidate a number of traits peculiar to Giraudoux's theater. It explains, among other things, why the speeches in *Littérature* (1941) or those in *L'Impromptu* show so much concern on behalf of a "literary theater." It will be recalled that when Robineau, in *L'Impromptu,* mentions the term, words fail Jouvet for the first time, and it is the entire cast that replies, starting with Renoir:

Dear Mr. Robineau, if in Paris, the public has run the risk of losing the notion of the theater, that is to say of the greatest of arts, it is because a number of people connected with the theater have aspired to court only that public's effortless compliance, and thereafter, its vulgarity. It was a question of pleasing by the vilest and most common means. As the French language, when it is properly spoken and written, resists such blackmail of its own motion, and obeys only those whom it respects, it is against that very language that the offensive was launched, and it is then that was found for the plays in which it was neither abused nor rendered slipshod, an epithet which corresponds, so it seems, to the very worst insults—that of literary plays.

This literary theater, like the *jeunes filles* of the novels, is an esthetic creation, something designed for its own sake, a part of the "show": this too is theater before the public. *Sodome et Gomorrhe* might be a serious treatise on the incommunicability of love, and *L'Apollon de Bellac* might be a light piece about the utter communicability of beauty—but in neither is there even the motion or peripeteia that people (or ideas more dramatically limber, as in the exceptional *Electre*) might execute. The witty play of the idea is performed through the language used on stage, and through no other part of the stage world. Indeed, Claude-Edmonde Magny (*Précieux Giraudoux*) is justified in saying: "The world of Giraudoux is perhaps the most perfect example of a universe created entirely by language."

The sets are as conventional as the characters are not, for the sets too are absolutes which the spectator must accept— there is no need for him to move beyond the footlights to create them (and on occasion, Jouvet collaborated with Bérard—as in *Ondine*—to overwhelm even the very least imaginative of spectators). But alongside these material objects are the same quintessences as were found in the novels—quintessences that exist because of the atmosphere which they dispense rather than because of the function which they serve. But neither will these demand that the spectator do anything more than remain where he is. Victor-Henry Debidour (*Jean Girau-doux*) has noted: "It is in the publicity pages of *L'Illustration* dating back a quarter of a century that are found the properties that he disseminates here and there throughout his novels: Innovation trunks, Burma jewelry, Yale locks, Brot mirrors. . . ." The same is true of the atmosphere disseminated throughout the plays. This is truly the savor of Paris, or generically, of all of France. This flavor is inherent in nearly every one of his plays, be it the biblical *Sodome et Gomorrhe* with its Cartesian inhabitants and its Parisian women, or the Gallic court at Troy. In one of the rare instances of atmospheric failure, the adaptation of Margaret Kennedy's novel *Tessa* (*The Constant Nymph*) in 1934, the very nature of the young girls does not render a Giralducian ring.

This recurrent flavor of France serves instead of another flavor ever lacking—that of humanity. Even the social protagonists of *La Folle de Chaillot* (1943), busy fighting evil magnates, are an utterly classless lot blended into the equalitarian haze of the author's fantasy and wit. Indeed, Giraudoux has never taken his ancillary characters too seriously—and even his protagonists, when they are off duty, come in for his raillery. "Luckily, humor is there," says Debidour, "that posture of the soul (ranging from cowardice to heroism, with all of the intermediate possibilities) that indicates that one does not entirely believe in what one is doing." Note that this is never the "posture of the soul" in a *character*—and that it is an excellent indication to the spectator not to commit himself too strongly either.

But the very broad area of this raillery is also that of the author's intelligence at play, and therefore, his supreme moment of identification with the spectator whom he has chosen.

The method, in Debidour's words, is "to give all those who appreciate him the fallacious pleasure of feeling in themselves a finesse, a moral elegance that is, however, his alone." Plays like the one-act *Supplément au Voyage de Cook* (1935), which is characteristically a new version of what was once Diderot's philosophical discussion, the *Supplément au Voyage de Bougainville,* are little more than a sprinkling of literary allusions. Fellow literati have already expressed their joy at having detected the learned winks in *La Guerre de Troie,* or in any number of Giraudoux's other writings. These are of course the gems of his intellectual creations, but in order to satisfy the less sophisticated, they are set in a coarser context, that of the unpretentious puns and the clichés that shock no common beliefs, as the English in the *Supplément au Voyage de Cook,* the Jews in *Tessa* or *Judith;* as once a dozen definitions lightly tossed off by a little girl in *Suzanne et le Pacifique* or by any one of her sisters.

And for those who might disdain, or might not be competent to play such games, there remains the vast domain of what Magny has called Giraudoux's *féerie.* And so, with hardly any people, a theater has been built, one for the ears, for the mind—but for hardly anything more.

3

Further Perils of Debate

Claudel

GIRAUDOUX'S UNRESOLVED dramatic form stands midway between two complementary and partial visions of the stage: that of the dramatists who see it as an exclusively recreative place or one for the performance of material magic, and that of those who think of it as a place for the establishment of a merely philosophical debate. Since each concept envisages a perceptory apparatus that is both sensory and intellective, each is valid to a degree. Both err in contemplating only parts of a totality, and hence, in working but with a part of the total stage. Still, it is the magician who builds on safer grounds: his are the inert, material, tangible properties of the theater; he works with what exists beyond question or debate. He furthers that part of the play that is illusion by restricting his focus to what must necessarily remain physical: the illusionist is not a visionary here but a technician. He performs within the security of acknowledged realms. His detractors can indict only his prudence.

The playwright who places a debate upon his boards sacrifices a greater part of his chosen medium since that medium furnishes him with a physical implement for which he has no use. He fashions a self-contained unit on stage into which the spectator is not granted entry, and in so doing abdicates mesmerism in an act that is by nature one of suggestion and intuition. Those who believe that a play exists only to the extent of its visual properties, and those who wish an intellectual apprehension, alike *exclude* the spectator as performer, though, of the two, the intellectual proponent charts a more perilous course in that the mind is capable of independent constructs and is less passive than the eye that apprehends directly and responds to intimate suasion. Both methods court doom, but the artificer enjoys a margin of success usually measured by the duration of the performance.

Ingenious reasoning has been advanced in France to defend the philosophical play against those who consider it an offspring of the *pièce à thèse*. Reasoning of this kind, when it merely defends argument in the theater through argument without, twice ignores the irrelevancy of the process. Paul Claudel, who offers Catholicism as the substance and basis of his writing, finds drama to be a natural form of Catholic expression. His defense rests largely on the brief articles written in 1914 ("Théâtre et religion" in *Positions et propositions*) after he had completed the major part of his dramatic opus. The strength of Christianity, says Claudel, resides in its principle of contradiction—its apparently unreasonable demands are in fact the only ones commensurate with man's strength and reason. The necessary principle of contradiction in art establishes a primary affinity between Christianity and drama. Moreover, the demands of the dogma never mutilate: they are Catholic, that is to say universal—and this universality achieves another requisite of drama. Even the authority of Saint Paul can be called upon, with but minor change of terms, to view man as "constantly in the arena, upon the set." Every one of man's acts thus becomes a living parable in a world that is an act before God. The Christian life enacts, in dramatic terms, a precise drama, with a denouement and a meaning.

In as much as every self-searching turns life as it is lived into drama, Claudel's concept of an essentially dramatic Catholicism can be allowed. But should the instance of a man questioning himself within the bounds of a dogma be transferred to the stage, it is apparent that the solution must ultimately frustrate the search, or, as here, that the universality must revert to mere Catholicism.

For the purpose of this examination, Claudel's conversion, adumbrated by the figure of Rimbaud in 1886 and confirmed by that of Baudelaire in 1890, is a literary manifestation, an esthetic protest against the materialism of the naturalists. Claudel is a poet, and the occasionally magnificent sweep of his language contains in such moments its own dramatic germ before the birth of formal drama. These formal elements will, in fact, hamper the innate power of the word in the same way that the transference of an experience to the stage for didactic reasons will tend to change what is naturally dramatic into theatrical artificiality, the urgency of life having been replaced by the demands of the synthetic play form.

Understandably, Claudel's first dramas are not the statements of individuals but rather of a collective force. *Tête d'or* (first version 1889, second 1894-95), though it tells of the conqueror whose victories turn to dust even as he grasps them, makes the central Simon Agnel ("Tête d'or" in combat) a reflector to be directed at a pageant of morality figures. The bulk of these, the "numerous male and female walk-ons," are the unredeemed multitude: Le Pédagogue, Le Tribun du Peuple, Le Moyen-Homme, etc. Two others turn the reflector back upon the unregenerate Tête d'or: Cébès whose obsessive fears are mystically dissipated as he dies, and the hereditary princess whose ultimate act in life is a gratuitous gesture of love for the dying Simon Agnel. More clearly, *La Ville* (1890 and 1897) becomes the symbol of the unsatisfactory shell, this one built by Lambert and Isidore de Besme, figures of political and scientific pragmatism. The shell crumbles under the blows of Avare so that the final lesson might be spelled out: the city cannot live if it refuses God. The apologue, transferred to China, is repeated substantially in *Le Repos du septième jour* (1896).

These plays are not the acts of Christians before God, especially as these are not accounts of personal acts. What personality the performer is granted seldom transcends that of the morality figure, of the symbol that is inert before the sign, since his reason for being is to give evidence of that inertia until the sign either redeems him or signifies that his time has passed. The actor upon this stage remains ancillary to that sign, to the manifestation of the conclusive truth. The spectator, in turn, remains passive and isolated before these sealed figures. He must accept the impersonal evidence of the sign as the action's only justification, and, if the totality is not to be rejected, he must accept it in all its attributes. As for the drama of the Catholic actor, extensible in its universality, that drama remains unborn along with its protagonist. The stage has not been granted the one universality of which it is capable: the form of a man.

Between 1893 and 1894, Claudel, who was translating the first part of the Oresteia, Aeschylus' *Agamemnon,* wrote *L'Echange,* the sober tale of four people in the heathen lands of the Eastern seaboard of the United States. Within the span which the French still think of as classical—a single day—Marthe sees her untamed husband Louis Laine turn to the actress Lechy Elbernon. But through her suffering, an older wisdom born of an older continent brings peace to Marthe and enables her even to reach Lechy's husband, the materialist Thomas Pollock Nageoire. Henceforth, people move onto Claudel's boards. *La*

Jeune Fille Violaine (1892) grew through a second version (1898) into *L'Annonce faite à Marie* (1910), a splendid evocation of the medieval ground upon which is wrought the sacrifice of Violaine. The heroine, born to a greater happiness than that of the earthly things of which she is deprived by her sister Mara, achieves saintliness through denudation that she might in turn dispense blessing upon those who have thus worked her salvation. *Partage de midi* (1905) likewise withholds salvation from Mesa until he lies dying, bereft of all earthly hope by the adventurer Amalric. It is then that he sees Ysé return to him, the woman whose fleshly embrace could keep no promise, and the mystical revelation is accomplished anew.

The harsh clash of people whose corrosive action ultimately purifies a victim, is afforded leisurely expression in Claudel's trilogy *L'Otage* (1909), *Le Pain dur* (1913-14), *Le Père humilié* (1916). Here, the degeneration, after the French Revolution, of the aristocratic Coûfontaines is shown as their no longer generous blood is mixed in order that it might be born anew. To free the "hostage"—the Pope—who has taken refuge upon her lands, Sygne de Coûfontaine must marry the prefect Toussaint Turelure, son of a vassal. The pride of the aristocrat that will not allow her to redeem a man whose love might have been an instrument of that redemption, starts the evil wheel turning. The unwanted Louis-Napoléon Turelure, ruthless son of a ruthless father, rises against old Turelure and kills him in *Le Pain dur*. He is abetted by two women, the Polish exile Lumîr and the Jewess Rachel Habenichts (Sichel) whom he marries. It is their blind daughter, Pensée, who at last brings the curse of Sygne to an end in *Le Père humilié*.

Claudel's luxuriance of plot and people reaches its baroque apogee in *Le Soulier de satin,* written between 1919 and 1924.

Here, in a make-believe Spain and various parts of the old and the new world, during some indefinite time in the sixteenth or seventeenth century, Dona Prouhèze and Don Rodrigue are denied fulfillment of their earthly love that they might achieve salvation in the usual Claudel manner. This drama, called "huge" by the author himself, not only repeats the lesson of *L'Annonce faite à Marie* and *Partage de midi* but its proliferation of scenes gathers in a dramatic legacy many of Claudel's other motives, such as those concerned with the ethics of conquest (*Tête d'or*), the frailty of temporal kingdoms, the emergence of a spiritual dominion (*La Ville, Le Repos du septième jour,* the trilogy), the notion of the individual's ultimate and redemptory peace (*L'Annonce, L'Echange*).

In summary form, every one of these plays becomes a clear apologue and a simple statement of the author's purpose. But within plays, which are manifestations of particular stances and reactions, the statement can be explicit no longer: it is parceled out as the reactions of a number of stage people, and its synthesis must await at least the prior analysis involved in the crediting of these individuals—an exercise whose hazards have been noted already. On these terms, Aristotle's pity and terror will be objectified—if indeed this is possible—only upon reflection, as a post-theatrical experience. In the theater these emotions are self-pity and fear for oneself, a distinction that Giraudoux failed to understand. Pity for the protagonist by a spectator not in self-mourning would be little more significant than terror conceived as revulsion instead of contamination through the protagonist's own terror. Catharsis might thus be a belated benefit, but Plato was right in condemning the spectacle for the time of its duration during which it enslaves the beholder.

When he entrusts the thesis to action of his people, Claudel encounters these difficulties since, the form of his drama notwithstanding, he continues to consider the ultimate apologue more important than the fate of any stage individual. Working with the motion and emotion that constitute a play, he remains committed to the pre-eminence of the impelling motion while his spectator can respond directly only to the resultant emotion. If Violaine is merely admirable in achieving martyrdom as she loses to Mara her patrimony and her lover, the morality triumphs but the character Violaine dies. If her humility is to affect the spectator, he cannot find it any more admirable than she does: he must instead live that humility. One might surmise that the person Violaine is less appealing when she effects only such intellectual acts: contrast her leprosy and her blindness that short-circuit debate through physical immediacy, impeding the possibility of reflective admiration and facilitating the spontaneous intimacy demanded of the stage.

The immanent dramatist Claudel appears recurrently in characters whose power and importance make them aspects of a scheme vaster indeed than that for which they were designed. The dialogue between Mesa and Ysé does not so much lead the spectator into an intellectual awareness of mundane vanity, the renunciation of which portends salvation, as it draws him into the simple, timeless, and truly poignant story of two lovers. Viewing the play as a spectator, Kenneth Cornell says (*Yale French Studies,* 1950):

It is quite possible that not all the spectators fully felt the message which Claudel was seeking to convey in *Partage de midi*. Until the lyric last scene of the play, the human emotions of the characters are so powerfully presented that the hand of God does not always seem to dominate the action.

The successful play dissipates the morality in drama; the apologue recedes while the characters grow.

Sainthood and martyrdom, because they are more admirable than desirable, and because they are moreover difficult to achieve, are likewise difficult to conceive. And should the spectator be capable of such comprehension, it is doubtful whether he will choose to do more than comprehend. Man is saved from cataclysmal visions by the minute dimensions of his eye: on stage such limited perception acts for the preservation of characters too overpoweringly superhuman; the figure admired will no longer be subject to contamination, either good or evil. The illustrative morality benefits therefore from presentation on a stage so long as it does not become a play. But halfway between such detachment and the complete absorption of the successful play is the esthetic distance that merely preserves from contact with that which is perishable. Mesa and Ysé are the closer to the very temporal since in point of time, action, and dress, they are committed to the physical area of the spectator. Except for their language, since Claudel remains essentially a poet, the properties and the circumstances of the character—the steamship upon which they meet, the mines they exploit, the native uprising that traps them—give them a specific stamp. *Partage de midi,* rooted in the present, is appreciable especially when contrasted with a morality vehicle such as *Tête d'or,* set in a nameless, timeless place.

The three plays of the trilogy extend these faults by reason of their resultant prolixity and because of an unfortunate reliance on vulgar symbols that demand more than historical coincidence for credence. After the still relatively simple and somewhat expository *L'Otage, Le Pain dur* becomes an especially grievous catalogue of conformist beliefs and clichés. Its

motor is money, an agent as corrupting theatrically as Claudel
would have it be morally. The conflicts of the characters turn
around the awkwardly paltry figure of 10,000 francs, twice
stated. It is first the sum that Lumîr has given Louis-Napoléon,
who has unprofitably invested it in Africa though it is a part
of Poland's national patrimony. The sum of 10,000 francs is
also the amount that old Turelure has received from Ali
Habenichts, Sichel's father, for the sale of the ancient lands of
Coûfontaine. This miserably superficial symbol is used by the
author to indict materialism in the aspects that he imagines
post-Revolutionary days to have engendered. He trusts the
symbol as only a bourgeois of peasant stock might, and backs
it with the usual train of clichés. Amongst these, the anti-Semite's picture of the Jew enables him to cap his maudlin vision
with the scene in which Louis-Napoléon sells the bronze
Christ to Ali Habenichts, the same Christ which, in earlier
days, Sygne and her nurse had brought back to its dominion,
"walking barefoot through the night." The haggling between
the two men that finally establishes the price at four francs a
kilo leaves the onlooker with the feeling that Claudel himself
has entered into the bargaining.

Thereafter, it will be hard to credit Sichel as "all of Israel"
abruptly released from bondage and coveting nothing less than
world dominion. The curse of Sygne extends even to Pensée in
Le Père humilié, as her lineage, once the simple illustration of
materialism, now requires elaboration sufficient to illuminate
the thornier questions of Christianity's filiation. What had
been a simple borrowing of the spectator's most common and
superficial terms is now inadequate for the postulation—and
resolution, in this moral drama—of metaphysical or philosophical debate. Rather than afford significant apperception,

this sort 'of complacent reliance by the poet upon the unquestioned stereotype will call to mind Claudel's occasional pieces,
such as in his *Poèmes de guerre* (1914-16), the chauvinistic
"Tant que vous voudrez, mon général!"

It is curious to note Claudel's dependence upon the commonly accepted symbol when he is establishing a morality that
attempts by definition to draw its objects away from common
acceptances. His use of base currency will hardly encourage
reflection, but as the particularization of any allegory tends to
focus attention upon the item individualized, figures drawn
from the spectator's most immediate areas of familiarity will
further encourage the spectator's affiliation. This is a manner of
flirtation reminiscent of Cocteau: the expectation that a part
of the drama initially prostituted might effect, in its loftier
totality, the ravishment of the spectator.

Claudel's drama is dependent to a great extent on such
mechanical figures. Devoid of the author's warmth, they remain hermetic—figures of heraldry or of laughter according to
the light trained upon them. An exclusive use of the latter in
certain of Claudel's plays and radio sketches makes these comic
vehicles. Such are *Protée* (1913) and *L'Ours et la lune* (1917).
The first is a *drame satyrique*—properly a drama of satyrs and
satirical: its performers are monsters, the word designating all
those removed, through constitution or chronology, from
Claudelian salvation. Brindosier, a nymph, tries to escape from
Protée by showing herself to Menelaus in the blue-garbed shape
of the Helen that was. But the real Helen wears ill the red of
autumnal wisdom and sells her identity for a few button snaps.
Scarcely distinguishable from the pagan divinities whom the
Christian cannot credit, these people are perfect embodiments
of the intellectual comic vice. Claudel uses them as such, occa-

sionally having them step out of character to become his mouthpiece for a casual jibe that underscores the mental nature of
the play. It is Claudel again who is heard in their magnificent
language. (The play was originally published in 1914 as part
of *Deux poèmes d'été*.) Thereafter, the figures are set dancing
to Darius Milhaud's music: having given up their every chance
of coming alive within the image of the spectator, they now
fall back on their sole remaining *raison d'être* in the theater:
like Cocteau's magical objects, they become the mechanical
properties of the spectacle.

A spectacle similarly built around a hollow center appears
with *L'Ours et la lune* in that here the performers are avowedly
marionettes. The author has signified his own detachment by
calling "farce" this curious midsummer night's dream shot
through with a scenic madness that prefigures even Cocteau.
For although it is the dream of people whose torment makes
them real, that dream as it bursts upon the stage spills forth
only marionettes—automatic agents par excellence—whose
satirical purport makes them once again morality figures.

Alongside such elementary effigies that include, in addition
to the mean and avaricious Jew, the superficially wise and
lustful Chinese, the savage Negro, acquisitive and libidinous,
etc., stand the primary figures of perdition whose subtlety is
that of the few layers concealing their atavism: the Indian in
Louis Laine, the barbarian in Tête d'or, the serf and pagan in
Turelure (son of the sorcerer Quiriace), the Moor in Don
Camille (*Le Soulier*). These too are specialized figures, and
their very names become labels: Mara, the Hebrew word for
bitter water and anguish, but also a homonym whose harshness must have stirred visions of bloodshed and of desecration
in Claudel's mind; Ali Habenichts, the heathen Oriental and

the Germanic Jew destitute of divine grace; Turelure, the shallow refrain; Lechy Elbernon, the adulterous actress.

Facing these are characters unremittingly good—Marthe, Violaine, Musique—the reverse of coins stamped by identical dies and intended for identical use. Jacques Madaule (*Le Drame de Paul Claudel,* 1936) calls Pierre de Craon "the messenger of God" because he is the sign awaited by Violaine, the catalyst in this Christian drama. In that their creation was meant only to instance a specific flaw—or virtue—all these people are similarly messengers. Though they are by no means Christians living a Christian drama, they are morality figures personifying vices and virtues according to Catholic doctrine: they are, properly, Gothic frieze pieces. Their life is confined to that of the mechanism into which they have been fitted: it is little wonder that beside them, such unordained figures as Mesa and Ysé flout the morality and achieve a catholicity that outdistances Catholicism.

These prehensile characters, whose multiplication is climaxed in *Le Soulier de satin,* are an indication of Claudel's increasing concern with a potential spectator, the author's protests to the contrary notwithstanding. Even though *Le Soulier de satin* has been used as illustration of Claudel's magnificent contempt for the stage—akin, we are told, to Shakespeare's—it is well to note that even *that* sprawling play has found its way onto the stage—and, for that matter, with little more difficulty than Shakespeare. Among its characters, however, the aforementioned Dona Musique introduces a new dimension that is in fact characteristic of the play.

Though once again an impeccable image of goodness, Musique is cast in the improbable figure of a charming young girl who leaves her earthbound family and the prospect of a degrading marriage so that she might seek a wholly mythical prince—whom she effortlessly proceeds to discover and wed. This bright summation of innocence and faith, later sobered by the image of a pregnant Musique praying for the redemption of strife-rent Europe, is a creation scarcely more realistic than the morality figures scattered about her in episodic parts. But contrary to these lifeless shapes, it is through conceptual freedom that she attains dramatic salvation: she conforms but to her own truth and demands no rigid frame of reference. Her symbolism is not constrained; rather, she is a fluid note in a fluid play designed for the harmonization of such people.

In a cosmos that borrows its lay terms from the sciences, the elastic dimensions of *Le Soulier de satin* are those of a ceaselessly expanding universe. The image of Spain extending its empire across the world provides dynamic tempo and pomp. Claudel has insisted upon a stage especially suggestive of itself whose essential changes would be made within sight of the audience: "Everything must appear to be provisional, in motion, hastily slapped together, incoherent, improvised upon the spur of enthusiasm!" Not only is the world of the stage to suggest by its flexibility the restless forces in motion upon it, but its appurtenances are intended to obliterate entirely the here and now so as to free its characters that they might invite the very broadest measure of receptivity.

Such receptivity extends the characters beyond the control of the author. Dona Prouhèze will respect in didactic fashion the sacrament of her marriage; she will even renounce Don Rodrigue voluntarily once Don Pélage has died—and all this presumably because the Virgin upon the door still holds the slipper she once gave her with the prayer, "When I attempt to rush on evil, let it be with limping foot." But Prouhèze, a laughing girl from a sunny corner of France, recalls too easily the symbols of the star, of love, of all things futilely attempted and recollected in gentle sadness. Alongside Musique, she is Dona Merveille, and though her very name might bespeak theological realms, its immediate appeal is that of the most elementary symbol sublimated through desire, hope, tenderness.

The ethical consciousness that will keep her apart from Rodrigue blends with the torsional forces that shape the age: the Christian ethic does not appear as clearly as the physical sign premonitory of any tragic wind. Along with the vision, the technical language of Catholicism becomes that of an era and an accepted part of its cast: ironically, it helps to remove the set from the physical present and in so doing releases the eternally young performers. In the same way, the shadowy figure of Joan of Arc adumbrates the medieval scene in *L'Annonce faite à Marie* more than it echoes the obscure martyrdom of Violaine. There is no Emperor's staff here sprouting the branches of a cross as once there was in *Le Repos du septième jour.*

The principals in *Le Soulier de satin* escape stigmatization because they are human beings: proof through contrast is offered by the caricatures of lust and stupidity—Jobarbara, Alcochete, Hinnulus, Bidince, etc.—and by the relatively limited use made of the Bergsonian laughter of exclusion which they call forth. If Prouhèze recalls Lâla (*La Ville*) in her femininity, Sygne in her pride, Violaine in her devotion, she also represents more than these because what was an exclusive symbol in the others becomes in her the complexity of a human. On the somber side, even Don Camille's Moorishness remains scarcely more than innuendo: but for Rodrigue's groping spiritual ascension, he is a physical match for the hero in a drama whose physical aspects are much of its people's spirituality. A joyful current thus runs through the play—the sap of common and receptive life: men in other than heraldic poses, girls within the dawn of springtime, a vigor of action that is heathen in that its power defies argument. The sensuous poet completely belies the apologist. Better theorists suffered from being lesser poets: Henri Ghéon who admired *Ubu roi* as an instance of *théâtre pur* and who demanded of the playwright only "that he tend toward gratuitousness and that which is absolute as much as he can" (*L'Art du théâtre,* 1944), found his most spontaneous vehicles, his farces, constrained for having cheated gratuity by adding to "entertainment" and "art" the notion of "edification." The sensual communion which he felt bound to discard was the blood that his coldly entertaining creatures needed to evoke their latent warmth and that of the audience. As it is, he was forced to set them in a world too antiseptic for even the germ of laughter; they remained colorless and inhibited through constant fear that a gusty breath from suspiciously terrestrial regions might fling the very devil's salt upon their words or raise a stiffly starched skirt.

Fears of this sort are alien to Claudel, that robust creature of the loam: his style is as fleshly and palpable as the nature it bespeaks. Tonquédec (*L'Œuvre de Paul Claudel,* 1917), a cleric whom such primal life occasionally frightens, says of Claudel, "He rips out whole pieces of reality and places them within your hands" and recalls from the plays moments during which the stage becomes an image of nature untamed: the blast of heat at high noon upon the Indian Ocean in *Partage de midi,* the hymn to the moon in the strophe and antistrophe of Cœuvre and Lâla (*La Ville*), or again the instant in nearly every play when tangible life in field or flower, stream or storm or beast, is evoked by the son of Tardenois farmers. Such pantheism cannot remain within pre-established confines: at the beginning of the third day in *Le Soulier de satin,* the prayers of the saints and of Dona Musique become a detailed winter scene by Breughel.

The people of such a vision become, when they are not the mental caricatures of an ill-tempered mind, creations as complex as the spectator's recognition of them, and their breadth exceeds Claudel's stipulated limitations. The joy that Prouhèze dispenses to *Le Soulier de satin* has a theological significance, but the benighted sinner will confound it with what joy he knows and curtail the lesson thereafter. In *L'Annonce faite à Marie,* the play of the seasons upon the medieval land will affect the senses more tellingly than will the medieval miracle.

This direct and sensual perception of life becomes immediate drama when given words by the poet. In days when both apprehensions were one, such intimate and dramatic knowledge might have evoked concomitantly the presence of God. But while the sensual knowledge remains a common endowment, its theological association has long developed into a special exercise: to attempt the exercise through the natural impulse involves an extension of immediate perception into realms accessible only to the specialist of good will—a specialist, incidentally, for whom such extension would be needless. Likewise, when Claudel states "Whereas in life one believes that it is the characters that imply the action, here a foreordained action explains the characters" ("Introduction à quelques œuvres," quoted by Jacques Madaule in *Le Génie de Paul Claudel,* 1933), he is giving a Christian meaning to the older concept of fate, making little allowance for the Aristotelian man who fought the mark of the gods within him. If he were sufficiently inarticulate to succeed in the creation of such plays, Claudel would achieve his purpose through the destruction of his characters. Or, if he wished them to escape such destruction while still not granting them autonomy, he would have to resort to the heraldic figures of huge proportions that sever all ties with the spectator to whom they merely impart an admirable but abstract lesson.

But the poet's creation eludes the calculations of the theorist: any apperception of man other than intellectual will be assimilated in the form of an intimate experience and given the shape of the individual who grants it. The responses of the poet that are universal, his sensuousness, what Samson (*Paul Claudel poète-musicien,* 1947) has called his "music" cannot be narrowed to serve as the exemplification of particulars: Mesa, who realizes in terms of his own terrible love that God is love of superhuman strength, speaks for the benefit of spectators who will have sensed his love through the power of their own and who will thus understand Mesa more easily than God. In like manner, a more discerning craftsman—André Obey—will use the biblical myth of *Noé* (1931) in its most naïve explicitness, in order that from such specific details, the well-intentioned spectator might recall worlds of his own and thus participate in the most general, most simple, and most profound of experiences—what Fergusson has termed "in miniature, as it were in a colored stereoscopic view, the perpetual death and rebirth, the tragic rhythm, of human life" (*The Idea of a Theater,* 1949).

Claudel's is an art of huge dimensions that devours all things whole. In the theater, it demands every resource of the stage—ballet, music, scenery, color, unlimited space (this is truly a theater of the outdoors)—no less than it does the pungent reality of the author's native sod. The poetic torrent, the life force made word, has power sufficient to sweep away much of his poor taste—his stereotypes, his common prejudices, his jargon. *Christophe Colomb* (1927) demands motion pictures for its backdrop—everything, says the author (and the word explains his immoderation as well as his strength), everything can be used for the glory of God. This youthful gesture of an older author will fade in time: the poet will survive more awkward attitudes long after more conscious theater experimenters—an Apollinaire or a Jean-Victor Pellerin—will have perished for having been of meaner artistic constitution.

In the first act of *L'Echange* occurs the passage which, though given to Lechy, has been cited often as the author's vision of the theater. Like Claudel, the actress also envisages a captive spectator:

I look at them, and the hall is nothing but flesh alive and dressed.
And they fill the walls like flies up to the ceiling.
And I see those hundreds of blank faces.

.   .   .   .

They listen to me and they think what I say; they look at me and
    I enter their soul as into a vacant house.

It is this reversal—the inadvertence that attributes to the merely suggestive form the functions of the seminal agent—that sometimes prevents giving life to what is stillborn on Claudel's stage.

Sartre

The poet in Claudel plays the devil's advocate, sometimes with skill sufficient to save for man what was to have been for God. The presence of an immutable and discouragingly omniscient divinity paralyzes debate and robs even Christian man of his free will. Only when dramatis personae are released from this vise can their search proceed in a way that is not affected by moral predetermination—offering no overriding vision to make their orientation less precarious, and, within the drama itself, allowing no external force greater than the character to step within his path. That path is the character's very delineation: his own groping must determine its pattern. This "action" constitutes the drama.

The infallibility of an intellectual god may be no worse than the tyranny of the author's own systems: the personages of the first and of the second will have to defer to a pre-established scheme. Their path will be prescribed to serve as the outline of an intellectual proposition rather than allow it to shape their own configuration. This is the part of the theater that attracts the moral novelist when his specialized vision turns to the stage. As a result, his drama always presents the somewhat contrived appearance of a grafting. Great writers, even such as André Gide, have been induced to err—and his case is significant in that he wavered for a long time between expectations of genuine drama (witness his attacks on the "modernity" of Cocteau's *Antigone* in 1922) and his own difficulties in remaining less than "modern" (only a few years after having taken Cocteau to task, his own *Œdipe* of 1930 gave as its version of the Sophoclean curse, "if I knew the swine!").

A little before this, in 1920, Gide had set down in his *Journal* his fear that the drama could not be a work of art. The fear followed logically from the belief of a writer who had examined in particular that part of the theater that is not artistic—if art assumes necessary subordination to the limits of the chosen medium. The use of the stage for purposes better achieved elsewhere overextends its function while slighting that which is properly its own. Shortly before the publication of his *Œdipe,* Gide wrote in *Le Journal des Faux-monnayeurs:* "There can be just as much life in the realm of thought, and just as much anxiety, passion, suffering." This statement repeats the error of Claudel who had believed that the edifying drama lived by the Christian could remain dramatic upon the stage. Drama within the realm of thought is indeed possible, but thought is not the stuff of which formal drama is made. The theater used as a moral projection of the author's self for the purpose of thematic illustration, in even the relatively many facets of a Montherlant, diverts the life of the drama for the specific needs of the theme. If James McLaren (*The Theatre of André Gide,* 1953) can conclude of Gide's plays that they are devoid of esthetic compromise, is it not true that Gide has discarded the aspect of the theater that would have made his drama acceptable? A Cocteau, or with more significance, a Pirandello, are closer to dramatic essence for having worked first of all with the instruments of their craft.

The playwright dealing with ideas fails only to the extent that he effects godlike manacling of his people. The philosophy of a Jules Romains—his well-known *Unanimisme*—expresses such a general idea about collectivism that it can hardly constrain any story meant to illustrate it. Those ignorant of the author's aims will not have less understanding of his plays for having failed to read his manifesto in *La Revue Bleue.* In a somewhat different manner, François Mauriac's characters revert to the bloodless standards of the commercial stage because the over-explicit nature of his plays leaves no aspect that the spectator might enlarge upon within himself. The latter's contribution is thus frustrated because the surface of the drama has been made assertive in order to represent a specific idea through a specific surface.

The tenets of existentialism would appear at first glance to offer an auspicious area for the development of a successful drama of ideas: its philosophical nexus is dynamic rather than static and, in atheistic existentialism at least, God is eliminated as a manacling force and is absorbed completely by the existentialist hero. The usual assumption that men are of the essence Man is reversed, leaving man free to choose his essence, the species Man being voided in favor of the freedom to choose. Choice is everything—it is the existentialist's escape from bondage and the profoundest assertion of his being. His choice of himself, his "becoming," distinguishes him from the inert and static object that merely "is." He broadens this differentiation and the gap between his own dynamic consciousness and the "consciouslessness" of the object's *en-soi* by the constant need to renew his life-dispensing volition. Freedom thus becomes at once an absolute and an ultimate necessity, sweeping aside heretofore accepted codes and standards, and scrapping God incidentally with the dross. Antiquated notions of good and evil vanish and the equally outmoded Deity gives way to a human embodiment of Descartes' God, a creature bound neither by truth nor by good, but generating both— good being equated with the loftiest surge of freedom. The existentialist's world is in every sense the one in which Dostoevski believed everything would be possible if God did not exist.

However, the concept leads to consequences that Dostoevski probably did not suspect. These are implicit in Sartre's definition of freedom as total responsibility in total solitude. The total responsibility is brought about by the fact that, in this system of compulsive ethics, the existentialist is first of all responsible for what he is, and logically—though more pointedly—for what he is not. But responsibility has here an extended meaning. Revealing a psychological aspect similar to the idealism of Berkeley or that of Hume, it asserts that since acts exist only outside of us in the measure that we *feel* their import, responsibility is perforce part of a cosmic interlinking and hence *total*.

No concession is granted the individual in this harsh theology: he lives only during the time that he remains supremely conscious and honest. The fraudulent patterns of daily existence conspire to detract from the individual's true nature by making him their "pseudo-center." This will enable Sartre to expose—and in so doing to live—a nearly Pirandellian situation, *Kean* (1953). The familiar theme of the actor for whom the boundaries between acting and living are ill-defined is taken to symbolize an aspect of the existentialist's anxiety: the agonizing search for the self through the snares of that which is not "authentic." The interlinking of truth and illusion is interestingly extended, in that Sartre's play is, in reality, another aspect of that of Alexandre Dumas the elder (whose own play, in turn, was suggested by de Courcy's): the tenuous world of truth remains an illusive presence amidst tangible assertions of deceptiveness and fraud. Using the idea on dummies that serve especially as figures of topical satire, *Nekrassov* (1955) allows Georges de Valera, an international crook, to fabricate for himself the personality of Nekrassov, a Soviet official erroneously reported as having fled from Russia. Valera is primarily a man filled with existentialist pride, and in this gross buffoonery, his point of honor lies in his ability to sell himself as Nekrassov to a reactionary newspaper. But when he wishes once again to assert his volition, to reclaim his own being, he finds that it is he who is in fact being used by the government whose interests will not allow him to become Valera again.

If the deception is not accepted, total and oppressive solitude fastens inescapably upon the clear-sighted existentialist. The constantly present but nonexistent world comes to life through the onlooker's consciousness thereof. But again, this concept turns to a form of death in the mind of its creator because, ineradicably a social animal, he finds himself *living* the concept in the midst of others similarly living it. Therefore, society—or the relation of any such consciousness to any number of others similarly conceived—is perpetually generating "conflict." It might lead to hatred, or murder, neither of which can in any way affect this conflict or put an end to the individual's freedom. Love, all-powerful in more romantic days, it just as unavailing. Being an attempt to absorb another's freedom, it is doomed to failure as it cannot effect the total fusion which the success of such an attempt would require. It fails in the form of seduction, an a priori destruction of the relationship brought about by an altruistic attempt on the part of one of the lovers to turn "object" for the greater benefit of the other. It fails as masochism, a chronic and debased form of seduction. In *L'Etre et le Néant* (1943) Sartre seeks out all the other possible forms of love (sadism, sexual intercourse, etc.) and shows them to be each equally futile. Even though these instances do not exhaust the reasons for the existentialist's "aloneness," they are sufficient to account for Sartre's definition of freedom inasmuch as it also means total solitude.

Solitude of such intensity, beyond the reach of witness, reward, or deception, turning man entirely upon himself as his sole arbiter and ultimate conscience, is that of *Morts sans sépulture* (1946). The five Resistance fighters captured by the Germans and locked in a garret are "dead" in that no one sees them. Their acts thus assume absolute gratuitousness whose only redemption is their own frame of reference, the self—a frightful illustration of Heidegger's *Grendzsituation*. Each character has reached the outer limits of conventional human behavior and stands beyond every disguise, forced at present, even against what might be his innermost will, to question and to judge himself. Thus, the coward Sorbier knows at last that he is a coward and his curse becomes that of those Sorbiers in the fraudulent world outside prison walls who will remain ignorant of their own cowardice. And so for each of those within the real world of the garret, there is left only irrecusable awareness and the need to make a choice for which he must answer solely to his own inexorably lucid conscience.

The fraudulent patterns of everyday life make the existential responsibility and its quest all the harder and the more imperative. Sartre is thus led to define the revolutionary act as the free act par excellence. Sartre's play of revolution is *Les Mains sales* (1948). Hugo Barine has been entrusted by the Party he has joined to do away with one of its leaders, Hoederer, whose present policies appear to be going against the best interests of the Party. Having met Hoederer, however, Hugo gradually comes under his spell and by degrees weakens in his resolve. It is only upon seeing his wife in the arms of Hoederer that he performs in a flash of anger the act which he had been unable to accomplish until then. He is sent to jail on a minor sentence for what appears to have been a *crime passionnel* and released before the expiration of his sentence. Upon his return, he finds that during his imprisonment Party lines have changed to conform with the views of the man he has killed. Thus, if he acknowledges that he did away with the former leader in a mere fit of jealousy, he will be free of the stigma that presently weighs upon him and he will be allowed to return to the fold. In an outburst of existentialist assertion, Hugo chooses to give his act meaning and, at the price of his life, he claims it was intentional.

The ideas that underlie this plot are considerably more complex, and in a large measure, they are so because of the very complexity of the man upon whom the existentialist operation is being performed, Hugo Barine. (It must be remembered that since the existentialist author is not interested in essences, his fiction will not attempt to isolate the universal aspects of any crisis but will exploit instead only those particularities present in relation to a specific individual upon whose mode of existence he is, in effect, experimenting.)

Hugo has joined the Communist Party out of a desperate need to assert his own being to himself. The bourgeois life he has given up had found him as wanting as he gradually found it to be. But because he is an intellectual, "an amateur," no one takes him too seriously here either. He is relegated to putting out the clandestine newspaper, a job which he does conscientiously, but one whose tameness plagues him with a growing feeling of impotence. It is finally through the leonine Olga that he is entrusted with his mission.

His wife Jessica, who accompanies him, is interesting in her own right. She is a young woman who has never been allowed to live. She is not prepared to help Hugo, for her personality does not extend to the levels at which Hugo's anxiety exists—though, more superficially, she is able to save him from physical dilemmas. The only result she achieves thereby is to make Hugo realize that even such a creature is more fit to act in this world than he is. Thus, to a basic lack of comprehension, new torments caused by mutual contrast are added to stifle any love that might have grown between the two.

It is apparent from the start that Hugo is incapable of killing Hoederer. He is not afraid to die—this life has offered him too little for him to regret it—but he is too keenly aware of the physical existence of Hoederer *existentially* and, according to a more conventional code, too conscious of the human value of the man's life. He is an intellectual: he thinks too much. He postpones an act he was committed to perform speedily. The existentialist must act: Hugo is not yet a *man*. To make things worse, he is abashed by the sheer stature of Hoederer, who, in contrast to Hugo, is the complete man. Hoederer is virile, but human withal. He loves men "for what they are," pathetic, naked, and afraid. This allows him genuine understanding of those he leads and enables him to define Hugo: "You're a kid who's having a bad time reaching manhood." But he holds out promise for Hugo "if someone smooths your way."

The reality of Hoederer reveals to Jessica the tangible quality of life: his strength is a reality from which she had been kept until then. It is she who forces both men to confront each other openly. More perceptive than her husband, for her lack of any affiliation does not muddle her judgment, she knows that Hoederer will be the winner. Hoederer wins easily, and after demonstrating to Hugo that he cannot kill him, generously turns mouthpiece for his existentialist author in a short sermon reminiscent of Camus' *Mythe de Sisyphe:* acts transcend their results; victories are unimportant as the dignity of man is salvaged in the effort. Hoederer will now assume the burden of Hugo's education.

But, for the necessities of the dramatic action, a nearly classical fatality haunts Hugo. Jessica gives herself to Hoederer in a scene which, because of the very romanesque hue of her ideas and the honest warnings of Hoederer, appears to be nearly coercion on her part. It is at that moment that Hugo re-enters the room. The words "if someone smooths your way" which Hoederer had so humanely spoken take on a poignantly ironic meaning for Hugo and yield their full bitterness. Betrayed once again, as he believes, Hugo seizes the gun that Hoederer had taken from him only seconds before and momentarily expiates a lifetime of frustration in the three shots he fires at him.

The years Hugo spends in prison thereafter teach him nothing. If he has aged, he has done so only in terms of the bitterness of his confinement and his ruminations. In the existentialist sense, he is still an incomplete man, deriving no benefit from his act in that he has not as yet made a conscious choice or assumed any responsibility. Olga will reopen the door for him. Hoederer has become a hero during the time of Hugo's confinement. Since Hugo is not sure of his motivation, why not allow it to be one of petty jealously—he will be *récupérable,* and will be able to resume his former life with Olga, who has become his prop since the shooting, instead of Jessica. But within this proposed solution Hugo has the revelation of a more sublime salvation. He had accepted his mission because he had believed Hoederer was wrong. He need now but assert the volition of his act to assume at last a definite responsibility which he will then seal with his life. It is a man free at last from the fetters of groping and indecision, exultant in the feeling of his responsibility finally shouldered, who kicks open the door to his executioners, shouting his deliverance: "Non récupérable!"

The mere outline of plot shows Sartre to be, in the French

tradition of dramatic craftsmanship, an effortless creator of the well-made play with no loose ends—the sort of play that raises no logical objections. Plot delineation for its own sake, that of a Scribe or a Sardou, supposes a character who is not substantially different from the one subordinate to a theorem or an intellectual postulation: that character remains in bondage until the spectator is satisfied that reactions which he feels to be natural have given the dramatic events their particular turn. A philosopher, in whose hands the theater is but a tool skillfully used, Sartre finds himself in further danger of debasing his characters once he abandons the safe criteria of universality in order to exemplify particulars. The redemption of Sartre will be that of Claudel since no character can indefinitely serve two masters and will instead lend itself to the spectator, granted certain favorable conditions.

In his statement for *Theatre Arts* ("Forgers of Myths," 1946), Sartre has sketched aspects of his stage views for the benefit of an American audience. He recalls that his first dramatic experience was as a prisoner in Germany in 1940. He staged a Christmas play "which, while pulling wool over the eyes of the German censors by means of simple symbols" was addressed to his fellow prisoners. The remarkable silence and attention of the latter gave him a realization of what theater ought to be: "a great, collective, religious phenomenon." Although Sartre refuses to give up esthetic distance, he believes that for the purpose of such communion, the playwright "must create his public [. . .] by awakening in the recesses of their spirits the things which all men of a given epoch and community care about." Sartre thus confirms the temporal nature of the play and allows his characters their first step down to the level of the audience. Once they have crossed from his world to that of the spectators, the characters will be able to retain their functional value only in fortuitous moments.

Interestingly, Sartre does not acknowledge this. The written word, which he sees as a social fact, cannot be an instrument ("Qu'est-ce que la littérature?" in *Situations II,* 1948). The existentialist who writes must observe an esthetic distance which is a sublimation of his emotions. This allows the reader to react by means of similarly "free emotions," his existential catharsis being in fact his ability to apprehend the esthetic object through objective feelings. It is therefore possible for the existentialist to write about man within this world while avoiding the confinement of the historical moment, just as his creation existing in the "Imaginary" escapes from the everyday absurd. In this way, the existentialist is not subject to the "bad conscience" of the bourgeois writer who is caught between social commitments and the desire to create non-contingent art —which, according to Sartre, does not exist.

Whether or not the one who apprehends a work of art is capable of such dissociation from his usual self, or whether he can legitimately be asked to effect such dissociation, this writing has attempted to show that in the theater at least it would be both unnatural and antidramatic for the spectator to thus objectify his relation to the play which is after all not a "pure" esthetic entity but one deeply contaminated by the human presence that shapes it.

Hugo Barine has been called by Rabi (*Esprit,* 1950) "the Hamlet of Sartre, but in this sense, that his character participates of that double interpretation through his fear of the act and through his feeling of the inanity of every act." Such groping is in fact not exclusively that of an atheistic existentialist: Hamlet has implications considerably broader. Similarly, to

Hugo's final revelation (one not granted Hamlet) might correspond the necessary insight that precedes the ultimate abatement in classical tragedy: understanding need not be qualified in any way to be valid.

According to a Kierkegaardian ideal, the existentialist play is designed to do away with the philosophical textbook. But the play handed over to the spectator will become property of the spectator, who effects an unconditional and inevitable appropriation. For the philosophical play, this transfer presents danger in that postulations unspoken threaten to grow stealthily at the expense of the relatively few formal notions which the philosopher is able to develop. Hugo is conceived alone in the spectator's own loneliness. A further step (post-theatrical) is demanded to effect the existentialist synapse. Hugo's conflict with Jessica is first that of ordinary people, before even implications of general incommunicability are suggested. To establish them as protagonists of the existentialist conflict demands the interpretation of a specialist. Yet it is this *malaise existentialiste* that sets the necessary psychological climate for the acceptance of its philosophical tenets. Because it represents a cohesive action, the play cannot reduce itself to the existentialist *absurde* without negating the formal items of its message. To make things philosophically worse, the people in *Les Mains sales* do not appear to be robbing each other of their essential personality for atavistically selfish ends. Set as they are in a Communist cell, they give instead an impression of human solidarity, as evidenced by that of the persistently humane Hoederer or by Olga, a character who should have been an impersonal gear in the party machine but whose devotion to Hugo destroys her philosophical meaning, on both the dramatic and the existentialist levels.

If Sartre refuses to recognize emotions, it is in part because depersonalization is necessary for the correct development of a thesis that must remain free from the unpredictable human quantity. But the spectator reinstates those very elements that make for philosophical inaccuracy. Sartre is already at fault when in his theoretical writing he illustrates abstract thought by means of concrete images: the material detail invites argument which the axiom opposes. Reliance on such "tangibilities" is the less permissible as, in theory, Sartre rejects them himself as being part of the deceptive and fraudulent vagaries of everyday life.

Sartre, already a victim of the spectator's misappropriation of his symbols, will similarly find the spectator likely to misinterpret the moral aspect of any question he treats existentially. For the existentialist, the attribute "moral" is replaced by "coherent." Acts need only the sanction inherent in spontaneity—"The profound choosing is one with the consciousness that we have of ourselves" (*L'Etre et le Néant*). Sartre points out that the painter is not required to paint according to rules confirmed by tradition: his artistic value and the basis for his judgment depend on the "coherence" of his work. This acceptable idea cannot apply, however, to the writing of plays if their author has chosen to speak a language of the past, for he will then have to illustrate new terms through old values. The acts of the existentialist hero might thus conform to patterns externally similar to those of people whose motives may differ from existentialist ideals. Are not the participants in *Les Mains sales* too static—even as revolutionaries? And yet it is Sartre who demands permament revolution, whereas the Marxist works toward the stabilization of an order (and thus comes under existentialist fire). Hoederer "loves" when love as such, or his expressed humanity, has no meaning. Sartre rejects characterization in terms of pre-established essences: "The people in our plays will be distinct from one another—not as a coward is from a miser or a miser from a brave man, but rather as actions are divergent or clashing, as right may conflict with right" ("Forgers of Myths"). Yet the clan represented by Hoederer and Olga is exponential of a *good* idea, whereas the prince and Karsky pitted against them have evil connotations. This situation is the more damning in that these avowedly meaningless terms are taken here in their simplest, oldest, and most conventionally moral sense. Sartre has indicated that the Marxists are not changing any basic values but simply eliminating certain of the old values (such as God) in order to abide by the very same moral directives as before the useless amputation: they are in fact adhering to a very positive and stable order of ideas. But the problem remains insoluble for the existentialist as long as he must express values for which there are no ready-made terms while using symbols familiar in another form to the audience he is attempting to reach.

It is thus curious to hear, in "Forgers of Myths," a call for esthetic distance, though this follows logically from the thesis developed in "Qu'est-ce que la littérature?" But indeed, after attacking Baty's 1942 production of *The Taming of the Shrew* for using steps that led into the audience (and indeed, after those steps in his own drama down which Sartre's characters descend into the audience) Sartre says:

We are very far away from such concepts and methods. To us a play should not seem too *familiar*. Its greatness derives from its social and, in a certain sense, religious functions: it must remain a rite; even as it speaks to the spectators of themselves it must do so in a tone and with a constant reserve of manner which, far from breeding familiarity, will increase the distance between a play and audience.

The idea of a rite is that of an intimate association of initiates participating in a single ceremonial: this explains the use of Baty's steps. But Sartre's nostalgia for detachment has its roots elsewhere: quite obviously he regrets the contamination that debases his necessary symbols.

Sartre had made an early attempt to circumvent this contamination in *Les Mouches* (1943), by transposing the philosophical issues into symbolic drama. The myth is admirably suited for the purpose, presenting a given aggregate of material and moral data, within which the hero will effect his personal development: in the same sense, Claudel had used the inflexible postulate of God as his framework. Sartre uses the Oresteia in such a way as to let Orestes find himself existentially. The hero as he returns to Argos has not yet made the existential commitment: he is seeking himself aimlessly, believing that a personality is made of home, friendship, memories, and all the customary notions which accord with the notion of an empty freedom that he has learned from his pedagogue. A stranger to himself and to the world, the hero comes home impelled by reminiscences of former ties. Argos is at present a thing of Jupiter, the conventional god who feeds on contriteness and who hopes by this device to keep man from discovering his singular freedom. Jupiter's foreman in this enterprise is Aegisthes who keeps the year-round contrition alive by appropriate ceremonial. The sole dissenter is Electra. She revolts in limited ways, as best she can, while awaiting the return of her brother who, she hopes, will do away with the murderous Aegisthes and his villainous accomplice, Clytemnestra.

Orestes' decision to stay is badly motivated at first: "I want my memories, my land, my place in the midst of the men of Argos [. . .] I want to be a man who belongs to some place, a man amongst men." Though the reasons are bad, the stay gives the hero a context which will become his responsibility: he has chosen the area of his action, the action must needs follow. Still, while he wavers, his gestures are without meaning: they are not his. His very victim Aegisthes remains hostilely passive: "I will not defend myself. I want you to kill me." The emphasis is on *want* and robs Orestes of what might have been his act.

Freedom must have "exploded in the heart of a man" before he can effect his regeneration. Orestes is presently contrasted with Electra who falls prey to Jupiter and to remorse, though the Erinyes (the flies, *les mouches*) loosed against both rebels are unable to penetrate the magnificent isolation of the hero. Against Jupiter, Orestes has understood his own autonomy— the neo-stoic has grasped his own immortality and invulnerability. Jupiter gives up the fight and speaks the epilogue: "A man was supposed to announce my twilight." A pied piper of collective guilt, Orestes leaves the city trailing a wake of symbolic flies, having at last transcended his people as their conscience.

Orestes is here the existentialist culmination of a long line of lucidly auto-analytic characters on the French stage; throughout his entire development he remains clearly aware of his inner self:

You have left me the freedom of those threads which the wind tears from spider-webs and that drift ten feet away from the ground; I do not weigh more than a thread and live in the air.

．　　．　　．　　．

I am neither the master nor the slave, Jupiter. I *am* my freedom! The moment you created me I ceased belonging to you.

．　　．　　．　　．

[We shall go] towards ourselves. Beyond the streams and the mountains there are an Orestes and an Electra waiting for us. We will have to seek them patiently.

Perhaps it is because of such unveiled sentences that Sartre has emphasized the element of spectacle in the play through the grandiose mob scenes, the suggested ballet which the Erinyes perform, etc. Nevertheless, the lay audiences run into difficulties on seeing the performance. Unless they are existentialists already, they have no way of bridging the discrepancy between Sartre's contextual inferences and their own. Atheism, for example, must be accepted as a Sartrian, self-evident premise. Otherwise the awesome Jupiter who rolls the temple walls away and reveals the revolving stars, intoning that he is the Good against which Orestes has transgressed, seems quite convincing and bids fair to steal the entire show. Orestes, thus cast in a somewhat dubious Nietzschean light, grows even more ambiguous in the closing scene where he takes on Christlike appearance and terminology:

I had come to claim my kingdom and you cast me out because I was not one of you. Now I am one of you, oh my people, we are bound in blood and I deserve to be your king. Your faults and your remorse, your nocturnal anguish, the crime of Aegisthes, all are mine, I take it all upon myself.

But this is to be placed in the proper frame of reference spoken by Orestes at the start of the action and dispelling Christian implications: "Expiate? I said that I would take unto me your repentance, but I did not say what I would do with this screeching fowl: I might wring its neck."

Orestes' "anxiety," though existentially correct, further clouds his portrait since it makes him appear to be at once in revolt against God and the Good, Christian in his atonement for his fellows' sins and at the same time fearful—though obviously undaunted by the sacred powers. The ambiguity extends to metaphysical areas wherein the philosopher is once again betrayed by the stage limitations that twist many of his ideas out of their original shape. In a play even as broadly symbolic as this one, there remains danger of distortion by what is unavoidably concrete. The murder in *Les Mouches* conforms to plot and lore, but through its very being tends to destroy vital and undisclosed problems of existentialism: the universal implications of the individual's acts. Orestes' preoccupation with his own freedom must make his acts symbolic, very much as Giraudoux's Electre must remain only a symbol. But if this interpretation is accepted, the drama is no longer one of "right against right" for his victims are of no consequence. If they should be, the scope of Orestes' selfish quest assumes proportions scarcely acceptable since his "right" has been set against another equally valid. Marjorie Grene has remarked (*Dreadful Freedom: A Critique of Existentialism,* 1948) that the truth of a physical proposition is no guarantee of the truth this same proposition might have when elevated to the status of an abstract system and considered out of its justificatory context. On stage, this means that Sartre will be forced to condone an act with no justification in the body of his ethics, an unfortunate dilemma for one who has chosen as communication the medium whose virtue is directness, for which it sacrifices the more explicit but more hazardous bypass of the mind.

Should the lesson of *Les Mouches* be properly understood, however, it will be derived from the change in the quality of Orestes' isolation that evolves from that of a superficial distance (which might be deceptively bridged) to that of the

hero's final commitment when he is alone *positively,* beyond
the reach of man or God.

The dependence of God upon man for His realization, and
the refusal of man to allow this realization, will be illustrated
anew by Goetz in *Le Diable et le Bon Dieu* (1951). This medieval hero makes at first the usual false assertions: he proves
what he considers his freedom through plunder, theft, and
murder. The priest Heinrich, the advocate of God, suggests
that a harder challenge lies in the doing of good. Goetz, cheating at the cast of the dice, accepts that challenge. He now
spares lives that are at his mercy, distributes land, preaches
brotherly love. His acts remain without echo and, physically,
they turn against him. Goetz has thus failed in the service of
good and has proved the inanity of moral terms: evil or good,
right or left, nobility or the peasants—all alike are deflectors of
the truth which the hero must seek within himself only. Goetz
is allowed a few penultimate hesitations—brief visions of the
havens of love, of submission—but these are short-lived: "I
will remain alone" is his last resolution and his culminating
vision. The war he now undertakes on behalf of the peasants is
one that answers only his own innermost conscience. He will
act henceforth before the judge within him, having spoken the
moral of *L'Etre et le Néant:* "God does not exist if man exists."

The play is weak as a dramatic vehicle, not only because of
its great length, but especially because the philosopher over-
powers the playwright. Sartre, whose language consistently remains that of a mass idiom, here reaches what Thierry Maulnier has called "blasphemous violence, with a sort of alacrity."
The tone makes the play an explicit pamphlet: Sartre is *engagé*
—committed to an extent that leaves little room for his characters. Goetz's isolation is more easily understood than felt. Nor

is God a presence: the feeling of a superhuman menace is replaced by a single word—and one used so frequently that on
occasion even the thesis seems to become a tirade. Were it not
for this, the play might have been considered an existentialist
success; the act within the given situation so conforms to the
situation that the spectator is afforded little chance to establish
his own potentially different situation. The theorem succeeds
at the expense of its people, as had already that of *La Putain
respectueuse* (1946) in which a wholly spurious American
prostitute was placed in an unconvincing South to illustrate,
through the racial problem, existentialist questions of freedom
and of commitment. The play disappoints more than does *Le
Diable et le Bon Dieu* as the latter relies less upon its characterization. In both instances, however, Sartre's dialectic dominates characters that remain intellectual propositions devoid
of the animal truth which transcends these propositions in
much of the author's drama.

In contrary fashion, a play like *Huis clos* (1944) absorbs the
most patent statements of existentialism and remains one of
the best arguments in favor of the modern tragedy that would
probe universals through a psychological drama in depth.

Three people, Garcin, Inès, and Estelle, are locked within
the usual closed area of a Sartre play. Here, it is a hotel room,
Hades, which they will make their mutual hell as each in turn
finds that communication with the others is impossible. To
this immediate failure is added the eternal memory of failure
in their recent lives, lives which are now ended and beyond
their power to amend. Garcin, upon whom the analysis cen-
ters, is pondering the events immediately preceding his death.
Do his actions indicate that he was a coward? Cannot his paci-
fism be interpreted as heroism? The equation of his guilt with

that of his two cell mates, a criminal homosexual and an infanticide, provides the inescapable answer. As each of the characters plays hangman to the others, the existentialist marrow of the play can be expressed plainly:

GARCIN: I did not dream that heroism. I chose it. One is what one wants to be.

INES: Prove it. Prove that it was not a dream. Only acts determine what one has wished.

GARCIN: I died too soon. I was not left enough time in which to accomplish *my* acts.

INES: One always dies too soon—or too late. And yet, there is life—ended; the line is drawn, you must add it all up. You are nothing else but your life.

For the necessity of demonstration, these people are dead. But the successful play cannot exhume a character who has made his statement fully and irretrievably before appearing on stage. It is with people fully alive that Sartre's spectators will achieve their identification. Estelle has killed her baby in a former life that belongs but remotely to this action. For a while at least she is a young and pathetic girl who longs desperately to return on earth, for only a moment— to dance. Even the forewarned critic will be led astray momentarily. This is but an instance of the variety of human emotions— love, shame, anxiety, etc.—upon which Sartre has been forced to draw. Each is a "fraudulent" detail in that the existentialist pith exists in spite of and beyond it. Sartre's people are rich with a wealth of feelings and moods that allow far more than merely a doctrinaire interpretation of the story which they enact. Only personages of obvious comedy, such as those in *Nekrassov,* remain as rudimentary and as functional as the author wishes them to be.

The author notes that significance was found in the Second Empire furniture with which he decorated his room in Hell (*Le Figaro Littéraire,* June 30, 1951): such attachment to the concrete should be an indication to him of the extent to which his characters will be appropriated by spectators heedless of his intent. Partisan differences may have influenced Heidegger's exclamation, "Sartre? A good writer but not a philosopher" (*Le Figaro Littéraire,* November 4, 1950), but it is a fact that critics like Bentley and Fergusson have been able to analyze Sartre's drama perceptively while completely neglecting the existentialist core—Fergusson going as far as to establish a curious preliminary: "It would be a mistake to dismiss his plays merely because his existentialism is so feeble as ethics or epistemology" (*Partisan Review,* 1949). Conversely, Sartre has been able to view all postwar French drama as existentialist—saying of Anouilh's Antigone, for example, that she is "a free woman without features at all until she chooses them for herself" ("Forgers of Myths"). On the basis of that interpretation, the classical hero does as much—and in the same article Sartre indeed claims a title to the Cornelian inheritance.

There is in such an all-embracing view of life a breadth that will not allow it to become a statement of particulars. In "Qu'est-ce que la littérature?" Sartre has written:

Reading is an exercise in generosity; and that which the writer demands of the reader is not the application of an abstract freedom but the gift of his entire being, with his passions, his prejudices, his sympathies, his sexual temperament, his scale of values.

The key word is "freedom." The "gift of his entire being" is not one offered by the reader for manipulation by the author. Rather, it is the gift of a being antecedent to the esthetic experience in preparation for which it must be cleansed. But in the theater where the author's characters, if they are to live at all, will live only *in* the donor, the objects that are proposed for esthetic transmutation are much more likely to be shaped by the spectator than they are to transform him. Whether or not their collective action may thereafter transpose the spectator to a more esthetic plane is a different and subordinate question. Through the living actor first of all, and then through every concession which he has made to the times, Sartre has given up the majority of his creations to his public: it is henceforth in that public's life and mode that theirs must be found. Should ever an existentialist consciousness be that of the spectator, Sartre's people will be recognized in the element for which they were designed. Until then, and long after the slang of a mid-twentieth century and of communist cells have passed, people of Sartre will still be enacting a significant drama, more simple and more profound than the vagaries of mores or philosophies.

4

Commercialism Reconsidered: Anouilh

BECAUSE OF Jean Anouilh's occasional arbitrariness in classifying his plays as *noires, roses, brillantes* or *grinçantes,* and for the purposes of identification and chronology, a five-group division can be established for the twenty-one plays here considered (that is to say, all his published plays up to the time of writing, except for the fragments, sketches or otherwise incomplete statements that do not bear on this discussion: *Humulus le muet, Mandarine, Attila le magnifique, Le Petit Bonheur, Oreste, Episode de la vie d'un auteur*). In each of these, and disregarding an occasionally misleading title, a figure either born pure or striving against his native and environmental impurity can be isolated and considered to be the hero. It is then possible to view each play as this hero's quest for salvation or his acceptance of the world, and it is possible to summarize the central action in terms of the principals concerned.

The first group, the largest, comprises those heroes whose redemption is achieved in death.

L'Hermine (1931), a play not unlike Sartre's *Les Mouches,* portrays Frantz in love with the young heiress Monime, whose rich and haughty aunt will never consent to their marriage. Frantz kills the aunt and, though he has escaped detection, assumes the responsibility of his act when he finds that it has cost him the love of a less strong Monime.

Eurydice (1941), is the Orpheus legend, the story of Orphée, an ambulant musician eking out a miserable existence with his unregenerate father. He meets a similarly burdened Eurydice with whom he leaves, only to lose her when the car crashes in which a weaker Eurydice was running away from him. Through intercession of the agent of death, a certain M. Henri, Eurydice can be his once more if he will not look into her eyes before morning. But when she is with him again, Orphée cannot keep his word because his tortured and uncompromising mind will not allow him to wait. Unable to countenance the unredeemed life which is his with the now definitely departed Eurydice, Orphée calls on M. Henri once again to be reunited with her in death.

Antigone (1942) is the brief tale of the defiance of Créon by Oedipus' daughter and of her death in spite of her uncle's attempts to save her. At one moment Créon gains the upper hand: when she gives a *reason* for her act—justice—he can counter with the reason of his logic: both the body she has tried to bury and the one that will receive the state's honors were so mutilated that he himself does not know which is which. But when he presses this advantage by showing Antigone her prosaic life thus regained and which must be its own justification, she once again breaks loose, claiming sole possession of her act, scorning every reasonable argument. In this play, Hémon is converted to her intractable point of view and accepts her solution—death.

Roméo et Jeannette (1945) has Frédéric as Roméo and as Juliet, *Juli*a and Jeann*ette,* two sisters belónging to a ramshackle family that includes the usual father and a once unhappily married brother, Lucien, who acts as chorus. Frédéric has come with his bourgeois mother and Julia to meet her family prior to his marriage with her. This is not Julia's idea for she, through reaction, has become the living antithesis of her kindred. Frédéric falls in love with Jeannette and this once promiscuous girl responds in kind to what is for her a meaningful and hitherto unknown experience. But when Julia's attempted suicide causes Jeannette to lose Frédéric, she marries the richest of her former suitors, a hasty gesture which she soon regrets. Dressed in her symbolically white bridal gown, she returns to Frédéric, offering to die with him since they cannot live together. Frédéric refuses, but when from the car in which he is leaving with his mother and Julia he sees Jeannette wading out to sea, he understands and runs after her to join her in death.

Médée (1946) is a one-act version of Euripides' play. In this, Médée dies in flames of her making symbolic of her temper that cannot envisage the prospect of a subdued Jason given over to the sham of respectability and convention.

L'Alouette (1953) is the story of Jeanne d'Arc left to the lonely victory of her martyrdom after realizing the hypocrisy of a brief recantation. The play ends with a recapitulative scene of Jeanne in her glory during the Rheims coronation—the usual cliché that serves to incriminate the audience along with the stage participants who have abandoned the saint in her moment of travail.

Ornifle, ou Le Courant d'air (1955) equates the symbolism of death and truth in a curious way. Ornifle is a successful poet whose verse once stood for what was most fresh and vibrant since Apollinaire. But now, facile success and superficiality are betokened in him by the pearls which he is given to wear by ladies who have found that his skin has rejuvenating powers. Ornifle foregoes a fancy-dress ball because of the premonition of a mysterious heart condition that doctors are unable to detect in him. Fabrice enters at this point. He is one of Ornifle's numerous unknown sons begotten by former mistresses and is intent upon killing the man who deserted his mother. This attempt fails because Marguerite, Fabrice's fiancée, has removed the bullets from the gun. But the meaningful shock of the experience brings on an attack and Ornifle faints. When he recovers, he recovers also a part of his former self. He now discovers a "soul" not only in himself but in those about him. As a result, he starts redeeming and explicating Machetu, his materialistic friend; Mademoiselle Supo, his old maid stenographer who has loved him these ten years; his remarkable wife, whose meaning has long been lost to him; his son Fabrice, whose youthful stiffness must be made supple to reveal an ideal that is yet too rigid; his future daughter-in-law Marguerite, in whom the "kitten" must be made to understand the love which it disguises; his friend, the Jesuit priest Dubaton, in whom charm and friendship will reveal the "illusionist" of religion. But in the final act, the doctors dismiss as illusory Ornifle's sickness and the poet returns to what he was when the curtain first went up: he tries to seduce Marguerite, abandons Machetu to his superficial nature, deserts his son. The hero goes off to meet a paramour in a hotel across the street from which comes news, a moment later, that Ornifle has died from the stroke that doctors had been unable to anticipate.

Two more plays are related to this group in spirit though their resolution is not specifically stated, or is tangential to the main action.

Colombe (1950) primarily concerns Julien, the rebellious son of Madame Alexandra, a famous actress and the habitual bad mother. Colombe is the very young flower vendor whom he one day meets. When he leaves for the army, Colombe, now his wife, is entrusted to Madame Alexandra and falls victim to the corruption that surrounds her, finally ending in the bed of Armand, Julien's brother. The play ends on an ironic flash-back: the scene of Julien and Colombe's first meeting.

La Répétition, ou L'Amour puni (1950) begins as the story of the aristocrat Tigre rehearsing a Marivaux play, *La Double Inconstance,* with the assistance, and for the entertainment, of his highly artificial and rarefied milieu. He meets in this syn-thetic world the usual poor young girl, Lucile, who looks after the orphanage located in a corner of Tigre's chateau. The countess, Tigre's wife, together with his mistress Hortensia, contrive to crush Lucile, Tigre's first true love. The scheme ultimately settled upon calls for Tigre's best friend, Héro, to seduce Lucile. Alluding to the supposed faithlessness of Tigre, Héro succeeds and thereafter Lucile flees from the castle—though Tigre leaves in search of her after learning of her de-parture. Starting with the seduction scene, however, the play is centered about Héro, who explains that years back, Tigre prevented him from marrying the girl he loved, causing her subsequent misery and death and his own present degrada-tion. Having completed this last gratuitous act of seduction, Héro attempts to die in a duel.

The second group of plays is made up of those that propose a relative victory, or at least an ultimate resolution, through life.

Jézabel (1932) is the unsatisfactory statement of Marc's brief battle and degeneracy. He is afflicted with the prototype of these leprous families—licentious parents. The mother, more-over, is a drunkard who poisons her husband. The contradis-tinctive Jacqueline, to whom Marc is engaged, represents salvation which he congenitally cannot reach. When she offers to remove him from the corruption that has so long been his, he, finding no arguments that will deter her, takes upon himself the murder which his mother has committed.

La Sauvage (1934) reverses the sexes in that a girl, Thérèse, is the poor young musician, marred and manacled by the usual family and sordid surroundings. Although engaged to the successful and perfect Florent, she, like Marc before her, cannot accept the sort of life that is here represented by Florent. She too attempts to destroy it by dragging into it her indecorous father. When she fails in this and other artificial attempts to bring about a break, after a fleeting moment of illusion, she shuns further excuses and of her own accord assumes once again her old life and the sordid integrity of its acceptance.

Pauvre Bitos, ou Le Dîner de têtes (1956) is summarized in the pun of the title which Jacques Prévert had already used with similar intent, *dîner de têtes* being taken to mean either a dinner at which the guests have their faces disguised, or one during which victims will have their heads put on the social block. Bitos is a poor and graceless upstart. He has been invited by resentful ex-schoolmates, who are either rich or well-bred, to a party meant to ridicule him. The theme of the masquerade is the French Revolution and each guest assumes historical features that fit his character, Robespierre's fanatical puritanism being assigned to Bitos. In the too faithful re-creation of the historical incidents, Bitos is nearly shot by a wartime delinquent whom he had condemned to a stiff prison term. To divert his anger and to make him even more ridiculous, Bitos is pressed into continuing the party in a local dive. At this point, Victoire, whose blue-blooded father had angrily refused her hand to Bitos that very afternoon, warns him of the plot and urges him to return to his native world of harshness and intransigent poverty. Bitos learns his lesson instantly, warning Victoire, "If I can ever take vengeance on all of you, I'll start with you!" And as he departs, Victoire speaks the concluding line, "Poor Bitos. . . ."

The third group of plays contains three near-comedies in which the hero is allowed to escape from the sordid reality of his past into the world of his vision.

Y'avait un prisonnier (1934) tells of Ludovic, a big business man who has just spent fifteen years in prison for unethical practices. The scene of his return is the yacht of Barricault, who represents the perverted society Ludovic left for jail. When Ludovic finds that he will never be able to re-enter that society, he jumps over the railing with a fellow convict whom he had brought with him, and heads for the shore upon which might be established a world different from that on the yacht.

Le Voyageur sans bagage (1936) is a certain Gaston, a victim of amnesia, and in reality the warped and cruel son of the Renaud family. When he discovers that as Jacques Renaud he stole his brother's wife, maimed his best friend during a quarrel over a seduced servant, and had a mother who quelled a possibly redeeming love affair of his, he disclaims the Renaud family and chooses instead to become a member of another family of which there remains only a little boy, about whom might be centered his own, more pleasant image of himself.

Le Rendez-vous de Senlis (1937) is an occasion planned by Georges to deceive Isabelle, the young girl he has recently met and whom he loves too much to soil with the reality of his ugly environment. He rents for the evening of his date an old family home which he furnishes with an ideal family to be created by paid actors. Georges' friend Robert and Robert's wife Barbara

(Georges' mistress) are parasites living together with Georges' family on his wife Henriette; they presently intrude upon the idyllic setting while Georges is away. But Isabelle and Georges resist this intrusion of the past and remain together to attempt the dream.

The fourth group consists of four comedies in which a better heroine (though not of the usual epic stature) redeems a weaker hero.

Le Bal des voleurs (1932) takes place at a spa where a bored Lady Hurf, her two nieces Juliette and Eva, and a senescent Lord Edgar encounter two older thieves and their young apprentice Gustave. Juliette and Gustave fall in love, but although Gustave wholly agrees with Lady Hurf that such a match cannot be, the candid but determined heroine sets about to change his mind.

Léocadia (1939) was an actress who had utterly fascinated a bored prince, and who left him disconsolate upon her death. His aunt, the duchess, discovers Amanda, a little milliner, who is Léocadia's physical image, and brings her into the fake world made up of all the props used by the prince and the actress during their brief encounter. The reality of Amanda collapses this world and destroys the ghost of Léocadia.

L'Invitation au château (1947) is a fairylike comedy of errors. The identical twins are Frédéric, engaged to Diana Messerschmann, and Horace, who knows that Diana has consented to that engagement out of spite because, though she loves him, he has turned her down. To thwart Diana and to protect the innocent Frédéric, his bitter and ruthless twin brings to the castle a beautiful but poor young dancer, Isabelle, and her stereotyped mother. By the time Diana discovers the plot, Frédéric has come under the spell of Isabelle and after a disentangling of the comic plot, the two sets of lovers are harmoniously paired off.

Cécile, ou L'Ecole des pères (1949) is a Molièresque *bluette*. Araminthe, Cécile's wise companion, persuades M. Orlas, Cécile's father, that his daughter will no more sin in marrying her lover than he will in marrying her.

The last group is that of the two farces, *Ardèle, ou La Marguerite* (1948) and *La Valse des toréadors* (1951), both presenting as a central figure general Saint-Pé, though the first play derives especially from his sister's illicit love and the complications and comments issuing from it. *La Valse des toréadors* is wholly the story of the general, still tortured by his invalid wife Amélie and who, on the verge of salvation through Ghislaine de Sainte-Euverte who has waited for him for seventeen years, loses her to his secretary with whom she has fallen in love.

ANOUILH'S IS a drama of shame. A voice variously named Gustave, Thérèse, Eurydice, Julien, Isabelle, Julia, repeats throughout this theater, "I am ashamed . . ." Until the supernaturally inspired Jeanne, every hero acknowledges his shame at some juncture of his life. Such junctures are focal points of his misery, the fulcrum upon which balance his overgrown pride and poverty.

Pride and poverty, the distinctive polarity of these people, point to the respective worlds that make up this polarity, the interaction of which fashions the hero: that of the illusion which he demands and that of the reality into which he has been inescapably willed.

The chorus that concludes *Antigone* remarks, "Without little Antigone, it's true, they would have all been resting easily." The remark is a valid one to make about the personal tragedy of the majority of Anouilh's heroes: without their cantankerous vision, always diametrically opposed to their reality, there would be little in them to arouse excitement. But excitement is the whole of these true creatures of illusion —it is their unique claim to stature and their sole effort toward salvation. Their illusion becomes a reality at least to the extent of their formidable anger.

Aristotle's tragic protagonist was an ideal projection but for the one, circumscribed area of his failing. His ills thus grew from him organically without disfiguring him. Anouilh's protagonist is conceived disfigured but for that clamorous pride which must shield his true being from the world and, for a while, from himself. The moment of his dramatic life is measured by the time required for the individual to destroy this shield.

Physically, the creation is fairly uniform. The hero—generally a heroine—is poor. The young Anouilh, that of *L'Hermine, Jézabel, La Sauvage,* remembered his own poverty, and unregenerate, material, abject penury—the sort caused by money and its want—establishes the area of the conflict. Yet even for Marc, in *Jézabel,* some of the indigence transcends that of money—he is poor, he is destitute of Jacqueline's world, and briefly, as will so many of these people, he tries to cheat: "I do not have any such [memories]. So, naturally, I use yours." The world of Jacqueline, vaster than that of wealth, but based on wealth in Marc's rudimentary analysis, is now tangibly established: the ambivalent hero will attempt to become a spiritual part of it while setting against it the physical truth of his own world until the hard fact of reality has worn away the spiritual illusion completely.

Before its collapse, that illusory world is one of unmixed purity. Frantz, the criminal who kills for money, is *L'Hermine* which, when cornered, lets itself be captured rather than get its pure-white coat sullied. The judgment of the world that would indict Frantz for precisely those acts from which his presumed salvation emerges cannot reach him since the world that formulated that judgment is not his—his world encompasses merely the gestures of his redemption and exists only in antithesis to the other. The tacit recognition of the conventional world which this deliberate antithesis implies troubles the hero no more than do any of the outer world's remonstrances—moral or logical. For Frantz there is no discrepancy —there is in fact a subtle linking—between the statements of his two beings. The first attempts integration on the terms of the physical realities into which he is thrust: "Why do you always believe, all of you, that something underhand is implied when one speaks of money, when, on the contrary, money alone affords isolation from what is underhand?" The second is spoken by the hero who has finally cast off the world: "If I killed her, it was not for her money, it was because her money, in the mysterious balance of things, was the exact price of our purity."

Since the evils of this drama are the world and its various excrescences, all symbolized by massiveness—the mark of that which is hard, extended, durable, gross, and insensitive—the hero will be physically frail. Somatically disqualified unless they happen to be felicitously fragile, male protagonists give way to women on this stage—or, still more frail, to *jeunes filles*. But these, contrary to those of Giraudoux, are physical beings suffering the dual weakness of the term: they combine the frailty of youth and of girls. The Anouilh *jeune fille* is "tiny" (Thérèse), "skinny" (Eurydice), "that frail little body" (Jeanne)—but also "more hard than the others" (Médée).

The hardness of the heroine derives from this delicate frame. No part of her body will allow the physical, and hence the moral, unwholesomeness of softness. Though frail in structure it will be redeemed by the moral toughness of the character into whose likeness it will develop. *La Sauvage,* Thérèse, is the prototype of such bodily assumption when she leaves the stage "hard and lucid," as would have been the ideal Colombe in Julien's mind, "hard, demanding, closed."

The flesh and its softness will be ever-yielding, ever-secretive, and unknown—symbols of weakness and deceit, along with the falseness of accompanying frills and finery. The skeletal heroine of Anouilh remains morally transparent in every physical attribute and goes about as Isabelle, Lucile, Amanda, Juliette, "completely naked" but for an equally ascetic cloth dress. The figure whose flesh reveals a woman, like Jeannette or Colombe—"with a bosom this big"—is the agent of a specific evil or, more subtly, prefigures the moral slackness through the physical: Amanda, the otherwise perfect replica of Léocadia, is just a little too *thin* for the part. This ideal of leanness denies youth, which it mocks just as it mocks, through parody, unattainable old age, thus bestowing upon each heroine tenderly called "little old lady" the ironic solace of an unrealizable dream.

Absence of the flesh means absence of carnality and establishes another opposition to the conventional world. These women, in whom everything denies their sex, respond to another ideal. Instead of their body, they bring to their men (whom they will inevitably dominate) the blessings of the anti-flesh, those virile qualities of hardness, intransigence, and purity as merciless as the corruption whence they issue. Through the intercourse of what Hubert Gignoux (*Jean Anouilh*, 1946) calls "a sort of [. . .] boy and girl scouting," the slight Thérèse becomes Florent's "little man"; the thin Eurydice, Orphée's "little brother"; the frail Jeanne, La Hire's "pal" (*copain,* not *copine*); and the hard Médée's intimacy with Jason is that of "the little soldier and the captain."

The relationships of these people are just another aspect of the inability of each to accept the normal conditions of his being, and together with the word "little"—which indicates that some sexual distinction still exists—it points to the inevitable collapse of the dream. That collapse is already more than adumbrated by the being that has been hidden since curtain rise. Thérèse and Eurydice are from almost the same milieu: it has soiled the first and perverted the second. And although the national saint of France, Jeanne, occupies a privileged position in this drama, the Euripidean sins of ruthlessness and murder do not suffice Médée who must achieve her entry among Anouilh women through carnality perverted and faithlessness.

Incontinence in the women, the vice out of which will grow the mythical, antipodal virtue, is matched by assorted vices in those males who are heroes. Just as Frantz is a murderer, Ludovic (*Y'avait un prisonnier*) is a dishonest and convicted magnate, Marc steps out of the past of Thérèse and Eurydice, and so does Georges, who will try to make of *Le Rendez-vous de Senlis* the exact inversion of that world. With money, Georges and Anouilh both have found the world as grim as that which was bereft of material wealth.

Helpless creatures of the mire from which they can derive but a brief and contrary illusion, they wholly give themselves up to that illusion and fiercely damn those who do not recognize it. Thereby, they temporarily achieve a mirage sufficiently convincing to cancel the ugly reality out of which that mirage developed, and announce the state of their ultimate assumption after the bodily remission of their stage life. "You will remember my tears and my great thirst for purity," says the criminal Frantz as he goes off, escorted by policemen, to the final transcendence of his physical wretchedness. In the same way will go Thérèse and Eurydice after having similarly canceled their promiscuity, Ludovic his malfeasance, the cheat Gaston (*Le Voyageur sans bagage*) his botched and brutal youth, Médée her sins of nearly every denomination.

Barring the previously sanctified Jeanne, only a comedy character like Juliette in *Le Bal des voleurs* can exclaim, "I am not ashamed" (though even she is known to be a "terrible and sweet little girl"). Even those agents of erosion, those materializations of the hero's ideal against which he will wear away, are either functional creations about whom nothing more is known, like Marc's Jacqueline or the Isabelle of *Le Rendez-vous de Senlis,* or they too are incriminated by their past. Colombe's Julien, that other Isabelle (*L'Invitation au château*), Lucile, in *La Répétition,* messengers of salvation though they be, carry some of their antecedent being with them, as Julien and Isabelle carry their mother, and occasionally acknowledge their bitter kinship as when Lucile tells Héro, "One does not die of shame so easily, believe me."

Wholly dedicated to such an ideal of ruthless intransigence, these creatures rarely have any of that weakness, human warmth, that would attract those within their orbit—and the public. Their virtue demands instead isolation and admiration. "Pride," which they all have, insufferably, is too abstract a trait. Because their physical angularity demands a moral reflection they are, like Antigone and Julien, simply "bad-tempered." Because their isolation is a virtue, their general obnoxiousness which facilitates that isolation is of course a positive characteristic also. Anyhow, it is directed against the world which can be postulated as evil since it is the counterpoise to their dream. Ludovic, after his release from fifteen years of confinement, attempts to find out from his once best friend Marcellin what the latter has done with his fifteen years of freedom. The point here attempted by the play is that Marcellin's freedom has kept him more confined—since he enjoyed no belated revelation—than was Ludovic by his imprisonment. Actually, it is Ludovic's revelation of his sudden superiority over a rejected world that must make him dismiss as futile Marcellin's acts, no matter what they might be. Ludovic is now a hero, superior and isolated but for the targets of his infallible judgment and his rebellion.

No part of that world, however, is too futile to be rejected since each of its parts can provide opposition. Julien has rejected convention: "No, I do not want to be sociable!" Lucile rejects logic that might ensnare her: "I do not want to be reasonable." Ludovic won't work, Antigone has compacted all of her being into the single word "no." Ornifle is a swan upon whose back water leaves no trace. It makes little difference what they refuse. In *L'Invitation au château,* Horace, in musing about his "sergeant during the war," is able to raise an army camp cliché to the dignity of a moral standard: " 'I don't want to hear about it!' There was a man!" Thereafter, the hero can remark with varying degrees of bitter pleasure, like Machetu to Ornifle, like Lucien (*Roméo et Jeannette*), the general (*La Valse de toréadors*), the banker Messerschmann

(*L'Invitation au château*), "One is all alone." And Orphée will discover that even as lovers one remains "two skins, two envelopes, well sealed."

Very soon the hero's revolt turns into an orgasm of refusal. The very last glimmer of Antigone's detested "rotten hope" is snuffed out. Jason, who speaks with the objective clarity of the anti-hero (and who here echoes that other anti-hero, Créon, speaking to Antigone), says to Médée: "The more of us there will be to judge you, to hate you, the better it will be, won't it?" For a while, hope of materializing the illusion enables the hero to grasp at something beyond himself and slows him in his descent. But once that grasp is broken, he acquires quickly his tragic momentum: he comes into his own. In the words of the chorus of *Antigone:* "So there it goes. Little Antigone is caught. Little Antigone is going to be able to be herself for the first time." From now on the orgy of negation will destroy everything about him until there is nothing left in the hero's path but the shame of his own being. It is then that he commits that last murder, his own.

Marc and the cheat Gaston use nearly identical words in describing this process: "It is a horrible feeling to be killing someone in order to live," says the latter. But his words have a somewhat different implication. His, like Ludovic's, is a fraudulent suicide—the shedding of his old life for a new one. Similarly, Amanda will kill the ghost of Léocadia and Georges (or Isabelle) will kill the Georges of before what develops out of *Le Rendez-vous de Senlis.*

But Marc's is a recurrent form of suicide in this drama which, because it steadfastly and pointlessly refuses remedy, truly merits the name of masochism. It is that exacerbation which Anouilh notes for his ambiguous heroine when summoned by Orphée: "Eurydice now answers him with the same eagerness to tear herself." Only rarely does the hero's inverted sense of life and death find sufficient sustenance in the physical mire for the illusion not to require suicide: Thérèse having found Florent's world to be "as if one existed no more" drags her typical life, personified by her objectionable father, into the very sanctum of Florent so as to seal it off from her conclusively. The meaning she confers upon her own life, in contrast to that of Florent, redeems what had been for Marc abject and meaningless suicide. In the same manner, if he is to find any salvation, Bitos must accept the rejection of society and assume fully the traits of Robespierre.

But the more normal pattern calls for the hero, in *Médée's* words, to resume his virginity—that is, to give up establishing the illusion in this world either through the suicide of a return to his former being, or through the consecration of death in which the dream will endure. That is why so many end in a debauch of self-disfiguration during which words flow like blood from a gashed artery until the victim is dead. Only in death (that of non-believers) can the sham, the shame, and the world that made it, cease. Only in death will the illusion be reality. Here is truly Montherlant's "thirst for nothingness."

Death is reconciliation. It is the end of this blackness and this isolation. For Eurydice and Orphée, it is the one secure and permanent meeting. Their haste to reach it is echoed by others. "At last," sighs Antigone, and Frédéric says to Jeannette: "What is soothing is to have arrived somewhere, be it even at the end of despair." Death is truly the bright resting place of which Thérèse speaks: "Right at the end of despair, there is a pretty white glade where one is nearly happy"; this is Robespierre's "glade where, finally, we will be able to rest, all of us," in *Pauvre Bitos*.

On occasion, attempts have been made to redeem Anouilh's inhumanity and to find leniency in his black outlook through mitigation of his heroes. Edward Owen Marsh (*Jean Anouilh, Poet of Pierrot and Pantaloon,* 1953), indicts Médée, for example, to show in Anouilh increasingly "humane" feelings. (Mr. Marsh's book was published three years before the performance of *Pauvre Bitos.*) Once the spotlight has been removed from Medea, Mr. Marsh believes he can claim that: "Anouilh here for the first time casts doubt on the virtue of rebellion, asserts that the constant refusal of other people's values is a vain attack on humanity." In support of this, he quotes some of Jason's words to Médée. In his translation:

Yes, I shall forget you. Yes, I shall live. And tomorrow, in spite of the blood you left behind after you had been at my side I shall start building up again my wretched little human framework beneath the indifferent eye of the powers that be.

One wonders whether that last pathetic sentence does not considerably detract from Jason's stature alongside that conception of Médée which, according to Marsh, admittedly "follows broadly the same lines as Euripides." Living is still a sinful compromise in the view of these intransigent characters, and so long as they die thus convinced, without leaving behind anyone more purposeful and significant than the residual Jason, that conviction must be presumed to belong to the author.

Robert Champigny ("Theatre in a Mirror," *Yale French Studies,* 1954) finds that in *L'Alouette*: "Though the ideal of romantic, narcissistic purity can still be felt, it is now challenged by a more 'adult' humanistic trend [. . .]. Social contact is not described as so necessarily alienating. The main enemy is religious fanaticism and hypocrisy." Social contact is indeed not necessarily alienating (presumably "alienating" the purity of the heroine) in this play in which, through Jeanne, Anouilh appears to recant:

Nothing is a sin, La Hire, in that which is real! I was a fool, I tormented you too much; I did not know. Big old bear of mine, yours is the good smell of hot sweat, of raw onion, of red wine—every good, innocent smell of men. Big old bear of mine, you kill, you swear, you only think of girls.

Still, it must be remembered that La Hire will abandon Jeanne as will all the others and that Jeanne will go to her martyrdom alone. How long the human contact is sanctified remains questionable.

Moreover, the enemy does not appear to be religious fanaticism but simply another impediment in the way of the hero's self-assertion. His characteristic and prerogative "no" is opposed by what is here termed the anti-man and represented—in this lay drama—by the Inquisitor. Is Jeanne's ultimate triumph not that of still another Anouilh heroine gratuitously refusing and is it not the reason for the Inquisitor's rage that makes him sound so much like Créon?

Do you need to question her further? To ask her why she threw herself from the top of that tower in which she was a prisoner, to flee or to destroy herself, against the commandments of God? Why did she leave her father and mother, put on this male dress which she will not give up, against the commandments of the Church? She will give you the same answer, as a man: "That which I did, I did. It is mine. No one can take it back from me and I do not disown it. All you can do is kill me, make me yell anything at all on the rack, but to make me say 'yes,' that you cannot do."

Notwithstanding some superficial religious terminology, all of the protagonist's usual traits are sketched: the need to escape from his constraining world which must end in flight or in death; the masculinity of the type; the sanctity of the hero's acts; and the sublimity of negation.

If this were an anti-religious play, would such Sartrian lines be given to Bishop Cauchon who has himself spent seven months trying to make Jeanne say "yes": "But it is in this solitude, in this silence of a vanished God, in this animal need and misery, that the man who continues to hold his head high is great indeed. Great all alone." Is this not merely another play about the greatness of man alone and in revolt?

Admittedly, the choice of a previously sanctified heroine would appear to indicate a change in Anouilh's perspective. Nevertheless, his ability to make even that figure follow the same path shows only a refinement of his craft. If Jeanne has been humanized, it is only to the extent that other protagonists have been humanized (as since 1945, with the appearance of Jeannette), an Antigone in her revolt, her refusal of easy ways out, of compromise—but one who had achieved some human warmth through sin. Or, since 1949, when words usually ascribed to the villain were granted the congenial count in *Ardèle:*

No, no. It is more important than you think. We are too demanding, Aunt Ardèle. Life is made up of nickels and dimes and there is a fortune of these to be made by the ones who can collect them. Only we despise nickels and dimes. We are always waiting for life to square up with us in the form of a thousand dollar bill. And so we remain poor. . .

But such peripheral gloss, though it may enrich even the hero, fails to change his substance which remains, through *L'Alouette,* the harsh chastity of quasi-gratuitous denial.

With a hero created in such direct opposition to the terms

of his necessary re-creation, there are interlinking contradictions that extend into his curious mythology. Mention has already been made of the theoretical discrepancy inherent in the urge to impress upon a rejected world the validity of that rejection—a discrepancy enlarged by the fact that the physical part of the arguer belongs to the physical area which he refuses. This brings about a reliance for dramatic characterization on wholly intellectual evidence that denies the physical portrait.

Another aspect of such self-engendering conflict stems from the hero's strength, substituted for morality, customs, logic— the usual arbiters—which must be the main justification for his rejections, since his very strength derives almost wholly from the totality and the intransigence of those rejections. Negation of such sweep necessarily rejects terms essential for the very expression of the hero. His re-appropriation of these terms is achieved through a personal redefinition of them with the further weakening of the debate normally consequent upon such resolutions.

Underlying these dramatic and dialectical difficulties is the author's predisposition to center the philosophical thesis upon the fact and the symbol of sexuality. The advantage of such a postulate lies in its immediate projection into the vast reaches of love, human communication, and purity. But the hero's need of these expressions, without which he himself stands accused by his indictment of others on identical counts, questions the value of his fundamental assertion—that of his ruthless virginity.

An initial threat to the hero who remains sexually abstemious comes from the possibility of being equated with the common of mankind for whom the act has likewise lost significance—though for precisely opposite reasons. The hero, who must ultimately discover that his utter scorn can subsist only through his utter availability, is now forced to transmute a basically repugnant symbol. That is why, although sexual potency was one of the many traits left in his prison cell by the Ludovic of 1934, subsequent "little fellows," "little brothers," "little pals," "little soldiers," come to synthesize genres, though not always without awkwardness since such an achievement is more easily effected as a vision in the wake of failure than as a fact. Characteristically, the clearest statement of this synthesis occurs as the result of mere day-dreaming by the general in *La Valse des toréadors*: "That joy, that very simple joy of no longer being alone in the world, of having a little comrade-in-arms, one that is silent and tender and who undresses at night and changes into a woman." But since all ideals of contact have already been doomed in this drama, love becomes no more than a corroborative statement and another aspect of the hero's sublime isolation. His lucidity on the subject will help further to differentiate him from the weak for whom love remains a persistent and deceptive opiate.

Even when feasible, the temporary changing into women of these "little comrades" can represent at best but a partial statement of the more virile, more positive and more complete ideal of friendship. Gaston (*Le Voyageur sans bagage*), a hero exceptionally granted a new life of his making, states on the verge of choice: "Before asking you what women were mine [. . .] I feel it is far more urgent that I ask you who was my friend." In his mind, there is no doubt as to the relative importance of each—the pejorative plural of the first is humbled by the uniqueness of the second. In like fashion, the most virulent indictment of love—that in *Ardèle* ("We are calling love to account")—is in terms of its incompatibility with friendship: Nathalie will forever love Nicolas but will never give herself to him because when her husband, Nicolas' brother whom she never loved, took her on the very night of her wedding, in the pleasure of the flesh she forgot Nicolas. And again, in *La Valse des toréadors,* the general loses Ghislaine in an hour, after waiting seventeen years for her, because in that hour his secretary made love to her and removed from her mind the seventeen-year dream. The semi-humorous equivalent in *La Répétition* (significantly subtitled *L'Amour puni*) provokes an exclamation of the countess whose spite is nearly sublime: "You mean to say that you don't mind that he should love her like a little boy?" This is true mortification of the flesh in contrast to the positive aspirations which the equally illusory dream of friendship induces. Both Gaston, the friendless victim of amnesia, and Georges (Isabelle notwithstanding) have composed their respective dreams of identical ingredients. Each involves, significantly enough, the sacrificing of a girl by or for the friend, and the saving of the friend's life. Even in its evanescence, friendship appears more dynamic and more significant than love.

The attempt to achieve love can be, of course, a suitable explanation for a number of the hero's stances. The hopelessness of love matches the magnificent frustration of the central character, and its egocentric assertion closely parallels his (love is defined as "that evanescent little image of oneself" in *L'Invitation au château*). It can represent, moreover, that form of the unattainable harshly sought by people such as Jeannette whose quest and whose definition evince her kinship with Antigone: "That moment in life when good and reasonable things are no longer altogether fair." And in the end, even Ardèle is urged to love (by Nicolas) in defiance of all.

However, it takes the heedlessness of comedy (*Le Bal des*

voleurs, Léocadia, L'Invitation au château, Cécile) to credit love's success. The three plays that are not quite turned into comedy by its successful issue, *Le Rendez-vous de Senlis, La Répétition,* and *Ornifle,* are interesting exceptions that confirm the rule. The figure of love in the first, Isabelle, looms so frightening as to scare the victorious Georges into whispering, "You are a terrible person, Isabelle." Which she calmly acknowledges: "I am happiness. And happiness is always just a little terrible." This conscious symbol uses a word reminiscent of the "horrible" spoken by Thérèse, and so confirms the emotion's nature. In *La Répétition,* when Tigre at last repudiates his world in the hope of entering Lucile's, both these formerly principal figures are summarily discarded and attention is focused upon the tragedy of Héro, thereby rendering significant his heretofore irrelevant name. Héro's is a common experience, confirming Lucien's axiom—which he too has learned through practice—that love is something which exacts payment for life (a conviction repeated nearly verbatim by the wise count in *Ardèle*). In the end, love as a positive force is inoperative and of little consequence. In the words of the general in *Ardèle:* "There is love, of course. And then there is life, love's enemy." The remark is a capsule statement of *Ornifle.*

Bereft of human warmth, the lonely, isolating halls of this world echo an unending call, "Help. . . ." Though not always given this direct expression, as it is by Julia, the general, Diana Messerschmann, etc., the hero's fright and his weakness are evidenced by those parts of the myth wherein he seeks refuge from his world's emptiness—while claiming for that refuge, in typical fashion, improbable virtues and contradictory symbols.

The world of his chastity is, for Anouilh's protagonist, a

paradise lost, and so his present void is filled in a surprising number of cases by that image of his former innocence, his childhood. "Oh! if I were still a child. . ." sighs Ludovic and with him all those who tire of the fight or who rebel at the corruption into which they have grown. Each does so with his own voice and according to the particular view of the over-all pollution which is his. The entire moral spectrum is defined once again by this vision, which, in retrospect, is sufficiently absolute. Once it exists as a tangible point of reference, it will be drawn into the eternal monologue that cannot reconcile the futile voices of those who have accepted and the contempt of those who refuse. And should the comedy allow a victory, it is again thanks to youth—because youth transcends even comedy: once the fun is over for Lady Hurf (*Le Bal des voleurs*), she must remain alone like all anti-heroes to await a pointless extinction. But with the characteristic clear-sightedness of her part, she speaks of the young who have escaped: "The comedy has turned out right only for those who played it with all their youth, and at that, only because they were playing their youth, which does not always work out. They did not even notice the comedy!"

This fleeting ideal once grasped and then lost but for its significance, is, as might be expected, that of hero's apotheosis to be achieved in death. For the only one of these allowed a life which he himself will fashion—Gaston—the symbol of his new existence will be the little boy with whom he leaves the stage.

This symbol and the aspiration to which it points are curious choices since more frequently, and more cogently, children are the ugly sexual residue, the living tokens of anti-friendship. For each according to his temperament, the child grows distorted and acquires the face of a familiar evil. For the protagonists of *Roméo et Jeannette,* contrasted to the domestic Julia, as for even Julien, the child is the anti-poetic in their anticipations. Médée endows hers with her own violence and her particular resentment, that she might hand them a Euripidean fate. Ornifle hates them until at the moment of his salvation he is granted a child that is already a man. And for Héro, at last, they come to represent the whole abhorrent family whose impurity must stifle whatever pure vision might have been contemplated.

The hero who views his present corruption does so because of an attempted or successful regeneration. The identical corruption of his parents is not similarly graced, and in contrasting the romantic image of his youth with his present state, his parents appear as the logical agents of his own perversion and are thereby thrust into the enemy camp. His plea for a return to the lost pristine life frequently becomes the fervent wish for the warmth of a family, and in moments of lofty flight the hero may unaccountably settle on such prosaic images more worthy of the bourgeois which he is than of the sublime figure which he claims to be. Even Hémon will incriminate the world which Créon represents by confronting his father upon the ground which once they shared, that of his own youth, of whose promise he now claims to be the sole depositary: "All those books full of heroes, to end up this way? To be a man, as you say, and all too happy to be alive." The world of candid youth, if it ever existed, existed for the hero alone. Thereafter, families are evil and their excrescences the symbols of evil. In the ever widening clearing about the hero, the family too must be felled. Negating the existence of his mother, the tyrannical Madame Alexandra, Julien offers Colombe a luxury: "You married an orphan—I wanted you to enjoy every possible advantage of such a match." And when the clearing is completed, when it has become the sought-after desert, it echoes the death wish which is the ultimate formulation of the hero: "To become at last an orphan, an orphan without memories!" Marc's wish, when granted, will provide the usual grace, the resolution of not only these contradictions, but of all those out of which the hero and his world have evolved.

The preceding has attempted to show that rather than black and rose, Anouilh's theater is frequently just black and white. Black and white are the terms of the conflict, black and white is the hero's elementary complexity, both terms being derived from the same harsh reality and the splendid illusion which it enfolds.

Face to face with these white and sinful heroes are the black and not-so-condemnable non-heroes. Their constitution is as simple as that of the heroes, of whose same cloth they are cut. More than a physical affinity, theirs is in nearly every case a veritable kinship to the hero which is meant to signify emphatically the hero's effort to get away from himself. As noted, the villains in nearly every one of these dramas are the mothers and fathers dressed in the garish robes of their auto-da-fé. Their stigma and their differentiation lie quite simply in that they have suffered no epiphany. They remain cheerfully consonant with their physical being and surroundings, thereby giving up the leaven of conflict—and even trading it for that of laughter when their blind equanimity persists in defiance of of manifest catastrophes. Their basic cheerfulness is such that in order to change the stern drama into comedy, the author need only allay the virulent hero.

As hard and as absurd as life is for the hero, it is insipidly pleasant for the non-hero who can close his eyes. His cheerfulness becomes a characteristic contrast to the hero's gloom. The mother of Eurydice sounds like the fathers of Ludovic, of Georges, of Jeannette, in her summation: "As for me, what I can't understand, is why everything should seem so sad to these kids." Bitos' enemies may be worse than he is, but they have charm.

Physically, the secondary characters are embodiments of those vices against which the hero is reacting—and as his reaction is strong, they are generally quite corrupt. By the hero's choice, the general domain of their degeneracy is that of the sensual, the women especially bearing the full brunt of their sexual symbolism. Their lives, in contradistinction to those of the principals, are enacted for and within the temporal, and are significant in terms of such values only. Even Créon will find little more than arguments drawn from such spheres to offer Antigone—or to justify himself. These materialists' lives are as wretched as the hero's, but for them, every aspect of the illusion provides a satisfactory lie to be eagerly grasped. They are given to common joys and to common appetites, and only occasionally does the vice grow to the point of monstrosity, revealing a Jézabel in the mother of Marc or a Madame Alexandra who, together with her many vices, is evil enough to become the prototypal miser created by Anouilh.

These types are cowards and weaklings, petty cheats and thieves, but mostly, their sins and the extent of their damage appear venial because of the circumstances of their existence—although their blindness may of course allow the propagation of more serious evil. The Prologue defines them through the guards in *Antigone:*

They are not bad fellows, they have wives, children, petty annoyances the same as everyone, but in a moment they will lay hold of the accused without even blinking. They smell of garlic, leather, and wine and they are utterly devoid of imagination. They are the auxiliaries of justice, always innocent and always satisfied with themselves. For the time being, and until a new and duly sworn-in chief of Thebes orders them to arrest Créon in his turn, they are the auxiliaries of Créon.

Their sensory limitations root them irremediably to the earth and this further weakness finds expression diametrically opposed to the hero's. "I want to live!" is the cry of Marc, of the young Frédéric, of Médée's nurse—of all those who must find out that in this particular view of life it is simply not possible, or who must die pointlessly unregenerate.

In depicting them, Anouilh remembered the physical image of his own mother, a violinist at the Arcachon casino, and in addition to the recurrent "second prix du Conservatoire d'Arcachon," he retained for the majority of his minor types the figures of poor musicians and provincial troupers, underprivileged in their circumstances and talent. Even alone, the word *artiste* mocks in this drama (Georges' father, Isabelle's mother, etc.), and is meaningful because generations of *ratés* tied their most materialistic needs, that of their daily subsistence, to art—that chance for evasion from terrestrial realms into those of the hero. Although he is as materially destitute as his father, Orphée is a good violinist upon whom his father depends for what meager bookings they can get—his own virtuosity consisting solely of memories and prevarications.

The frequently trifling nature of these characters' sins cannot always bear the weight of the severe castigation laid upon them. Even the occasional ones who are truly evil are not allowed to be as superbly evil as is the hero; moreover, there are fewer of the first. Their many areas of likeness to the hero and the attenuating circumstances of their weakness make the hero's vituperation all the less virulent and on occasion drag him down to the insignificant level of the one at whom the vituperation is directed. Moreover, in their weakness, they have what would appear to be at first glance a lovable trait: they are unable to hurt. "I cannot make anyone suffer," says the general in *La Valse des toréadors*.

The sin of these people is evidently that they lack that essential fiber of heroes—heroism. In this amoral concept, conventional virtues are replaced by intensity and the courage it demands. Once so endowed, the hero will redeem through contact all things that remain debased for the non-hero. Where the latter is pettily selfish, the hero is magnificently selfish; where tactless or ill-mannered, he is ruthlessly consonant; where Marc's mother poisons his father by failing to sort the mushrooms properly, Frantz kills in defiance of a despised society. If Horace and the general (and perhaps Créon and Cauchon) cannot stand suffering, they can be induced to compromise and there is no greater sin than that of transigence.

When made of more substantial stuff, the non-hero becomes the anti-hero. He may be drawn positively, as the embodiment of the hero's aspirations, in which case personality is sometimes lost for the sake of the symbol (Jacqueline or Georges' Isabelle), or his might be an evolution toward the redemption of the hero (Frédéric, or perhaps Tigre; or even Orphée, considered incomplete without his ideal image of Eurydice). In the figure of the latter occurs an interesting modulation, making Eurydice one of the few ambiguous presences in this drama. Truly, hers is a fluctuation between the equipollent forces of depravity and purity. She comes to represent through such oscillation the vicissitudes of an unsatisfactory world in contrast to the bitter permanence and ironic security of death.

A decade later, a similarly conceived but ultimately lost Colombe will testify by contrast to the continuing harshness of the author's view of mankind.

When drawn with negative characteristics, the anti-hero becomes the hero's formidable opponent. His sin remains, as in the minor figures, that of least resistance, of facility—of whatever might be tantamount to compromise. Bourgeois clichés of virtue mask the weaknesses of the secondaries; the anti-hero's true embodiment of conventional virtues makes him likewise objectionable. Florent, the man whom Thérèse loves, represents compromise brought on by such moral excellences: he has accepted, without questioning, the ease and success of innumerable gifts; he is good without exertion. The villainy which others have acquired because of vice and inferiority, he has acquired because of native virtue and perfection—his, no less than theirs, is the sin of sloth. Whatever moral arguments may be invoked, Thérèse's inability to come within the grace of Florent is metabolic: her constitution is dynamically acquired, whereas that of outwardly strong people like Florent (or Frédéric before salvation, or Orphée in the first flush of love) is passive and untested. And as already noted, Jason is another figure of compromise. Once the active and purposeful mate of Médée, he has grown weary of the outcast's life and craves the rest of society. He is little more than the mythological projection of any of the minor figures from whom the caricature might likewise have been removed.

One of these stands out sufficiently from the rest of the anti-heroes to have occasionally assumed the hero's title, his failing being generally more acceptable than the fortitude of the heroine involved. Before his encounter with Antigone, Créon is complete. He has been depicted without flaws by the Prologue

—with only those shades of doubt that guard him against blindness without enfeebling him. He is Giraudoux's Egisthe at his height. But in this positive and even congenial portrait, two strains of weakness have already been suggested. The first will become apparent upon Créon's first encounter with the hostile Antigone: he has accepted the constriction of a pre-established and external truth. The evening may awaken torpid doubts in the overstimulated and temporarily more questioning mind, but the morning's problems bring with them the ready standards of arbitration and peace—the peace of credence, the security of dedication to such outer strength. Créon has bought his compass instead of making it.

This shade of compromise is detected by Antigone, but because it is so very nearly imperceptible, the ill-willed heroine must acquire commensurate stature through gratuitous negation: "You have said 'yes.' You will never stop paying, henceforth!" This terrible young girl can sense in Créon the threat of more shadows moving across her ideal of immaculateness. Créon attains distant kinship to that other pathetic soldier, the general, through a similar weakness: he reasons (the same foible whose danger has already been pointed out by Lucile, Jeannette, Médée, etc.).

Antigone was postulated victorious by an author who had not as yet written his *Brandt*. Créon can only accede to the usual request of the hero by doing away with the hero's perishable flesh to leave nothing that will detract from the magnificence of the symbol. Thereafter, the epilogue belongs to the anti-hero. Bereft of that symbolism, which now dwarfs his pointless acts, and debarred because of his temporal and external allegiances from the confirmation of death, he remains an existentialist and lonely figure, but an insignificant one, meaningless even in the knowledge of his insignificance. The task was senseless and sordid indeed, and truly should have been left to one really coarse and fit for such work.

The postulation of such a figure, even one as big as Créon, is nevertheless the postulation of a character stillborn, and raises dramatic difficulties. The hero may alienate, and even appear ridiculous, because of his absence of restraint, but such overstatements tend at least to a definite, to an even bourgeois hope of achievement, of consecration. The negative overstatement of the secondary figures immobilizes them, occasionally rendering them incomprehensible. This sort of helpless automatism would reduce the secondary types to the functional level of foils and limit their interest to that of a few personal quirks. In a number of cases, they are saved from such sterility by becoming individual choruses. When debasement has not been sought for them in the form of specific depravity, when theirs is merely the fault of common sense in defiance of which the hero will become uncommon and gradually insensate, they occasionally define the hero with the words of that common sense. Such definitions by Jason and by Lucien have already been referred to. But the final indictment against all Anouilh heroes is left once again to Madame Alexandra speaking, with her temperament, for all the non-heroes: "Those who are terrible are the ones who prevent things from running smoothly on earth, those who simply have to force upon you their bleeding insides [. . .]. It's too much, by far. We are fed up!"

The historically detached hero would move in a timeless world, foreign to all particular ones and true only to its own prototypal reality. That hero would engage in no conflicts but those sufficiently irreconcilable to be indefinitely renewed. The

Anouilh hero indicates on occasion a desire for such immortality by seeing himself as an inevitable gesture in an undated act. *Antigone*'s Prologue arrives on stage with a complete cast momentarily frozen in the incipient motions which must inevitably be theirs once "the little shove for it to get started" has been given. They are all destiny's automata, fated and utterly passive: "In a drama, one struggles because one hopes to get out of it. It is ignominious, it is utilitarian. Here, it is gratuitous. It is for kings. And there is nothing to be attempted —at last!" Actually, there are no heroes at all, and no villains from which to distinguish them—there are merely sacrificed parts in a flawless and more important machine.

Such an idea is not an unusual one in Anouilh's drama. It accounts for Tigre's comment: "Everyone is guilty or no one is!" It reminds the spectator that Eurydice is likewise a very old myth: "Ah! here we are in a nice mess, both of us, facing each other, with everything that is going to happen to us already settled behind us." And likewise, Jeanne cannot be burned right away as Warwick would want it because she is first of all the exponent of an immutable ritual: "She must enact all her life first."

In such an absolute drama the timeless gratuitousness of the hero will be claimed also for Anouilh's minor figures with whom the principal enacts his Platonic gestures. "The people of [your] past," indicates the cast of *Le Voyageur sans bagage, Eurydice, Le Rendez-vous de Senlis,* etc., and states that theirs is no accidental occurrence that might draw the hero down to levels of contingency. These people intend to exist in relation to each other for the performance of a drama that transcends their several individualities. The question is whether such transcendence will be possible. Antigone has advantages: her quest is not questionable, it has no root in time or logic, and few material projections deflect it. She refuses consistently to fight upon the plane of those about her, in the end forcing even these to assume the lofty terms that are hers. Therefore, earth traits, such as her repeated concern for her "she-dog Douce," may be forgotten ultimately, along with her "bad tempers," her skinniness, her kid's shovel, and the rest of the opaque and mortal properties of the little girl who must be thrust into the eternal figure of the myth.

This may be a play for kings, but Antigone is not quite alone. There are first of all people who have been with the heroine all along, the inevitably soiled fringes of the ermine. Gignoux thinks that Anouilh may not have achieved tragedy with *Antigone,* "being attracted too much by the human reality." Then there is Créon, accused by his terrible niece of effortless reliance on the world's compass, who finds a remarkably parallel weakness in Antigone: "What a drink, eh, the words that condemn you? And how thirstily they are swallowed when one is called Œdipe, or Antigone." And the spectator leaning towards Antigone becomes uncomfortably aware that Créon is quite right. Her tragedy is, as usual, difference; and the mechanism of doom, as Créon suspects, is an inability to keep quiet. Characteristically, it is Jeanne who speaks the part of her voices. The inevitability of the tragedy thus becomes subordinate to an inherent trait in the character. That trait initially asserts the primacy of the individual over the abstract truth which he is supposed to convey.

A tragedy stripped for enduring action sheds the plot, ever in danger of becoming adventitious, for the naked crisis, and sheds perishable words for the poetic—hence abstract—rendition of that crisis. In defiance of his credentials, Anouilh's hero is rooted to the circumstantial aspects with which he contends and, because he can recognize no outer norm, finds that very contention limited to his own ill-tempered or shrill expression. Here, the physical individual is never an impersonal masque representing its own symbolism. Aspects of his awareness of the world around him have already been shown, such as the characteristically frail shape he develops in contrast to that world. And, in this drama that might have been gratuitous—"for kings"—that frailty is exemplified by many aspects of the hero's indigence. The symbol of poverty even assumes the base appearance of money—a token so evanescent as to have changed with the author's own lot. (Boredom has become everyone's cross by 1950 with *La Répétition,* or *Ornifle* in 1955, thereby extinguishing some of Thérèse's earlier fire, while placing that particular problem within its proper and limited perspective.)

The ermine character of a hero as magnificently contemptuous as Antigone is not easy to preserve. The awkwardness and the contradictions inherent in a sexual definition of the hero have already been suggested. Such visceral descent from the intellectual heights of tragedy cannot but limit the hero. And as long as the pure hero must exist as the result of a contradistinctive impurity physically expressed and fortuitously present, his physical contact with the symbols of his rejection weakens the truth of which he was to have been the abstract embodiment. Eventually, the remote dignity of the classical deuteragonist now gives way to the vigor of the flesh and blood puppet whose coarse reality will stand for the hostile world. He remains a constant overstatement so as not to fail the overstated hero built in his image. To justify the Gaston who rejects him, a young proto-Gaston suffers a past need-

when Léocadia's prince is) redeemed by the little *cousette* right out of fairy tales—the same who might have saved Gaston before his ugly mother put an end to that relationship. What curiously frail motives impel such level-headed heroines as Lucile or Isabelle (*L'Invitation au château*) to change their previously stated course for curiously anti-heroic traits discovered in their quondam opponents? And if it be objected that these are comedy types, one might ask how much weight the death of Ornifle imparts to his momentary sentimentality.

A pure Frédéric might come, quite naturally, to the soiled Jeannette of his salvation in classical tragedy—just as might a similar Orphée to a similar Eurydice. The postulation of such fate is a single statement and one conceivable when no further coincidences are required. But when the many contingencies of material circumstances must likewise be accepted, the aggregate coincidences become too burdensome to be credited. And likewise, evil itself steadily counterpoised becomes as suspicious as the drama's "good young man [who] might have arrived in time with the gendarmes." Not one of the people in Anouilh's drama relies honestly on the myth to give him his dramatic stuff. Each attempts to acquire that stuff on his own, through expressions that the public can be counted upon to understand. After virulent rejection of someone just like the public by a too exceptional individual, terms of reconciliation are sought to explain that too exceptional individual to the public. Therefore the hero is frail, and a young girl, and poor, and has suffered the conventional slings of a legitimately outrageous fortune. Or there are hints that a thoroughly unpleasant Bitos might grow in the shape of a grim but heroic Robespierre. The too exceptional individual might thus receive some of the pity freely bestowed upon the conventional underdog. On such terms, Joan of Arc, the peasant girl who goes from rags to riches and thence to great suffering, becomes an adequate figure of melodrama.

The danger of this flirtation has been pointed out. The permanent stature potentially belonging to the hero because of a noncontingent and intrinsic worth is instead dependent on the temporal symbols which he has assumed for recognition by a particular audience. And the temporal dress about the myth, that which was to have proved the endurance of an eternal lesson, is in danger of becoming an anachronistic barrier blocking comprehension of that lesson.

Ultimately, the myth itself becomes contingent. Orpheus counting money, Medea and Eurydice sleeping with men other than the one granted to each by the legend, Robespierre about whom there are rumors of sexual impotence, destroy their claim to the legend and invalidate the name they bear. They must now rely solely on their individual strength: they have forsaken the strength of the myth.

Once the norms are discarded by the hero, once Créon's compass is contemptuously cast aside, the world becomes meaningless as a coherent organism and turns into endless patterns of absurdity. Within these, the hero's striving is perforce nonsensical until he is able to establish a stable basis amid this self-willed chaos. That stability he achieves by becoming his own god and standard. Doomed because of external circumstances, he removes from them his valid inner self which he submits to the authority of a self-appointed order. He can avoid vacuousness if a volitional force informs his postulated nihilism—"Nihilism which [. . .] is, in the end, merely a new romanticism, the romanticism of despair," according to Serge Radine's definition (*Anouilh, Lenormand, Salacrou: Trois Dra-*

maturges à la recherche de leur vérité, 1951). The myth lost, he seeks existentialist grandeur.

Gignoux, Radine, Marsh are among those who have drawn attention to a prefiguration of Sartre by Anouilh. However, attention to the pessimism of Anouilh's formulation has often slighted what becomes the single element of optimism in this drama.

"All the people of [your] past"—the fallacious sentence that was to have granted the protagonist a homogeneous body of myth—discloses another and more important meaning as the expression of the existentialist's fundamental confinement. Because he believes that no one escapes being the aggregate of his past actions, the classical concept of the immutable gesture performed throughout time is confirmed by a philosophical credence that likewise assumes the inevitable antecedents of any such gesture. Just as the existentialist knows he cannot escape or in any way get rid of himself, Anouilh's hero accepts as inevitable and sordid his physical axiom, stressing it in the plays whose resolution is simply black, while accepting as securely innate his nonphysical and contrasting self in the plays whose resolution, though black, makes him a magnificently moral symbol.

The somber postulations of existentialism look to the inevitable past of the hero. But these should be only the ground for his coercive ethic and its concomitant salvation. He has been conceived as someone who must inevitably choose. By rendering this inevitable choice significant he may become significant himself. By remaining common, espousing forms illusory and facile, he robs the inevitability of the choice of all but its mechanical and oppressive power. To Gaston, who is still within the privileged sanctuary this side of choice, his ex-mistress Valentine speaks the villain's part and allows appropriate, if unconscious, irony: "Those of us who have a memory, we know that one is always forced to choose." But the one who makes a conscious choice, its conventional morality notwithstanding, is Gaston and not those who have bowed to an even easier, and hence a far less moral, convention.

Gaston illustrates the corollary of this ethic: he is the existentialist hero free to create his own values. He uses the proper terminology in asserting the incontrovertible and dynamic fact of his being: "Me! Me! I exist, *I* do, in spite of all your stories. . . ." This is a familiar averment charged with the usual claim to an egocentric freedom justified by the sole fact of the heroes' existence. Sartre's *disponibilité* is their self-assertion directed against whatever form of subservience or sclerosis hampers those about them. In philosophical terms, their purity is their unyielding need to formulate constantly their being regardless of external pressures of any sort. And Gignoux reminds us that Gaston is a mere aspect of a constant, variously termed Thérèse, Orphée, Eurydice, etc.

The unimpeded creation of these values and their assumption gives the principal his distinctive mantle of heroism and the strength of a nonfortuitous essence. Attention has previously been directed to the similarity that links *L'Hermine* and *Les Mouches;* both emphasize an existentialist morality in demanding the assertion and the recognition of one's acts. The Orestes of Sartre must carry his burden alone once Electra has proved too frail to follow him into the consequences of his act; similarly must Frantz when Monime reverts to convention. And an even clearer statement will be made by Antigone whose inspiration has kindled her sister Ismène just a little too late.

The hero's necessary isolation for the confirmation of his

dramatic stature echoes another existentialist postulate according to which everyone is alone as the result of that breaking away from the ties and bases which once gave the world an illusion of logical order and equilibrium. Such severing of bonds through the clear perception of their essential fallacy has irremediably isolated the hero (note the many statements by Lucien, the general, Orphée, Ornifle—or Messerschmann's, already alluded to "One is all alone, that much is certain. We can do nothing for each other but play the game"), and it has forced the discarding of the conventional world for the projection of the hero's.

That world can have but one meaning for the hero: it is a symbol of his rejection, goading him to establish his own. Life and death are meaningless alongside this striving, and that conviction occasionally rings out in expressions reminiscent of a younger Camus. "Death too is absurd," cries Frédéric, though his immediately subsequent actions bring the play to a sardonic conclusion. But that is because the conclusion was to be sought only in the gratuitousness of an unyielding assertion. And Cauchon, who has observed such stubbornness in Jeanne, echoes the same Camus in the previously quoted words that speak about the greatness of man alone.

THE PLAY courts two realities: its own, the spectacle or show—that which is properly of the stage; and that of the spectator, a non-simulated life upon which may act the suggestions of that stage in the manner of sympathetic vibrations producing a secondary but true sound in a receptive body. The strength of classical drama resides in its ability to discard the dead attributes of the stage, using it but as the convergence of a number of specific stimuli. The strength of any

extravaganza, *féerie,* pantomime, circus, etc., resides in its
ability to remain an end in itself, valid without the further
action of any external catalyst. The failure of the realistic stage
is derived from false premises: it has assumed that genuine life
might be engendered somehow within a synthetic realm by
the simple virtue of stage properties that look real.

The modern author who realizes how frail is the realistic
stage, and who nevertheless feels bound to preserve its being
in new forms, repeats the efforts and the errors originated with
that other hybrid creation, the neo-realistic hero, the protagonist
of such worlds. When, in *Le Rendez-vous de Senlis,* Robert
echoes the classical choruses of Anouilh's drama and his existentialist tenets—"now we are going to be forced to play [our]
parts to the end"—he is asserting a particular consciousness,
that of his own illusiveness in an experience which, for him,
can never be more than "play." Anouilh remained aware of
the impossibility of materializing the dramatic illusion upon
the boards, though he long felt reluctant to exchange that illusion for the reality of the spectator. This long-standing ambivalence indicates a significant direction in the author's development and the genesis of a form that modifies or cancels
former discrepancies.

Robert's realization of his nonexistence is by no means an
isolated occurrence in Anouilh's theater. It is, on the contrary,
a self-consciousness that extends and reflects the hero's concept
of the artificial world into which his circumstances have temporarily forced him. The awareness of this distinction allows
Champigny ("Theatre in a Mirror"), in opposition to a moral
critic such as Radine, to assert: "Whatever the personal philosophy of Anouilh, if any, may be, the pessimistic color of his
plays bears on the theater, not on life, at least not on 'real

life.'" The "real life" of the hero is his tragic epitome re-created in, or remembered by, the spectator. The tokens of his action and his stage surroundings concern him as little as they do the spectator who grants him life: they have a function of their own which, though it may be for the spectator, is not dependent on him.

The contradictory tones in so many of Anouilh's plays are due to the sharply distinguished worlds of the hero's cor-poreality and of his ideal projection. Hero and anti-heroes treat each other with a contempt that indicates their lack of faith in the world within which they move: each is conscious for rea-sons of self-preservation of the fact that he is merely acting within a play. The hero preserves his virginity, the minor pro-tagonist his necessary automatism, whether moral or comic. Little wonder that Anouilh's Antigone forgets, in such a con-text, why she is dying. Although these creatures evidence outer realism, the world within which they have been created re-mains illusory—the author hoping, through such evident de-tachment, to use the realistic surface of clay figures while hav-ing them generate the significance of tragic ones.

The role of these conscious puppets thus reverts to that of players within a play, and "Now we are going to be forced to play [our] parts to the end" becomes a scenic rather than an intellective statement, though it parallels intellective data as closely as it does the classical concepts of the chorus. In a num-ber of plays, the dream—the play within the play—is a manifest part of the action whose individuating nuance it de-livers. In *Le Rendez-vous de Senlis* Anouilh comes close to Pirandello by having his characters acknowledge on stage the theatricalism of their being and of their actions. In this play it is the hero Georges who attempts to give to his dream the physical dimensions of the stage, and the impossibility of such a contradiction will become at least a part of the derived morality.

The detachment of a conscious game played before the foot-lights affects other parts of the play and illuminates other aspects of Anouilh's tragedy. Non-heroic types employing Lady Hurf's expression "I am playing a part," come to signify a protagonist who has submitted to the sham, one who is in Sartre's view and expression a "swine." Messerschmann's "One is all alone, that much is certain. We can do nothing for each other but play the game," becomes the mark of his lesser stature; the hero, who is in perfect agreement with him philo-sophically, comes to a different conclusion: the "game" played throughout the duration of the *play* will be the definition of what must be given up at the conclusion of the equally ephemeral play. This drama is essentially carnival and defini-tion of the Lent to come.

Whereas the hero remains a reluctant actor bent upon prov-ing the nonsense of his presence to justify his final departure and to illumine his latent significance, the non-hero's symbol-ism becomes that of conscious nonexistence—the embodiment of that dead and transient part which the hero will reject. The many who are actors fuse their dual realities in the creation of what must be a willed illusion. They are hermetic figures, rooted to the fallacy of the stage, upon which their obtuseness becomes symbol and background for the character of the hero. As noted, they constantly "play a part" and where that part ends, so do they, their significance never enduring beyond the time of their physical presence. They are the wholly automatic clowns of the comedies whom nobody credits. They are Kant's comic figures aware that they are comic, natural subjects of laughter not only because of this postulated automatism but because of their cheerfulness which is another way in which they give physical evidence of their philosophical difference from the hero. Occasionally drawn to the lofty stature of the anti-hero, they nevertheless remain bound to the narrow and transitory stage, denied as they are the meaningful exit of the hero. Figures like those of Florent, Jason, or Créon may occasionally usurp part of the hero's mantle, but there is no mistaking the others who go off in a burst of laughter in a drama which, though artificially black (the temporary and false anteworld of the hero), is superficially colored with their meaningless mirth.

Moving in worlds that are primarily those of the stage, these protagonists can elect, in order to emphasize the theatrical illusion, an even more specious world, that of comedy. The latter kind is generally situated in castles, that convergence of nonreality, fairyland, and the lavish trimmings of gay, rich, and presumably colorful figures (this is truly the world of the stage, of the *show*). The nonreality of these plays is either emphasized by their position out of time, that *fin de siècle* atmosphere called by Marsh "A vague half-way house between the solid bourgeois confidence of the pre-Dreyfus decade and the uneasily self-righteous idiocy that followed" or locations even more remote. It is an anachronism that further isolates the stage and its action, as do the modern clothes of *Antigone* or the "Louis XV bourgeois costumes or maybe Louis XVI—but as spurious as possible" of *Cécile*. These departures from the reality of the action emphasize domains properly belonging to the stage and introduce other properties that further mock the action, such as music, ballet interludes, etc. Otherwise serious plays like *Le Voyageur sans bagage* or even *La Sauvage* and

Ornifle use music to mark moods more fundamentally pertinent to the theater than to the drama therein enacted.

In addition to their wholly scenic value, the secondaries become convenient pawns for a number of nonincriminating
constructions. They are truly puppets—not only puppets that
play, but puppets that might be played with for the sheer
pleasure of the game. Anouilh has spoken against the mere
weaving of plot through Tigre in *La Répétition:* "I have a
horror of detective stories. I find them to be the silliest things
in the world. To go to the trouble of embroiling artificially a
story so that one might afford the false elegance of unraveling
it in three pages at the end, is the pastime of a wag." This must
be considered, however, as mere reaction by the author whom
Radine quotes as admitting that the various parts of *La
Répétition,* a very complex weft indeed, "gave me a devil of a
time." For Anouilh obviously enjoys that "embroiling" which,
incidentally, is not the well-oiled and simple mainspring of
tragedy. Marsh and others draw attention to the pleasure the
author derives from "playing." This quasi-gratuitous pleasure
would appear to be the sole explanation conceivable for, e.g.,
the otherwise meaningless *Cécile,* an exercise in the Molière
manner, witty, and with—again—a clever plot, of which
Anouilh has said, "The author himself doesn't know [what
will happen.]"

There is further evidence that Anouilh considers—with satis-
faction—his nonheroic casts as colored glass to be used in the
creation of an intricate but flat mosaic. The secondary people
are visualized especially from the outside, on their surface:
they are genuine adjuncts of the set. They, as villains all, smoke
cigars, belch, physically evidence slovenliness and the ruddy
color typical of such cheerful unregeneracy. Occasionally, their

moral defects inform their body, La Surette's ugly wife
(*Colombe*), for example, finding in a harelipped lover confirmation for her faithlessness. This is the caricatural result of
the need already observed in Anouilh to project into tangible
figures the underlying idea—the heroines (rather than heroes),
their metaphysical skinniness, their purity that strips them of
even the hypocrisy of clothes, their "dark" pigment of hate,
etc. Characteristically, these same heroines are not uncom-
monly given the tangible aspects of a pre-established common
denominator: Amanda, Colombe, Isabelle (that of *L'Invitation
au château*) are called *Greuzes*. (In *Léocadia* the image is even
extended to the possible inclusion of Le Nain, while rejecting
Boucher.) Such attributes are visual extensions of the mental
device likening favorable stage action to Musset or Marivaux,
while consigning *ratés* to the performance of Hugo. (In
Eurydice second-raters play *Les Burgraves,* and in *La Répétition,* Tigre's wife exclaims "So much the worse if we play
Ruy Blas!") This last device is given a noteworthy twist in
Eurydice wherein the second-rate actor Vincent is allowed to
quote Musset—"It is I who lived and not a creature conjured
by my pride and my spleen"—only in order that such a dis-
crepant notion might underline the fact that even at this key
moment he is no more than an actor acting.

Physical attributes—the totality of these people—can be used
for the creation of a comedy of errors (the twins Horace and
Frédéric in *L'Invitation au château*) or for more subtle com-
plexities, such as those that enable the absorption of *La
Répétition*'s cast into that of *La Double Inconstance,* or that of
Bitos into historical figures which they help illuminate and by
which they are illuminated in turn. Anouilh may also use his
scenic dexterity to throw a particular light on the dramatic

statement being made. *Colombe,* a play characteristically set
in a theater and about a girl who ceases to be the ideal she once
represented because, essentially, she starts "acting," merges the
nonreality of the play at the beginning of the fourth act—that
being performed by Madame Alexandra and Du Barthas—
into the reality of the barren stage upon which the act will
end. This contrast allows a first semblance of reality: that
which is unreal marking off areas of reality. Thereafter the
naked stage, divested of the lies that are the usual scenic properties, underscores the climactic truth. That stage is ultimately
the area for the materialization of an intellective act, Julien's
meditation upon his first meeting with Colombe.

In *L'Alouette,* Anouilh's virtuosity develops on the several
planes of the trial, the historical and the intimate life of Jeanne.
This play, in which each performer is an actor supposedly por-
traying himself, acquires the directness of an authoritative nar-
rative. The fluidity of the action allows the participation of
the actors in the shaping of the scenes (with perhaps more
grace and skill than those of a similarly motivated Claudel in
Le Soulier de satin) and permits the denouement which substitutes for the expected climax—Jeanne's burning, already
philosophically achieved—the clashing irony of the coronation
scene. The spectator's customary vision of Jeanne (and perhaps
not Champigny's "play within the play which meaningfully
supplants the play" ["Theatre in a Mirror"]), allows him to
appropriate an ending that pertains to the world disavowed by
Jeanne and thus projects the spectator into the play, making
him and his vision part of, and participant in, the domain rejected.

Thus it is that the figures least important in Anouilh's
theater, the disinherited, enjoy the finest delineation and all

the play's color; they are in fact the one real presence of the stage on stage—that which must remain eternally, in defiance of final curtains and transient spectators. In this theater of purity and otherworldly glory, they are the heavy assertion of all that is coarse and solid. Alongside them, the principals remain thin, ghostly ephemerae, waiting to leave these too weighty antagonists, though hoping that their own off-stage substance will be sufficiently indicated by contrast.

THE ADJECTIVES *roses, brillantes,* or the laughter of the *pièces noires,* are admissions of uneasiness about heroes of such proportions as might be ridiculous were they to be wholly credited on stage. The creation of such a central character makes his dramatic life a meaningless hiatus and makes the plays built around him blank parentheses in his being since he will never attempt to enter the truth of those amidst whom he moves nor will he attempt to draw them into his. These people do not speak the same language and are in fact not made of like substances. Anouilh's drama until 1948 was essentially one of two completely different textures.

A prior attempt has been made to show how such utter difference and reciprocal scorn generally eliminated a genuine conflict and doomed the possibility of tragedy. The noncongruence of this world, viewed by the hero as an existentialist *absurde,* does not lend itself to tragic perception since even the hero's isolation is one born of superiority and entertained by unrelieved contempt. The words used by the otherworldly M. Henri in *Eurydice,* "This buffoonery, this absurd melodrama, is life," indicate accurately the nature of the onlooker's disdain: this is not somber and contaminating ridiculousness, it is mere ridicule fit to excite laughter.

The drama, then, develops on two planes—that of the fully delineated secondaries who occupy the stage during the entire performance, and that of the hero who does not enter into that performance. The first are a dramatic creation, the second is a mental concept. The word farcical (*cocasse*) finds its way as effortlessly into comedies such as *Le Bal des voleurs* as it does into a serious drama like *Colombe* or *Ornifle*. It indicates the affinity between the moral deficiencies of the world rejected and its laughter-dispensing properties, and points to the time when the exasperation of the hero (or of the author) at the absurd world around him will best be translated by the exasperatingly real Farce in its absurd flights.

The world of the Farce, lifelike in its integument and disfigured only to indicate that the integument is to be discarded for an inherent substance, is on many levels necessary for the projection of Anouilh's casts. The misleading polarity of the somber heroes, giving them not only figures similar to those of their antagonists but, as formerly noted, similar traits enhanced to a heroic scale, confuses the audience and is in danger of alienating it more than is the good-natured villainy of the minor casts. Similar difficulties encountered by Sartre, Giraudoux, etc., have already been noted.

The Farce, discarding the unilateral hero, will be first a homogeneous body—and one substantially humanized because of the intransigence thus removed. Thereafter, the occasional overstatement due to the brutality of an uncompromising view, a view that tends to caricature in the drama, may turn to drama in a world of caricature: the overstatements of the Farce are absorbed into its sustained power which becomes litotes in the Farce's lesson.

That lesson itself can now move into the realms of the

spectator, who has been forced until then to reject the equally false exits of minor and major protagonists, the first actually remaining on a dead stage from which he has never been raised, while the second enters into a necessary reality not yet defined.

For Anouilh, the fun of a world in which one "plays" might then be preserved without invalidating its substance. The laughter of, and at, the characters can freely echo in the music, the dance, the color, and all the attributes of the spectacle. These attributes concomitantly dissociate the morality figures from their superficial circumstances, as once did the stylization of the tragic masque, by making them simple stage properties.

Within these prosceniums, the secondaries have always been the gaudy figures of Farce, Marsh's "caricatures with a heart"— mechanical and variegated casings for eminently sensual organisms. Anouilh's world has always contained not only the standard clowns already encountered but many other identical figures of stylization: the comic old aunts and duchesses, the senile and automatic figures of male aristocracy (Lord Edgar, in *Le Bal des voleurs,* or Baron Hector, in *Léocadia*), the caricature of the Jew, another figure of materialism (Messerschmann), the replicas of every type—servants, valets, businessmen, parasites—of a physically sinful hero, but bereft moreover of an off-stage vision. These cigar-smoking, snoring, belching, libidinous people have always been present, if only through their ridiculous names designed to make them further butts of laughter—the recurrent Dandinet-Dandaine, Fripont-Minet, the dancing teacher Raspoutini, or the poet Robinet, or again the inane father in *Y'avait un prisonnier,* M. Peine, whose son will not bear such a silly name and who appears only as Ludovic. Also, the world of these protagonists, M.

Henri's "buffoonery," has long been recognized. A fierce inter-
jection of Ludovic situated it from the first: "Quick! Quick!
I must play my part in this farce. . . ." It was a world in which
pliable events easily shaped the story to fit the moral. But
especially, it was a world rendered farcical or ridiculous by
the contamination from the secondary puppets. Not until 1948,
when Anouilh for the first time removed the figure of the im-
maculate hero from *Ardèle,* was laughter to echo within
the tragedy.

Ardèle takes up once again the main theme of corruption of
what might have been pure and uses as its indictment—the
most fierce yet—the default of love. The central figure, but not
yet the wholly dominating one, is General Saint-Pé. His
setting is already established: the house to which he has re-
tired, his invalid wife Amélie whose dementia will be subsequently explained, a maid to whom the general makes love
surreptitiously, though she, in keeping with the general tone
of the play, derives neither warmth nor physical joy from it.
There is also a ten-year-old son of the general, the insolent and
clear-sighted Toto; and Nathalie, the general's daughter-in-
law, the wife of his eldest son, a rake now stationed in the
colonies.

The general has sent for his sister Liliane because their older
sister, the hunchback Ardèle (never seen in this play) has
fallen in love with another hunchback, Toto's tutor. Liliane
arrives accompanied by her husband the count, her little girl
Marie-Christine, and her lover Villardieu. The gross stage is
now set for the visual, physical projection of Anouilh's principal ideas.

The case of the hunchback in love recalls La Surette's un-
faithful wife, likewise a wretch who finds a physical counterpart

with which to make love. It suggests Eurydice's momentarily existentialist disgust: "What ugly things are gestures." Love is a "gesture," something ugly because rather than remain spiritual, it becomes an act of the palpable flesh—and the Farce, through externalization, renders condemnation tangible also. It is echoed by *la générale,* a hyper-sensitive creature who, like a coarse copy of Giraudoux's Lucile, senses copulation wherever it takes place.

The ridiculousness of the forms of love are given visual dimension by the countess Liliane who is but three years younger than her sister and who is forced to make of that slight difference a weighty argument. The other forms she invokes, those of propriety, are again graphically caricatured through the already encountered device of projecting morality into physical personalities: in this case, Anouilh specifies that the figures of her husband and of her lover are in fact identical.

Meanwhile, at the level of the conventional mirror of reality, Nicolas, the general's third son, finds that Nathalie whom he loves and who loves him, will not yield to him even though she is free. She at least will not debase the symbol, and pointing to the room of the love-making cripples she echoes Eurydice: "What an ugly thing is love."

The first part of the play is primarily taken up with the pleas of the participants before the locked door of Ardèle, extending and defining their respective natures. The Farce mechanism actuates this play and brings on its climax. Amélie suddenly rushes to the landing, shouting her obsession of all carnality and disclosing that Ardèle is not alone in her room. The men (even the kind count, thereby signifying the unholiness of this grotesque love of the flesh) attempt to break down Ardèle's door, a farce scene in which "they push each other about; it must be nearly a clown's act, in spite of the anxiety." Anxiety has never left them, knitting them into this drama that is not actually the drama of the invisible symbol Ardèle but their own, as the count had indicated before: "We have not left [Ardèle], general. Aunt Ardèle is love. If we can talk Aunt Ardèle out of giving everything to her hunchback, that is to say to herself, it means that we can all be cured." But this explicit lesson is inevitably the antecedent of tragedy, for it is futile. The door is broken down too late. Ardèle and her lover have killed themselves.

None of the themes, none of the dreams lost is given up because of the Farce. The fact that the characters have made fun of themselves by self-parody could not blind the onlooker to the significant flaw that occasioned the jibe. No hero is needed whose illusory portrait before or after the stage action will be assimilated by the spectator. That hero is replaced by the aura of these artificial people, and that aura in turn makes each of them significant for the spectator in whom they will become alive.

Such ironic tragedy is more convincing than those of the author's plays that merely treat the classical tragedy ironically by making it a contingent vehicle. *Ardèle* reverses the usual mechanism of Anouilh's drama—the importance of the dream beyond the stage reality—by stressing the ultimate reality underlying the stage dream. It thus permits the very sad conclusion of the count: "Luckily we are ridiculous, for otherwise this story would be too sad indeed."

Anouilh grew interested in the latent being of General Saint-Pé, the farcelike figure called "very Dourakine" in *Ardèle* (referring to the conventional figure of the general in the stories by La Comtesse de Ségur) and three years later he tightened the design of the Farce about him. In *La Valse des toréadors,* the figures from outer life, the young lovers Nathalie and Nicolas, have been eliminated; so have the male children and a number of supernumeraries. Instead of these, the general is still afflicted with the sad, satirical seed of love, two gawky daughters about whom he wryly comments: "To have so loved pretty women and to have brought that into the world in a moment of aberration." The Farce setting remains. The general is still plagued by his nagging wife Amélie whose repeated call interrupts the memoirs of happier days spent fighting the Moroccan War which he is attempting to dictate to his secretary, a very young man and a very innocent one. The general has, however, one friend (in addition to the usual house maid whom he pursues), the doctor Bonfant who looks after Amélie and in whom he now confides, explaining to him presently how his and Amélie's love has deteriorated into hatred.

The scene is definitively disrupted by the entrance of Ghislaine de Sainte-Euverte who has loved the general faithfully and from afar ever since they danced the Toreadors' Waltz at a Saumur ball seventeen years ago. She has now come to him with a passionate letter written by Amélie to the doctor, a manifest proof of infidelity and legitimate grounds for the general's freedom.

In this tragedy about ineffectual people and the ineffectuality of love, the general is fated not to leave with Ghislaine. He challenges the doctor to a duel, but the doctor who has obviously never had an affair with Amélie does not allow the general even this approximation of action and very soon settles back to his former role as the general's confidant. In talking with him, the general now determines again to act: he will face Amélie and then leave her for Ghislaine. But he promptly returns from her room: Amélie has gone, leaving a note that indicates suicide. Both men rush out after her. Ghislaine who sees this decides that the general must love his wife after all. She too will kill herself, and she will do it with the dainty pearl handle revolver which she has carried with her as a defiant symbol of her virginity for seventeen years. But no symbol can endure for such a length of time and the gun does not go off. She rushes upstairs instead and jumps through the window —but lands on the secretary who is resting in the garden hammock. In her daze she clings to him thinking he is the long lost figure of the general, and in order to humor her, the young man kisses her just as the general walks in with the equally unconscious Amélie. The general is furious, but it is too late.

Past the inevitable turning point which he refuses to recognize, goaded by his own desperation, the general rushes into his wife's room upon which the scene is now focused. Here, the horror and the power of the Farce reach their climax. Amélie will never let the general go, and she is the only strong one in this drama. She is one of the numerous *ratés* in Anouilh's theater, another former *artiste* but one vibrant with the full power of the Farce. Amélie heinously confesses that she has no love for the general but that she enjoys both the power she wields over him and her supreme sadistic pleasure in his inability to escape her, even in the grave. He is hers through fate and she recalls a similar Médée who once reminded Jason that their weld was not weakened by pathetically superficial gestures of emancipation.

The scene ends on the horrible parody of the romantic waltz by Amélie, no longer a cripple, who embraces the general and cries out: "I want this! And you want everything I want. Come dance with your old skeleton, with your old chronic sickness. Come dance with your remorse. Come dance with your love!" The moment of panic that overtakes all of Anouilh's characters now echoes in the general. He desperately calls back his youth, "Lieutenant Saint-Pé! Help!"

Amélie, the false invalid who has kept the general in bondage for seventeen years, now towering over him, erect on her sick-bed, crying out her implacable possessiveness, transforms the idea which she represents into a frighteningly effective image. And within the garish stylization and caricature of the Farce she very logically leads her husband to strangle her. The fact that he is unable to kill her merely prolongs both characterizations graphically.

The end comes as an anticlimax in the Farce, like the abatement of tragedy. The general has long since lost Ghislaine to his suddenly awakened secretary. When he discovers through the village priest that he was actually the young man's father, the unessential story continues yet a while but the protagonists have already walked their appointed rounds. There remains but for the general to lead the new maid into the garden for still one more dose of illusion—"It isn't that it means much, but still, one feels less alone in the dark. . ."—and for Anouilh to conclude, "They have disappeared, a derisory couple, in the garden's darkness."

The hopeless isolation no longer pertains to an ephemeral hero—but to the spectator. Solitude, the ineffectuality of love, of any reaching out, obliterate the color, the gross puns, the funny faces, the impossible scenes. These surfaces cast the spectator back into himself and into a genuine world—that of man's very unenviable lot.

II

The Pain of Laughter

5

The Belgian Current

THE FARCE REPRESENTED for Anouilh the culmination of a particular evolution. However, the apposition of
the terms Farce and evolution robs the former of a part of its
meaning. The Dionysiac quality of the true Farce, that which
would assimilate it to the elemental theater, would appear too
far removed from intellectual processes for intellectual acquisi-
tion. The huge, architectonic Farce, wherein communion
would mean orgiastic participation and of whose over-all
orgasm laughter would be a mere fragment, exultation through
exaltation—such Farce would of course be rooted to the essential culture of creator and participants alike.

Laughter on today's sophisticated stages is primarily peripheral or specialized, and, in that it thus serves a purpose, it
becomes less legitimate. Like the neo-Romantic hero which
it occasionally abets, modern laughter frequently lacks resonance; like his, its trivial attributes fail to make it an essential
part of the spectator whose favor it courts, and its mere extension does not resound as the ecstatic and supernatural voice it
might have been.

Mallarmé's theater, *lieu absolu,* now bows to the public and
becomes *lieu contingent,* and the modern self-consciousness
that rationalizes senses and soul, commonly transforms Bentley's "magical theater" into an intellectual one. However, one
French author at least, Roger Martin du Gard, attempted to

forsake the sophisticated literary canon of his day and revive a
more ancient tradition in order to sound, through laughter,
greater depths on the stage.[1]

Le Testament du Père Leleu (1914) and *La Gonfle* (1928)
ferret out the bestiality in man by magnifying the ungodly
traits that disfigure him. Laughter leaves the intellectual
sphere in which even a Jarry had kept it. Here, Farce becomes
the caricature of peasants who have in them only human traits
enough to render monstrous their animal substance. They
lack, therefore, like *Ubu,* many of the aspects necessary for
the spectator to establish the comparison with himself whence
will issue his revelation, his triumph, and his laughter. *La
Gonfle* certainly reflects a traditional formula but as the
wooden insides of conventional puppets are here rendered
fleshly, it will not always be easy to dispel the oppressive atmosphere of these two playlets. Although made of coarse
scenes, bastinados, situations impossible in society as it is generally conceived, and though spoken in a savorous dialect that
removes them from linguistic immediacy, these plays are Farce
especially because of the author's merciless eye that sees "no
regional picturesqueness."

The crudeness of a world gone by, so much less inhibited
than today's that it alienates the modern temper, suggests a
medieval inspiration. But the unpleasantness of these plays
stems not so much from their crudeness as from the fact that
this crudeness remains their essential motivation. To show
men as animals is to show only the mechanism of their doom.
It is the suprahuman in him and his effort to assert it that

---

[1] In contrast to the psychological analysis of a more conventional sort
to which the author was to return in 1932 with his last drama, *Un
Taciturne.*

give man his meaning and that give meaning, incidentally, to all drama, as that struggle remains the one significant source of dramatic conflict.

Roger Martin du Gard has drawn two forceful sketches of man, but they are static. Because he failed to state an essential conflict, he has either postulated characters incapable of arousing interest, or people about whom that which is interesting has been left yet unsaid.

As noted with reference to Anouilh, today's French dramatist fears the relative impersonality of the masque and attempts by diverse means to reconcile transitory aspects and an enduring substance. The prevalent emphasis by French authors upon intellectual forms that might render the creation objective makes *Le Testament du Père Leleu* and *La Gonfle* exceptional plays in their own country. In Belgium, however, the land from whose present boundaries presumably issued the first French Farce extant, another outlook prevails. Here, a more primal, more immediate, and yet supernatural understanding of fateful agencies replaces intellectual assimilation—sufficiently at least for the more vital author to feel laughter as an emotion no less significant than any other. Until he too flounders because of tangential demands imposed on him by the frequently finicking modern stage, a genuine Farce form readily shapes the Belgian dramatist's most essential vision.

His patrimony is that of a nation of peasants, of artisans, and of merchants—three classes given, each in its own way, to a meticulous scrutiny of surfaces. This culture effects a plastic and literary translation of minute realism: Belgium is the birthplace of the tales of Renard, of the portraits of Van Eyck, of the craftsmen who carved the wooden portals of the Beauvais cathedral.

This realism leads into a frankly sensual realm. Alongside the Arnolphinis of Van Eyck are the Helenas of Rubens. Perhaps this gradation is actually a spiritualization, the redemption of the realistic that might be accounted for were Flemish mysticism explained, because alongside Renard there stands Ruysbroeck. Jan-Albert Goris (*Du Génie flamand,* 1945) believes that this mixed impress distinguishes his countrymen from birth: "Mysticism plus sensuality is the very H_2O of baptismal water."

It is through realism, mysticism, and the senses that Belgium has preserved its heroes: the brothers Aymon, Thyl Uylenspiegel, Godefroid de Bouillon, or that proliferation of more humble legends sown in the days when God and his legions still walked the earth. To this day, the myth remains sufficiently intimate in Belgium to escape questioning. It has insidiously haunted even such sceptics as Charles van Lerberghe, Henry Soumagne, or Herman Closson, whose disbelief is expressed by the very symbols they reject. It is therefore understandable that the Belgian theater died out once the indigenous vein was lost and that its dramatic rebirth stems from the rediscovery of that vein.

To escape literary mediocrity, Belgium had to wait for the same strong gusts from the south that doomed naturalism in France. Its first signs were felt in 1883 when the younger generation of Belgian writers overtly paid tribute to Camille Lemonnier whose novel *Un Mâle* had been refused official recognition. (Against expectations, the academic rulers had not awarded him the *prix quinquennal de littérature.*) This action widened the growing breach between the official formalists and those in search of a less sterile expression. The subsequent revolution had its normal quota of excesses, vestiges of which are still visible in Lerberghe or Rodenbach's funerary claptrap, but it broke the obstructive surfaces of traditional realism sufficiently for the Belgian poet to rediscover his most genuine and most fertile strata. Six years later, Maeterlinck came to light, in Paris, with *La Princesse Maleine.*

In 1894, Camille Lemonnier was in the process of breaking with existing forms through a Farce-pantomime, *Le Mort.* Marguerite Duterme, an eminent Belgian dramatist herself, is quoted by Solvay (*Le Théâtre belge d'expression française depuis 1830,* 1936) as saying, "We fail in the theater because we are painters [...]. Action escapes us" (an interesting confirmation of the fact that Belgian theater is an immediately sensual and nonintellective experience). Lemonnier remembered that the Farce speaks through the variegation of the pageant and it is as a Flemish painter that he has illuminated in a slender plot *Le Mort:* ironic Fate in the mantle of the titular ghost pursuing two brothers, Bast (craft) and Balt (strength) who have killed and robbed their relative Hendrik. As befits the traditional Farce (allied in this instance to the visual concept of the pantomime) the types are stylized and symbolistic. The dead one is the familiar scythe-bearer in the medieval *danse macabre* who alternates here with garish kermess throngs and their coarse fun during Balt's wedding scene or the somber evocation of Flanders in the brothers' windlashed shack hunched upon the wretched land. Thus is the simple tale distorted into the supernatural perspective indigenous to Flemish poets, into that "other kind of beauty" of which the Belgian playwright Suzanne Lilar speaks (*The Belgian Theater since 1890, 1950*), "generated by hermeticism, having a predilection for everything fantastic, irrational, strange, disconcerting, weird."

This stamp is on all significant Belgian drama, comic or

serious. An essay concerned with the Farce genre would point
out the extent to which the original form has influenced Belgian drama, from the scholarly and poetic renditions of Robert
Guiette to the commercial adaptations of Charles Desbonnets
or of others still writing today. And if works other than those
written in French were considered, Flemish contemporary
drama as represented by Herman Teirlinck or Herwig Hen-
sen would be found to evidence interesting parallels to that of
Ghelderode or of the other Belgians here examined. One
might envisage new generations conceiving more universal
forms, but so far, the genius who might replace the mark of
his race with his own has not yet appeared. Instead, when this
Flemish savor is lacking, the dramatic potency is diluted to the
extent of implicating the author in the spectator's uneasy feeling of plagiarism.

The grim gothic realism used by Maeterlinck, Lerberghe,
Rodenbach, and the others as the setting for their otherwordly
emanations has become a widely adopted form for the present
day Farce, as exemplified by Ghelderode—alongside whose
plays those of his predecessors might well be called mirthless
farces. The modern Belgian dramatists may have developed, as
the result of the self-consciousness already noted in the French
—in the Belgian case, a desire to continue the type of drama
begun during their national *renaissance des lettres*—a type that
depends on laughter in order not to age. However, they initially stand upon the secure ground of their Flemish ancestry
whose hallucinatory world is etched in the same acid as that
of the Farce. For them, the world might well be informed by
laughter before secondary considerations are invoked. When
a truly national drama was reborn in Belgium, the rebirth of
the Farce was so obvious a corollary that this rediscovered

form was not always distinct from the rest. It is significant that Camille Lemonnier called his aforementioned pantomime *Farce tragique*.

In 1906, appeared Charles van Lerberghe's *Pan,* "satiric comedy in three acts." It is the story of the turmoil caused by gypsies bringing Pan with them to a Flemish village and into the home of the shepherd Pierre, guardian of the communal buck (the scapegoat). The danger of this atheistic intrusion summons the church and civic leaders. Farce scenes show them attempting to disentangle themselves from parliamentary procedure, choosing a pig, and later a cat, an owl, and a toad that will convey the soul of the devil as it is chased out of the village. The cheerful pantheism of Pan converts a good part of the village and the sexton himself who, drunken and disheveled, disrupts the august body. The latter decrees a set of statutes against Pan that will reduce him to a common symbol, but the panic herd routs the official body and brings the curtain down on a final outcry of mystical pantheism.

If the symbolists' influence is fairly evident in the music and the dances of the play, the Farce scenes must be accounted for by the Flemish inspiration and the legacy of the *sotternijen.* Just how strong that influence was may be gauged by the extent to which the original motivation—the panic hymn which constitutes the entire first draft—has been transformed. In its present form, the play is a gay, colorful, and tuneful ensemble (written with a musical score and choreography) conceived for the eye. The language occasionally burdens this play that appears overly loquacious and didactic—a common failing of Belgian drama, but one that also echoes a primitive need: the moment when a reasonable voice moves out of the Dionysian aura to address a sobered spectator. Nevertheless, the form of the modern Farce is established: a spectacle enfolding a latent truth.

After 1918, two noteworthy Belgian playwrights come to light, Henry Soumagne and Herman Closson. Each must be considered here for at least one play using the comic mode to make, through new forms, a significant dramatic contribution.

Fame came to Soumagne with *L'Autre Messie,* produced by Lugné-Poë in 1923. The play is a sceptic's *divertissement.* As it does in all his plays, Soumagne's own amusement appears in the stage direction to the extent of jeopardizing them. Such facetiousness, which must remain unknown to potential spectators, would encourage the belief that Soumagne wrote plays only to be read, were it not for the extraordinary scenic evocations which he achieves.

L'Autre Messie is a certain Kellerstein who comes back to his native ghetto after having become successful though his soul still harbors unquenched longings. Godlessness and frustration are symbolized to him by his failure to discover anywhere in the world a firm-breasted woman. Dmitri, the one Christian in the tavern that contains this action, offers to prove God to him. The aridity of the debate is turned, by remarkable stage mastery, into four amusing and hallucinatory rounds of boxing: the pub becomes an arena; the customers become handlers and spectators; the arguments are blows under which the contestants reel though they never touch each other.

Kellerstein is unfairly beaten (the blows below the belt are Dmitri's emotional and self-contradictory arguments). He acknowledges his defeat by recognizing that the innkeeper's daughter Rosi has indeed firm breasts. Then comes Kellerstein's task of choosing, and again the scene is visually rendered. The hero's imagination, a gaudy show girl who has seen better days, dresses the tavern's patrons in the symbolic raiment of all the gods that man has created and makes them parade before Kellerstein. The successive failure of each to establish a valid claim to the title "real God" leads Kellerstein to understand that he himself is God. Thereupon God the Father who has engendered all these phantoms through his marriage with the earth, appears and tells the hero to give men the new religion which they badly need while the multitudes echo the demand in the darkened pub.

Kellerstein, who has the answer to their cries in the cyanide which he carries in his dime-store ring, decides, after a short tussle with himself, to leave that truth for yet another God unborn. He will merely give them the more familiar false promises; having so resolved, he passes out, dead drunk, in the midst of the others.

The narration of this play conveys a false impression of shallow topical allusions and naïveté in that it renders only the expressionistic symbols which the author has kept purposely simple. The dress of these clotheshorses is Soumagne's important contribution. The smelly pub that keeps shifting between its realistic and its cosmic significance houses truly ingenious stage devices. Soumagne's understanding of the essential theater keeps the colorful and sensual spectacle amusing throughout. His most cynical directions also betray his concern to keep the play a show, while sheer fun is evident in his constant, and usually subtle, puns, wholly subordinated to the action. During the scholastic bout, Seltzberger who is "handling" Dmitri advises, "Hit him with your left. . ." which admonition is immediately registered by his fighter who hits Kellerstein with, "And what are the results of atheism?"

The Farce, realistic and surrealistic, trivial and yet transfigured, serves as the setting for a number of masks, most of
which are provided by the anti-Semite's concept of the Jew.
The deep sensuality which pervades them provides a link with
the audience and the atmosphere in which the germ should
have prospered. But Soumagne is plagued by that recurrent
ailment of the Flemish playwright no matter what language
he employs: he is more argumentative than the Jews whom he
blames for this failing in a subsequent play, *Madame Marie*.
Reminiscent of Jean-Victor Pellerin's experiments, this one
might have also called to mind Pirandello, had it not been for
the thesis which is intellectually debated—and hence seldom
felt—and which the very rich atmosphere cannot always redeem, as each is distinct.

The Farce, however, is an essential expression of the Belgian, and the didactic loquacity that frequently mars it is seen
as *a part of* the genre rather than as an effort to explain or to
excuse the genre. Soumagne's failing lay elsewhere, in his contempt for an essential drama that might have arisen from a
nonintellective statement. After *L'Autre Messie*, plays such as
Bas-Noyard, Les Danseurs de gigue, Terminus, reflect a growing concern with the mere mechanics of the stage, making
other concerns ancillary to a nearly arid stylization of scenic
developments. Eventually, the author himself tired of such
blind alleys and returned to a former training of his, devoting
himself henceforth to the recording of court scenes and of famous trials.

Herman Closson's work, though considerably vaster than
that of Soumagne, bears less directly on aspects here considered. Out of a dozen plays which he has written, only one is
a farce. However, Closson is one of those authors whose icono-

clastic temperament seems to have been fostered by the blatantly heretical taste of so many dramas written after the First World War. His first play, the unpublished *Sous-sol,* is the soliloquy of an elderly woman knitting while in a water closet —this particular farce seat having evidently enjoyed something of a craze in 1925 which was also the year of Crommelynck's *Tripes d'or.* Thus, right from the start, Closson made evident his desire to remove his works from temporality and to spring a very aggressive type of play from wholly realistic settings.

In the manner of Cocteau and the surrealists, Closson is a visual poet. Not only is his language fluent and ample but the vigorous phrase is echoed and sustained by the grandiose settings drawn to the scale of the protagonists themselves. An immense thirst, a lack of measure, is as characteristic of Closson as of his heroes—all truly his own flesh and blood. Another aspect of Closson that accounts for the personal flavor of his drama is a deep-felt sensuality. Aside from *Le Jeu des quatre fils Aymon* (1943) whose protagonists remain a little too heraldic for such frailties, not a single one of his characters is free from the most emphatic carnal obsession. The unsated flesh is merely one of the absolutes in whose pursuit the protagonists of Closson meet with ultimate frustration.

This verve and his particular concepts of the theater were to lead Closson eventually to the Farce. *La Farce des deux nues* (1935) is exactly the result one might have expected. The carnal illusion and the living presence of the flesh assume again their familiar place upon a vehicle which they first helped fashion.

Most of the action is set in a bawdyhouse to which has come the obsessed baron in search of the agent of fulfillment eternally haunting Closson's heroes. In this instance, the nobleman who rules the small town in which the story unfolds has exhausted the carnal mystery. The *maquerelle,* whose advice he seeks, proposes for his pleasure a Godiva who will ride through the deserted streets hidden from all eyes but his. Meanwhile, Astolphe, whose wife Yolande is cuckolding him outrageously, asks of the same counselor that she provide Yolande with a man known to him so that he might be able to confront at least *one* real presence (something of Crommelynck's Bruno and of his pathetic jealousy as *Le Cocu magnifique* are discernible here). The malevolent *maquerelle* knots the thread by deciding that the baron might do: she merely has to make Yolande play Godiva. However, the baron's wife gets wind of the project and trades places with Yolande. For a brief moment the baron's senses are roused, but the illusion vanishes when he recognizes his wife and the tragic knell is sounded as he vainly tries to retain the illusion, begging of a prostitute while the curtain falls, "Tell me that it was you, the Naked Woman?. . ."

The compelling ambivalence of carnality and its universality that make it at once myth, communion, and drama, actuate most of Closson's conventional plays. Here, the substance of funny puppets is again the unquiet flesh since, for Closson, the sensual mysticism of the Flemish, easily wed to caricature, readily suggested itself. The puns, the crude violence, and the titillation do not make *La Farce des deux nues* substantially different from Strindberg's *Countess Julia,* in which (regardless of extraneous implications) a similar flower grows from similar mires. Of course, Astolphe does not kill the baron once he has cornered the phantasm—and though his cowardice is also Farce, such weaker passions should remain first-act parts in a genre that moves crescendo. If Astolphe stops at murder, it is because Closson is after all a Latin and his great seething usually dissipates in words. But even the death's head can grin in Flanders: Fernand Crommelynck and Michel de Ghelderode, two of the century's important dramatists, were to prove this.

A GRIMACE that might be laughter twists every one of Fernand Crommelynck's plays. The author is a Fleming, a man whose outlook remains essentially somber though his eye sees grotesque appearances. Crommelynck is deeply moored in the gloom of that race whose scrutiny of ridiculous detail never lightens the oppressive awareness of man's absurd destiny and which makes it spiritually kin to the tormented among the existentialists.

By the time he was twenty he had already written three successful plays. In chronological order of publication, these were *Nous n'irons plus au bois* (1906), *Chacun pour soi* (1907), and the first version of *Le Sculpteur de masques* (1908). André Berger (*A la rencontre de Fernand Crommelynck,* 1947), in an endeavor to dispel some of "the bitter northern mists" with which André Bellessort has associated Crommelynck (*Le Plaisir du théâtre,* 1938), omits mention of *Le Sculpteur de masques* in order to point out that the author's very first play is a lighthearted *bluette* utterly devoid of gloom or philosophy. True, *Nous n'irons plus au bois* is a *bluette* and, admittedly, Crommelynck's next play is a farce with no underlying design, whose types and situations appear to imitate Molière while its language and tone sometimes recall Marivaux. However, it seems that if one is to speak of the author's initial endeavors, one cannot omit *Le Sculpteur de masques* (called by the author *symbole tragique*) which, notwithstanding its date of publication, was written in 1905. Even if some light piece should antedate this drama, it might well be remembered that at twenty the author was already preoccupied by the horror upon which laughing masks brood.

That by 1905 Crommelynck had definitely conceived laughter to be as huge, as grotesque, and as superficial as the mask, is confirmed by the fact that three years later, he expanded his one-act tragic symbol into a full-length play, and that his succeeding work, *Le Marchand de regrets* (1913), overshadows laughter with mysticism and human suffering, though at first glance the plot appears to be that of a farce. The *marchand* is an antiquary more in love with his antiques than with his young wife. The young woman ultimately elopes with the village miller. But there is a crime: the antiquary kills his pandering neighbor and *Le Marchand de regrets* acquires the fuller meaning of its tragic title.

Such had been the texture of Crommelynck's plots and people when his next play burst upon the stages of Europe. *Le Cocu magnifique* (1920), "Farce in three acts," was to link Crommelynck's name with that genre—though it is noteworthy of changing times that Hébertot's first postwar *reprise* (December 31, 1945) made it a *pièce triste*. Bruno, village scribe and poet, is in love with, and loved by, his wife, the simple, pristine Stella. One day, the malignant virus of jealousy grips him. In order to relieve suspicions that soon dwell in him stronger than any other feeling, he forces Stella into the arms of every male villager in the hope of discovering *the* figment that obsesses him. He ends by losing Stella completely though still believing, as she is carried out the door, that this is merely another trick to hide from him the "real one." Such

a plot, superficially related or superficially treated, would be
little more than an ordinary farce. The caricature which the
ageless Bruno has become by the end of the play is gross portrayal also. (When a hero's hair turns grey, it is usually an invisible function of tragedy; should he lose his hair completely,
in sight of the audience, a farcical note has been injected,
though both changes may be due to identical emotions.) Still,
no one placed within the play can forget that every line distorting Bruno's face is incised by pain.

Lest anyone be misled by Stella's poetry and the sincerity of
her love, Romanie, her old *nourrice,* early in the first act clouts
the *bouvier,* Stella's first suitor and her ultimate one, to re-
mind the spectator that blow-dealing leaves no marks upon
the tough surface of the Farce. This is the first bastinado, a
common activity on Crommelynck's stage. There are others
later in the play, when wrathful village women belabor one
of Stella's numerous lovers, but by this time something of the
play's harshness has gone into their blows and Farce has
verged on drama.

This element of bitterness communicates itself to, and redeems, many of the comic props. Those who escape and remain simple creatures of laughter are the unregenerate, the
occasional characters on whom tragedy has no grip because
they have been drawn as mechanical agents of mirth with no
further purpose. Such is the *bourgmestre* who reappears often
in Crommelynck casts, generally endowed with the braggado-
cio, cowardice, venality, and stupidity which are the traditional
Farce attributes of officialdom.

Types such as these pursue their course with no regard to,
with no comprehension of, the latent tragedy building up
about them. Their surface is scrupulously realistic but houses

no soul. They are, however, rare. Estrugo, Bruno's secretary, is awkward and funny when he must resort to pantomime, pressed for words which, in him, are always too slow in coming. At such times he is a clown. However, when his silence becomes fuel for the suspicions of Bruno, he unwittingly grows to demoniacal stature. The pains which the author has taken to paint him as "Bruno's double" suggest Iago living within the body of Othello. The comic symbol need not represent only those whose meaninglessness makes them amusing. Through his character, or through the situation in which he has been placed, a stage personage builds up an expectation of superficial emotions, actions, or words, which he then abruptly shatters according to the laws of some inner consonance. This sudden departure from what had been anticipated —and usually the departure is from the falsely sublime to the very prosaic—brings about a twist which is humorous and which, because it is so disrespectful of the elevated tone it interrupts, can act but as a comic trigger, very similar to Herbert Spencer's "descending incongruity."

The character, however, has not been necessarily robbed of a more essential fiber which the audience had singled out in him and which will lead him, or the over-all action, to a grimly significant and wholly acceptable conclusion. When Bruno, obsessed by his monomania, is warned by the *bourgmestre* that the whole village is after his wife, Bruno's persistence in his dementia might lend deep tragedy to his reply. Crommelynck, nevertheless, turns it into a farce speech by the tone and words used: "Ah . . . Oh! wild imagination. What will they invent next? *Bourgmestre,* your mind is as flat and as twitching as a monkey's ass. Begging your pardon, begging your pardon!" And thereafter, the author abets his comic figure of tragedy with the aid of the genuine Farce type, the official, who rises deeply stung to mimic and speak the following retort: "To a magistrate! (*He looks around him in fear. No one. He feels better.*) Mum's the word!"

Likewise, the tone of the Farce, that is to say the use of vernacular for humorous effect, frequently dominates the poetic language, spoken in this play chiefly by Stella and Bruno. The mob scenes, the choruses of men and women that enter towards the end of the play, are frankly crude and reminiscent of the similar scenes which Peter Breughel once painted. The difference between Crommelynck's and Breughel's colorful, lusty mobs is that they are agents of sorrow in the scenes of the Belgian playwright, a suggestion not always apparent in his compatriot's canvases.

Some of, or all, these superficial disguises of tragedy come back in Crommelynck's succeeding plays, though their paucity in *Les Amants puérils,* which he staged during the following year (1921), suggests that this play might have been conceived earlier. Yet even here, in this somber drama concerned wholly with the incommunicability of souls, Crommelynck uses comic characters. Such are the servants, notably Zulma with her heavy, naïve laughter, and old Quasiment, whose deafness occasions amusing pantomime. There is also a coarse, carnal tone, much more pertinent to Farce than to tragedy, and again it is granted to those traditional comic heirs —the servants.

Tripes d'or (1925) has often been linked to Molière's *L'Avare.* The link is slender: both plays deal with avarice, one of the oldest Farce themes, and through the intensity of the drama they convey, both have soared beyond the realm of mere laughter. The dramatic impact of Crommelynck's play does not prevent, once more, the comic elements from dominating. The very ludicrousness of the situation stamps the work as Farce. Pierre-Auguste Hormidas (the names of the main characters are frequently meaningful) inherits a fortune which soon becomes the cause of his nightmares and his insanity. Barbulesque, the cosmically wise horse-doctor who attends him, advises him to eat his gold as a cure. After a month's constipation, Pierre-Auguste can no longer keep the gold in his system and he dies—the masque of comedy has become death mask.

Clearly, such a plot is symbolistic, but the author has given the symbols humble life by placing their acts under the aegis of Folly, and one must fall back on the conventional *bourgmestre* for harmless fun. Beneath their superficial insanity, these people exhibit fiendish implacability and coldness in their acts, "logical as only madmen can be," in the words of Maurice Coindreau (*La Farce est jouée*, 1942). When Pierre-Auguste's manservant Muscar, whose name and cruelty are reminiscent of Ben Jonson's Mosca, brandishes a whip, he sends a chill through cast and audience, for there are tales of murder about him, rampant even before the play is fully under way. Froumence, Muscar's wife, the clairvoyant chorus whose insights are penetrating to the point of discomfort, becomes the nearly monstrous conscience of Pierre-Auguste.

In line with the rest, Barbulesque, the veterinary in attendance on the hero, is revealed early in the play to be as broadly omniscient as the Knock of Jules Romains. After narrowly skirting satire throughout the first two acts, he assumes cosmic significance at the last when he rises before the dying Pierre-Auguste, and "burlesquing a terrible menace," exposes in a horrendous version of Creation the futility of men's acts.

In spite of the otherworldly implications of these characters and their inevitable didacticism, Crommelynck has been very careful to remain *terre à terre* in most of his scenes (even relieving Barbulesque's rather terrifying apocalyptical speech with the image of "millions of little Adams fornicating throughout the world"). Where he might have had Pierre-Auguste eating his gold pieces as such, thereby placing the scene in a symbolic light, he makes the hero grind each piece into fine powder which he eats with a hash—the dog's, incidentally. Such painstaking realism preserves in the most meaningful moments a caricatural surface: insignificant details are magnified while the substance of the theme is understated.

Furthermore, faithful to his method, Crommelynck inserts fun into moments of greatest pathos. At the height of his agony, Pierre-Auguste makes puns. Talking of the gold he has kept in him for a whole month, he blurts out, sobbing, "And now I can hold out no longer. The microbes are waging, with modern weapons, an intestine war."

But the true quality of these people's laughter becomes apparent when contrasted with that of the unalloyed Farce character, the customary *bourgmestre,* in scenes such as that during which, trimming by trimming, he is bribed into performing a marriage by proxy for the price of a handsome uniform. However, his is indeed a feeble voice in the mad chorus assembled here by Crommelynck.

Carine, ou La Jeune Fille folle de son âme (1929) is not a comedy. The play is about a young girl who says, "I do not believe that there is a single natural thing in the world into which candor might not enter," and who dies when the brutal coarseness of the world finally breaks through to her. This brooding drama affords a glimpse of the self-conscious author unable to curb the superficial strain of his mockery even though the heavy gloom of the drama makes it an awkward echo. Flippant language burlesques the speech of many of the characters, if not that of the two protagonists, though the characters be normally as disquieting as the ominous and sexually perverted uncle whose veiled and symbolic speeches contain discordantly humorous fillips. Such language would not be called for usually in a play as intensely tragic as this one. However, it echoes distantly the farcical types that do circulate even here, such as the servants or some of the sillier young girls.

Even the sentence that Carine speaks about her young husband Frédéric, "Frédéric is not a man," though it is innocent in her mouth, soon becomes fraught with more lurid meaning when bruited about by a girl friend, and acquires singular resonance in that the misunderstanding which it brings about starts the fatal unwinding of the tragedy. The *quid pro quo* in tragedy, the tablets in *Hippolytus,* like the handkerchief in *Othello,* even if unseen, have the credible substance of tangible objects. It is more typical of the Farce that a similar mechanism be, if not unbelievably real, at least close to the shallow pun if it is not to jar the Farce tone.

By contrast with the semi-caricatures around them, the realistic Carine and Frédéric occasionally sound awkward and ultimately unreal. Divested of all humorous attributes, they have become overstatements of purity and this exaggerated realism makes them morbid counterparts of the missing *bourgmestre.* Crommelynck experiences here some of the difficulties that were to beset Giraudoux and Anouilh a few years later.

Thus, the lack of tonal unity by which Crommelynck had hoped to single out his heroes creates an unpleasant dissonance

and frustrates the communion intended. A Farce character
can be accepted as real no matter what his exterior if his fundamental conflicts are accepted, but a soul too heavily swelled
with its own pathos remains a vulnerable target for the pin
pricks of his Farce associates. Stylized figures of unrelieved
tragedy must dwell on their own stage if the spectator is
not to be encouraged to throw them off the precarious ped-
estals which they would assume on a stage that also allowed
comedy.

With *Une Femme qu'a le cœur trop petit* (1934), Crommelynck turns the subject of *Carine* inside out and gives the
Farce aspects freer rein. If these are less assertive than in either
Le Cocu magnifique or *Tripes d'or,* it is because there is no
tragic vein in this comedy, and the whole tone being subdued,
the Farce, which needs the full ferocity of tragedy to maintain
its exacerbated pitch, will be perforce paler also.

The situation is, however, farcical, for attempts to unbend a
prudish woman are bound to be humorous if successful.
Crommelynck has turned even the prudery of Balbine into
farce, since it is on this account that the servants are driven to
concupiscence, her solidly constituted husband to hypochon-
dria, and her stepdaughter to marry her timid lover. Balbine
dresses her evidently indecently exposed servant Minna, thereby repeating in her own household the trouble that followed
upon the original sin. Her steadfastly puritanical demureness
makes her husband conscious of his age and starts him taking
his temperature. She confuses Patricia's romantic lucubrations
with threats of seduction and drives her into the arms of the
agronomist who would have been too shy to act of his own
accord.

The comic situation is granted echoes of Molière in the two

servants, Minna and Xantus, and, as usual, the Farce actuates
what little drama will be vouchsafed this play:

BALBINE: Stand straight! There, you see: your knees are frowning
at me.

MINNA: Frowning, my knees?—Oh, no, Madam, I beg of you.

BALBINE: And you have nothing under that dress.

MINNA: I have nothing under that dress, I?

BALBINE: Nothing at all, my poor child.

MINNA *(proudly):* Nothing at all? Oh, yes, Madam, I have what
it takes!

BALBINE: What did you say?

MINNA: I beg Madam's pardon—I have what it takes, under my
dress.

BALBINE *(surprised):* What "what it takes"?

MINNA *(overflowing with pride):* Yes, Madam—but I have my
innocence!

And at this point, Balbine who finally understands, faints,
revealing her physical (and symbolic) weakness: a heart too
small to countenance the fuller implications of life. However,
in spite of these Farce devices, and others, such as the pantomime scenes enacted by the servants, and that performed by
Balbine herself, the archhousekeeper who goes about her
chores even while sleepwalking, this same Balbine, never
wholly farcical, never wholly tragic, sets the tone of this mild
comedy. The Farce crackles throughout, but never sufficiently
to kindle significant action.

With *Chaud et Froid, ou L'Idée de Monsieur Dom* (1934),
Fernand Crommelynck seemed to reach his apogee. Here are
blended elements of Farce, satire, and drama in the story of an
adulterous wife who is compelled after her husband's death
to become a vestal to his memory. When Mr. Dom dies, and

he does so early enough never to be seen, his wife Léona discovers that he had had a mistress. She is crushed when she further finds that this man, who was nearly an abstraction to her, loved another woman enough to find in himself unsuspected lyricism, images such as "Félie, your eyes are longer than the days in June, longer than even happy memories," or, "Your eyes, when nearly closed, just like a soft horizon, eternize the gentle sadness of a subtle twilight," which first stagger Léona and then start torturing her.

Meanwhile, Alix, the abnormal servant-girl of Léona, spreads the rumor that Mr. Dom died mumbling, "I have an idea." This "spiritual legacy" is pounced on by the *bourgmestre* and other leaders of the community, with the result that the colorless Mr. Dom starts living a truly epic life the minute he is dead. Humiliated, frustrated, Léona finds herself trapped between the intense public life that has suddenly been conferred upon her husband in the form of political factions vying for the support of his "idea," and his just as suddenly revealed private life personified by her husband's mistress, Félie. This dual development has been blamed by many critics, namely Bellessort (*Le Plaisir du théâtre*) as plot-padding. But Léona must be driven ultimately to the pathetic expedient of convincing others, if not herself, that her husband's love-words to Félie were really addressed to her. In order to achieve this denouement, Léona's jealousy and her frustration must first be exacerbated. This can happen only if Mr. Dom becomes formidably real after his death, a man of sufficient stature and sufficiently alive to flog Léona with humiliation she cannot return. The Farce lining of this drama confers that grandeur upon Mr. Dom and its non-farcical significance forces his wife into the submission which this ironic drama demands.

Notwithstanding the secondary motor-plot, the play escapes Farce appellation. The mental form of the humor and of its implications make this high comedy. But harmonious integration of the forms sprinkles Farce situations and types throughout the action. Relying solely on the stupidity of the official, Crommelynck has created here his most comic *bourgmestre*—a slow-witted individual whose laboriously contrived sentences are usually open to amusing innuendos. He is the inadequate character who is unwittingly drawn into the growth of the "idea" whose birth is reminiscent of a similar one in Jules Romains's *Donogoo:*

ALIX: He is repeating softly: "I have an idea . . . I have an idea . . ." (*Amazement. Alix leaves. The men look at each other, astonished.*)

EVERYONE (*on every sort of note*): An idea? An idea? An idea?

BELLEMASSE (*laughs mockingly*): Mister Dom's idea? Ha! ha! ha! can you imagine that?

THE BOURGMESTRE: Who can tell?

BELLEMASSE: It would be properly his first one and his last.

THE BOURGMESTRE: We must unfortunately admit that he belonged to no clan, to no group . . .

BELLEMASSE: . . . to no party.

THIERRY (*brutal, all of a sudden*): Not to yours, assuredly!

BELLEMASSE (*pale with rage*): Not to yours, assuredly!

THIERRY (*wild*): My party!!

BELLEMASSE: My party!!! You old cocoon!

THIERRY: You dung-beetle's crap!

BELLEMASSE: You fart's skin!

THIERRY: You rabbit's leavings! You jaundiced excrement!

BELLEMASSE: You moth dust! You microbe's rump!!!

THE BOURGMESTRE (*moves between them, arms upraised, indignant*): Gentlemen!!! (*The pitch has so risen that the Bourgmestre*

*intervenes. He takes from his pocket a small, golden bell, whose
ring is shrill and tiny, and shakes it frantically. This minor
melodic shower seems so unusual that it calms the antagonists, as
if by miracle.)*

And after this reminder of Métaphraste's bell in Molière's
Dépit amoureux, the second-act curtain will come down on
this note of mock exaltation:

THE BOURGMESTRE *(calls):* Amédée-Jacques-Louis Dom!
ALL THE OTHERS *(together):* Here!
THE BOURGMESTRE *(exalted):* Amédée-Jacques-Louis Dom!
ALL THE OTHERS: Here!!!

These are instances of Farce seeking the fun of its caricature
in a stylization that affords it, nevertheless, crude realism.
However, that same fun has more somber extensions. When
in the concluding moments of the play, Léona, who has alien-
ated Félie's affection for Dom by forcing her own lover upon
Félie, quotes to Alix a sentence purloined from Félie's love
affair: "Do you know, one afternoon, we were running together on the meadow, and as I was gaining on him, he
shouted to me 'Léona, you are cheating, your feet do not touch
ground!' " Alix's answer is grossly amusing: "You were walking on your hands, of course." But it is this same abnormal
servant in whom are detected undertones of sexual irregular-
ity and a devotion to her mistress which is more like possessiveness—this same Alix brings the curtain down upon an obviously pathetic Léona who has stolen only an illusion and
who stands bereft of all but this empty token, with the words,
"Yes, yes, you are his entirely."

What might be said about this play can apply in general to
the theater of Crommelynck. Here, the very deep frustration

of a central figure has been drawn from the broader element of the comedy, just as elsewhere a deep suffering ultimately is differentiated from the Farce setting. The plays of Crommelynck recall the fine, feminine hands Rodin has carved and polished out of the coarse stone which he left rough-hewn for contrast.

A CARNAL obsession lies at the core of Crommelynck's drama—in the words of Léon Ruth ("Fernand Crommelynck," 1922): "Everything in him is translated through the senses or mysticism." Although written in reference to *Les Amants puérils,* something of that appraisal is valid for the other plays as well. In *Carine,* one of the masks says: "What are you doing there, without a mask or coat? Come with me into the only world that is real—the world of faceless beings. No more brain, no more superfluous names! Good-bye, cares, torments of the mind, waiting and useless seeking. Put on your mask. Come to the park, come join the essential play of mankind!" This atmosphere fashions not only Carine's world but that of nearly every drama of Crommelynck from the earliest.

In *Le Sculpteur de masques,* written at twenty, the author had already sketched the hermetic nature of the protagonists in the larger carnal scene. Pascal has loved Magdeleine and now his own wife, Louison—Magdeleine's sister—is dying. Haunted by a sensuality which frustrates both art and sensitivity, Pascal dreams of a world that might integrate beauty and his own passionate drives. Presently, the symbol of temporal lusts, a drunken lot of bacchanals, breaks upon the scene. They are followed by a leper whose terrible isolation sets off the heavily voluptuous atmosphere. It is to this leper that Magdeleine's own seclusion and remorse finally draw her.

But even that contact is not to be effected for their worlds are already sealed. Meanwhile Pascal, whose longing makes him a supreme outcast amidst the others, falls prey to his horrible masks that become the mad Erinyes of his despair.

Giacomo Antonini (*Il Teatro contemporaneo in Francia,* 1930) has seen in *Carine* the inability of human love to succeed, doomed as it is by the libido of man: the Italian critic could have found substantially the same thesis in Pascal's torment. He could have found it also in *Les Amants puérils* that anticipated *Carine* by nearly a decade. This was the undoing of Elisabeth de Groulingen grown old under her make-up and the veil of twilight in which she hides. A "stranger" loves the ideal mask of her, the flesh which he imagines:

I have seen you dressed in wind, behind the silk of banners, between the clouds whose slow shadows stroke the ridge of the sea, and beneath the leaves of young poplars that trembled as you tremble against me, Elisabeth! It was you, I swear it, who danced upon the beach, in the transparent dress of the tumultuous sands. I have seen you a thousand times, reclining, warm, and altogether naked in the shadeless dunes.

But Elisabeth is old. The baron Cazou who is senile and broken was her lover in the days beyond time and its punishing. All the while, two children, Marie-Henriette and Walter, act out in counterpoint a similarly hopeless love story suggesting that the basic incommunicability of souls may be due to causes deeper than the barriers of the flesh.

The statement of this incommunicability is presumably more important than that of the flesh which is a mere vehicle. The flesh, although a latent presence in every play, will simply be used to describe different aspects of the failure of love, a frail agency, weaker than jealousy (*Le Cocu magnifique*), weaker than avarice (*Tripes d'or*), conceivably even weaker than fraud (*Chaud et Froid*). However, the vehicle has frequently obscured the statement. André Rouveyre ("Carine," 1930), who could not find very much to salvage in Crommelynck ("Let him be exported as quickly as possible; that will be best,") saw the Belgian playwright's drama as "Solely an object of venereal functions [. . .] that gives its characters the shabby aspect of maniacal patrons in a bawdy house."

André Rouveyre was not allowing, in such condemnation, for one of the primary attributes of Farce that dates back to days when coarseness was accounted for by the greater intimacy then existing between art and life. This part of the theater is properly its own and escapes mental confines: it is the primal spectacle whose communion harks back to the days of a more essential drama. Referring to Bruno's exhibition of Stella to Pétrus, Léon Ruth ("Fernand Crommelynck," 1922), has said with scarcely disguised enjoyment: "Not only Pétrus, but the entire audience as well partakes at great length of this spectacle."

However, this element of immoderation before the problems of the flesh is also part of a greater excessiveness—and of it, the same Rouveyre has said ("Le Cocu Magnifique," 1928): "The Crommelynck hero is, in a word, cracked, and cracked people are not funny on stage." This assertion calls for amplification and, especially, qualification.

Implicit in the remark is an admission that these characters are something more than mere vehicles for comedy since automata could not be disturbing. Those automata that do circulate on these boards are neither new, nor more debased than is the average subject of laughter. They are the servants, the *bourgmestres,* and occasional characters whose life-span is measured in terms of a few humorous cues. They are the recognizable descendants of the medieval Farce. They have no life of their own, they are stock characters, and for that reason could not be offensive even if they were actually "cracked."

Another category of Crommelynck personae comprises the tragic characters such as Pascal, Carine, or Elisabeth de Groulingen. These people never depart from the dignity which is a fundamental attribute of their flesh and blood reality. They never attempt therefore to create laughter, and can obviously not be the ones drawing Rouveyre's criticism. As noted, Farce context—if it exists for them—tends to rob them of their credibility: French authors such as Apollinaire and even Giraudoux had already experienced this.

In the third group are those mysterious hybrids, such as the *chasseur,* Carine's malevolent uncle, or the previously encountered Estrugo. They are obviously "real" people though their quiddity appears to be part of a vaster supernatural scheme. If they are crazy, they dominate their insanity and channel it with uncanny malignity. In them madness is not an oppression but a weapon.

The last, and most important body of characters in Crommelynck's dramatic roster, is made up of those true-to-life creations that go mad as the play progresses. These are the ones whom insanity subjugates—though to call them "cracked" is to indulge a hasty apriority that neither situates nor renders the true quality of their dementia. These, and the creatures in the third group, are presumably the ones that disturbed Rouveyre. They are Crommelynck's distinctive contribution to the theater, the types that recur most frequently in his later drama and consequently the ones that come to mind when one thinks of "the Crommelynck hero."

The hybrids, of whom it would be rash to say that they are actually mad, though they are clearly not "normal," have a symbolic value which accounts for the disproportionate shape they acquire at times and which might have been confused with madness by critics writing in 1928. Since that time they have become recognizable in contemporary drama thanks to certain of the mythological transpositions of Cocteau, Sartre, Giraudoux, etc. Notable in Crommelynck's work are Froumence, Barbulesque, the *chasseur,* and Estrugo.

Froumence, in *Tripes d'or,* starts out merely as Pierre-Auguste's very down-to-earth housekeeper. As Pierre-Auguste gradually grows more insane and more incoherent in his words, Froumence appears by contrast to be more and more tight-lipped and progressively more formidable, eventually towering over the insane hero as the silent but thundering voice of his conscience. She ultimately dominates the entire stage, making even the terrible Muscar, Pierre-Auguste's demoniacal shadow, cringe before his own whip which she now wields.

Froumence actually exists only in relation to Pierre-Auguste, and later, as a result of his death. She is more important as a presence than as a creature exhibiting autonomous life. The impassioned ending of the first act calls for her to remain immobile while the hero tries to disculpate himself from accusations never leveled at him: such and other instances throughout the play indicate a physical projection of what might have been a simple verbal or intellectual statement in a genre relying more on mental synthesis.

In the same play, the already-mentioned Barbulesque is a similar character with no intrinsic life. His function is that of an omniscient and satirical chorus, in the same sense as the beggar in Giraudoux's *Electre*. This fantastic horse-doctor knows the inner thoughts of all and, by exposing them divested of their social wraps, he enriches the play with incisive comment. It is he, at the end, who presides over the sumptuously grotesque death of Pierre-Auguste to whom he has ministered all along, following his degeneracy with the cool detachment of a doctor or an otherworldly judge, both of which he embodies.

The disquieting uncle of Carine, the hunter (*le chasseur*), is somewhat more disconcerting because the tangible part of his being, that part which is not symbolic, is fixed within the incidents of the drama instead of belonging to the more broadly sketched Farce world where his physical acts might have been discounted. He too knows the lives of everyone beyond the mask. When Nency speaks of Carine as "the young girl in love with her soul," the uncle asks her, "Is that what Carine was called in the convent?—And you, who have no soul, you have come to find out how roughly hers is being handled?" He thus shows an insight into Carine's soul (and into Nency as well) which even Carine's own fiancé will not attain until it is too late—Frédéric being able to achieve such comprehension only through her death. Yet the uncle appears as a wholly perverted figure when he ends the words of his insight with the following, "Ah! I love you, dear child." (*He takes her head in both his hands, draws her close and kisses her on the mouth.*) He is an anti-Carine, a wholly sensual organism. But if this is the drama of Carine, his suprahuman wisdom imperils her own symbolism.

Nevertheless, the hunter is granted the habitual function of such symbols—that of becoming epilogue—for he too comes back to stand over the deaths of the two principals. But this man, whom Crommelynck has created laughing harshly and saying while the calls of hunting-horns are heard outside, "Fury, disgust, terror, everything lashes my desire!" is by no means an abstraction in his final impersonation, since he has contributed to the pollution of the air from which Carine dies.

Solely for the comic aspects which it seeks, the Farce demands realism in detail; the discrepancy thus created by an unreal situation arouses unessential laughter. The drama can allow those same details to be unreal, but only if they, in so becoming, acquire symbolic value, because the genre demands a reality in depth—the note which must echo in the soul and marrow of the spectator. Therefore, in this drama, the hunter is a disturbing element since, truly, a hybrid, he is pure only symbolically while remaining corrupted by his physical action throughout the play.

Estrugo, Bruno's second self, is a clown until his slow-wittedness is given the amplitude and the significance of Froumence's damning silence. He is, essentially, the rejected part of Bruno's soliloquies. Like all Crommelynck's hybrids, he is only semi-real. These people are born on the stage as symbols, even though they may occasionally have one or both feet on the ground of the general Farce life. Inversely, the main protagonists—the all-important fourth group—appear as real people when the curtain rises, or at any rate people as real as is the surface of the Farce. They end up tortured, wracked, demented; figures of whom, when their realistic body has withered away, the truer significance is clear.

They are hypersensitive. This abnormality, enlarged to the scope of a psychosis, is the source of all their other infirmities. They are relatively weak until the moment when their full energy is compacted into the one obsession of their madness and the fury of their monomania powerfully exalts them. Until then, their hypersensitivity irritates their every nerve ending exposed to a world within which they cannot integrate themselves. But contrary to Anouilh's heroes, they achieve at least artistic integration in that a harmless prelude to their ultimate and significant madness knits them and the Farce cast from the first.

When they are passive, these inadaptable people, like Carine or Balbine, are ultimately stifled. When they are active, and this is more frequently the case, they are soon unable to keep their exasperation in check; their passions are intensified to such an extent that at the final curtain they escape from the physical framework of the drama.

It is by this uprooting, by cutting the individual adrift from all reserve, all modesty, all worldly conventions that might conceal a fragment of the true self, that Crommelynck analyses the ravages of an emotion upon the individual possessed. He is a laboratory technician isolating a mainspring of the human being in order to watch it as it runs down, unhampered, in the vacuum of an observation chamber. If this blunt removal clashes with the physical aspects of a more familiar world, the momentary laughter of such an awareness is Farce, but it does not affect the central concern.

Henri Clouard (*Histoire de la littérature française du symbolisme à nos jours,* 1949) has called this technique "the ripping out of what is real from the depths of the infinite." And Léon Ruth, ("Fernand Crommelynck,") a compatriot and a keen analyst of Crommelynck, details the method thus:

Take a man whose character is genuine and generous, cut him along an incisive line that frees him from the very first of contingencies, and then continue that line according to its own logic, work the dough according to its own consistency, and cut deeper, knead further, systematically, beyond existence, into the sheer and enormous truth, right in the midst of life pure and simple.

It is meaningless to say that these people are pathological. They might be pathological in a transitional stage, as when their disease first manifests itself, but such moments are those of dawn or twilight: very soon the character will become an abstraction—the essence of the vice from which he is suffering. Only a part of the individual, of the former physical individual, remains.

That part moves about in a world rife with the madness it has engendered at least to some extent and is surrounded by deceptive liaisons—the nonsymbolic part of the hybrid in attendance upon the nonsymbolic part of the hero, false contacts with a bygone world. That is the dolorous part of the individual, the memory of a lost being suffering from the distorting passion that feeds upon it—the sacrificed part that must nevertheless still bear the rigor of a meaningless present. Such is the anatomy of Farce: a garish masque bleeding to death.

In this world, the destructiveness of time continues, as does the corrosiveness of love, of lonesomeness—for like those of Anouilh, these protagonists always remain alone, though in this drama, both they and those around them attempt repeatedly to bridge the insuperable breach. It is this live outline of anguished flesh that gives the abstractions of Crommelynck their pathetic, their sometimes mystical appearance.

The typification of such a personage is Bruno. He is the embodiment of jealousy—"Jealousy [. . .] bursting suddenly, like a horrible, implicit flower, from a love that has simply become too strong, too expansive; the struggle of the hero with his suspicions" (J. Rivière, "Les Amants puérils," 1921). Bruno—ever seeking "the one who will not come, Him, the only One," losing his wife unconcernedly to all his neighbors while he lies in waiting for the ghost of his madness, *that* Bruno ends up logically and climactically insane. But the remnant of the old Bruno that loved, and that still loves his wife in moments when his lunacy assumes through some grotesque coincidence a posture reminiscent of his former self, that remnant nails the symbol to a suffering body.

Stella who prostitutes herself for the love of her husband, Stella, the ideal of love, does not for a moment understand her husband. She is able only to drive him deeper into his madness. Between the devoted Estrugo and the loving Stella, Bruno is helplessly alone. The hands they reach out to him and toward which he vainly strives can never extend into his hermetic world. It is Stella who becomes the true pathological type, for she is never to achieve martyrdom, that is to say abstraction.

Pierre-Auguste, the pathetic Tripes d'or, similarly lives in an atmosphere replete with demented people. He is in love with the never seen, and consequently ideal, Azelle. Once his gold possesses him, it forces him to give her up. When she has been driven away, there remains Muscar, disinterested and faithful, to whom he might turn for help. Unfortunately Muscar, the grotesque and terrifying jester, "whose untamed heart has never forgiven"—Muscar is mad. He is the one chosen to read the will, for who better than he can render the demented voice of old man Hormidas, its author? (The lines were spoken by Louis Jouvet when the play was first performed.)

Item, I give, yield and cede to the *bourgmestre* of the municipality,

my body with all that it contains, lean and fat, coarse and delicate,
inert and subtle, in a word, my earthly remains with all of their
dependences, incumbent upon him to have engraved atop my
tombstone the following epitaph:

> Here lies a sinner without remorse
> Who lived that he might diddle life.
> Now since in hanging, 'tis said, a corse
> Relieves the urge with which he's rife,
>> He hanged himself and gave up breath
>> That dying he might diddle death.

This Muscar is the man who remains the bond between the
Pierre-Auguste that once was and the world he has lost, and
who, through this semi-isolation within the pales of insanity,
preserves just enough of the hero's body for his delirium to
prey upon.

Carine enacts the tragedy of unmitigated sensitivity. Not
only is the coarseness of the world too brutal for her, the pure
ones about her are too brutal also, for she is seeking in them
responses to the most tenuous feelings of her deepest soul.
Marcel Arland ("Carine," 1930) has called this "The intimate
struggle of a primordial and unsullied chastity upon which
are forced, nearly inevitably, circumstances, traditions, the
character's aging, and perhaps some jealous demon hitherto
dormant within the very depths of his being." In analyzing
Carine, that demon might well be invoked, for is not her
world first created in rebellion against that which she has
rejected? And is not the area rejected again one of insanity—
specifically that caused by the flesh this time? Carine's hypersensitivity is more exacerbated by the incomplete comprehension of her very pure husband than by more objectionable
aspects of the outer world. But might one not assume that

through Frédéric, she is attempting to reach her mother, a pathetic madwoman fighting, like so many of Crommelynck's characters, the depredations of time and carnal love?

And here, of course, lurks the uncle, the one who *does* see through to Carine, but who is part of the over-all mania:

LE CHASSEUR: How goes your soul?
CARINE *(far away)*: Badly . . .
LE CHASSEUR: So much the better, my girl. Listen to this. In the Paradise lost, there was a proliferation of beasts and plants. Were they then mortal? For if they weren't, one of each kind would have sufficed. But let that be. Inevitably, then, these will be found in the Paradise regained. Thus, beasts have a soul. The lecherous dog, the lascivious ape have a soul—or you do not. Choose.

Perhaps these words are meant to save Carine. But there is of course no contact to be established with those who are sacrificed to a fixation.

The ambivalence of the attempted comprehension which is due to the dual nature of those closest to the central figure, and the failure of that attempt which further isolates the victim, are operative even upon as strong a character as Léona in *Chaud et Froid*. This is the already observed Léona, significantly named, who says to an outraged rival, "You have come to beat me. Strike! I am in a hurry." That rival, Ida, is one of the pathological creatures that surround every principal. She has momentarily lost her husband to Léona and comes to exact physical pain from her. (Later, when she has found that this has little effect, she will try mental pain. Such an instance shows how close are some of the Farce elements to the neurotic expressions of these people. Ida slapping Léona all through a fairly long scene is a bastinado whose bitterness has robbed it of its mirth. Similarly, uncontrolled women beat their husbands in *Le Cocu magnifique* and the tragic Pierre-Auguste beats his gold.)

The first evidence of a lesion in the tough Léona is a teardrop: a certain Félie has come to the bedside of the deceased Mr. Dom and "She is crying! She is crying with irresistably contagious strength," acknowledges Léona, who has never cried until then. It is the harsh Alix who presently tells her that Félie was the mistress of Dom. Léona fights the preposterous idea with all the fire of her past self-confidence: "Quiet! It is not true! Or I did not know Mr. Dom!" But evidence soon compels her to recognize the facts. Her reaction is a savagely violent outburst—for an instant, the atavistic woman is seen in the full grip of her madness. At this point, however, she wrestles the beast in her and subdues it. Though still quivering, she reassumes an appearance of normality but she is already alone. Odilon, ready to do anything Léona might command him (he had previously volunteered to kill Dom while the latter was still alive) and the supremely devoted Alix can reach only an exterior part of Léona, who, as a result, is locked within her incipient insanity.

The obsession of Mr. Dom's deceit is now building up in her to tremendous proportions:

ODILON: You were deceiving him too!
LÉONA *(carried away):* You lie by every hair on your body!
ODILON: With me!
LÉONA: You lie! Is that deceiving? I at least lived without a mask!

Perhaps because she is stronger than most of Crommelynck's heroes, she continues to fight. Her torment is measured by the fury with which she strikes her blows. She first attempts to destroy Félie's Dom with the Dom she knew. To the panic that grips her when she finds herself unable to break Félie's unruffled hold on her past is added Félie's unalterable serenity, reflection of the love which is a constant flagellation to Léona. A culminating blow is the reading of the will in which Dom has bequeathed to Félie a place next to his in the family vault. Mystically confident, Félie is about to kill herself. Should she die, she too will escape Léona just as Dom has. Léona is now a Cornelian heroine because of the choice forced upon her, and she will effect that choice in Cornelian fashion, for ultimately she must win her tremendous and pointless battle. She destroys Félie's faithfulness to Dom by forcing his mistress to accept her own lover Odilon. She slights the dead man just as he, from the grave, had slighted her. She exacts the right to be the sole keeper of a symbol that never existed for her. Exalted, like a triumphant Medea, she ultimately stands alone, drawn to the full height of her pathetic victory, having triumphed over an illusion.

In order that she might suffer, like Bruno, the full measure of her tragedy, Léona wins out over a figment. More mercifully created personages usually succumb, but it is always to a similar illusion, for there is little material interference and little essential action in these dramas for which the Farce is a separate shell indeed. But there can scarcely be anything humorous in the struggle which these people wage with the shadows of their own minds.

The part of the hero that laughs is the mortal part, that crucible not yet destroyed by the fire it contains. When it does laugh, it is in response to a Flemish atmosphere, which French critics like Clouard, Coindreau, Bellessort, Brisson, etc., have termed that of the *kermesse*. The word implies a world of boisterous, cheerful, rough, and rather primitive people—people already sufficiently detached from the polish of a more affected society to give the radically abstracted hero an initial modicum of credibility.

Discounting native biases, the atmosphere of the *kermesse* with its farcical implications might nevertheless be questioned as a dramatic medium. The quest for "the sheer and enormous truth" undertaken by Crommelynck provides one of the reasons for the choice. That truth can be found only in an archetype whose divorce from standardizing patterns is complete enough to make it an absolute. Such a figure lies beyond everyday normality, of course, and, in the case of Crommelynck's creation, even beyond everyday abnormality, so sharply has he been cut off from all avenues whereby he might have approached assuaging norms. Placed in a realistic drama, this character would have been bound to the limitations and the leveling of realism and those necessary compromises would have altered his make-up radically.

Moreover, any hero who corresponds to an excessive vision might easily grow beyond the spectator's reach, as have, for example, Carine and Frédéric. Dramatic logic calls for this kind of character to perform in a world of similar exaggeration wherein he can more easily assume his symbolic value, enabling the spectator to establish new links within an intellectual sphere.

Lastly, the very excessiveness of such heroes might be open to question. However, should they achieve beyond the stage the sought-for integration of their symbolism, their superficial stage life becomes part of the life of the theater—the often-stressed spectacle, its color, and its fun. In this realm, ambient insanity is justified in that it affords artistic homogeneity, blending the act resulting from comedy with that brought about by folly. But although such laughter integrates the world of the hero and that of his surroundings, it is never directed at that which is essentially tragic in the hero.

All through the drama of Crommelynck that hero will suffer, but usually within physical surroundings as mad as are those who people it and as funny as will always be the incongruous object to which no moral stigma can be affixed. Ferocious in his damnation of gold, the author has it kill Pierre-Auguste in the midst of bodily pain that adds to the latter's obvious mental pain. But the hero's Gethsemane is the most grotesque of seats—his *chaise percée*. In the broadly sketched world of the Farce, logic extends beyond its normal limits. Death is exacted by tragedy. The Farce indicates the place of death.

Mr. Dom who comes back from the grave to thwart the lovers Léona and Odilon, and who exacts from his wife the life-long faithfulness she never granted him during his own lifetime, is very reminiscent of the commander's statue in *Don Juan*. And yet he is an unreal presence, the creation of the abnormal Alix. And his ectoplasm is given reality by the frantic, and not altogether sane, leaders of the community. Everything around Mr. Dom is tragedy except his very real, though posthumous, self, which is unmitigated Farce.

Bruno allows a body obviously separate from his mind to become the principal Farce figure in a play wherein his substance is the titular hero. Like the clowns of Rouault, this one is transfigured in spite of his stage paint. Yet his most desperate cry in the play belongs to the over-all Farce. It rings out when, masked, having brought Stella to the verge of giving in to him, he comes tumbling down the stairs, screaming, "With me! With me! Estrugo! With myself, if I had wished it! Es-

trugo! I am cuckolded as much as one can be!" He is a forceful reminder that, originally, the Candaules myth was not a
farce.

The mysticism of the Flemish, that curious admixture of the
flesh and the supernatural grotesque, establishes a world that
is close to the medieval atmosphere of the original Farce. It is
fixed on the canvases of Jerome Bosch. It is apparent in the
work of Charles van Lerberghe and of Michel de Ghelderode.
Just as naturally, it seeps through the tamer writings of Maeterlinck. The French—including the French mystics, such as
Claudel, or even Péguy or Jammes—are usually more urbane,
and even when primitive seldom tend towards caricature.

Although Crommelynck has, on occasion, disclaimed his
Flemish heritage, it is in Belgium that he learned the theatrical trade, and, in interviews that Belgian newspapers have
published, he showed himself less anxious to reject the country in which he was brought up. The meticulous attention
which the Farce pays to details stamps Crommelynck, for in
his work these are Belgian. No draughty castle halls here, as in
Maeterlinck, subject to otherworldly rustling and temporal ridicule. Rather, these are opulent Flemish interiors, never very
different whether farmhouse, living room, or mansion hall,
with a door ever open onto the real world—the bedroom.

Water, symbol of Flanders, canals, and the endless passing
of time, is seldom far away. It is specifically indicated or implicit because of the action. The Belgian Northland is sketched
in the solidity and the cleanliness of the sets, such as that of
Tripes d'or—"Heavy oak furniture that is well polished,
painted earthenware, copper, and pewter utensils." Similarly,
Léona's interior is one of "luxury, order, stability." If the notation of order and cleanliness is absent, there is someone dusting

or decorating as the curtain goes up—diligent hands of *huis-vrouwen* are ever present.

Inevitably, this setting of regularity and bourgeois solidity is disrupted by the entrance of more significant symbols, but these grotesque intruders remain as Belgian as the surroundings they invade. True to another Flemish vein that fuses what is coarse with what is sublime, the most incensed of these performers will see a light in moments of desperate aspiration away from the direction of his madness. Such is the symbol Azelle, towards whose soothing sanity the body of Pierre-Auguste still strains. Such are the drives toward their past in Elisabeth, Bruno, or Carine. Ever does the aspiration remain within the individual; outer forces are never called on or brought into play. Evil is in the blood, salvation in the past— and the hopeless pattern within which these people are mured is ceaselessly repeated.

In this hallucinatory world, love is not one of the primordial forces as in Maeterlinck. The great forces are the primal passions that have endured since a much earlier drama and that are not subject to social or superficial psychological contingencies. The only ambient atmosphere strong enough to contain them is that of the flesh, the essential world that antedates morality. But if a moral might be derived from dramatic foundations, it might well be that taught Balbine: the senses whence flow all spiritual values are necessary rather than evil and are an essential constituent of the healthy, sane, and full individual. They have given birth to the Farce and its tragedy: they are now the spectator's to assume.

IF THE tone of these plays leaves an impression of earthiness, their language remains poetic in the main. The combination of these qualities has been called by André Belles-sort (*op. cit.*) "a coarse and precious style." "Coarse," this style is indeed, as are unpolished the people who speak it. If "precious" refers to the constant images through which their words express their immediate concerns, then this preciosity is indeed an attribute of lyric style. Expressions of the tragic and of broad farce are intermixed as naturally as are the genres. "Lyricism elbows bestiality. And even within the figure of the public scribe Bruno, poetry does not disdain to appear, though it may be suddenly interrupted by a burst of laughter that mocks it" (Jean-Richard Bloch, *Destin du théâtre*, 1930).

The achievement of Fernand Crommelynck has been to maintain poetry even through the coarsest passages of his work, so that the melodic flow seldom appears to be broken. It was this aspect of his drama, coming at a time when the taste of theater-goers was still accustomed to the language of the naturalistic play, that occasioned some of the *littérature* accusations that were leveled at him as they were at Giraudoux. Crommelynck replied to these in the same manner as did Giraudoux. In 1934, just before the Belgian première of *Une femme qu'a le cœur trop petit*, he declared to a journalist: "The drama that will be performed must first be a written drama. There is in language a plastic beauty that will have spoken value only if it has written value."

Maintaining these dramatic ideals, Crommelynck was, by obtaining recognition, one of the very first able to free the French stage of naturalism by creating a language—as well as a world—of the theater. J.-R. Bloch (*Destin du théâtre*) placed Crommelynck's *Le Cocu magnifique* alongside Giraudoux's *Siegfried* in listing plays which, he believed, were leading the French drama into new and more spacious realms. He saw in these plays a confirmation: "The public is desirous of and expects a dramatic *style* whose architecture will be at once ideological and imaged, with diamondlike poetry and terse prosody, fit to remain in the spectator's mind and able also to create its own aura."

Crommelynck's men are usually artists or are sufficiently cultured to warrant an imaged expression. Barring such innate distinction, the supranatural significance of the protagonist soon confers that right upon him. The women are, of course, essentially lyrical. The deep sadness of Carine's last speeches to Frédéric is spangled with poetic visions of the past, and her language makes her a sister of the prototypal Stella. It also echoes the speech of those naturally poetic people, the young, the lovers, the dreamers that are found in nearly every one of Crommelynck's plays.

Even the more sinister people in this drama couch the unpleasantness of their symbol in agreeable terms, and it is noteworthy of the author's gift for words that even his buffoons use a rich imagery in their harshest moments. Their adjectives are meaty, concrete, and smack of the fertile loam. Their speech comes effortlessly in a flow whose amplitude echoes Rabelais more convincingly than does that of Jarry for at such moments there is no intellectual notation intended—whether humorous or ideational.

Like Baudelaire, like Valéry, Crommelynck might be called the painter of the feminine body, so thoroughly are all of his people steeped in the essential flesh. But the extreme sensuality of the language hardly ever detracts from its beauty, though, on occasion, Crommelynck's poetic verve needlessly extends certain scenes. This fault parallels, and stems in part from, the garrulity and the argumentativeness of the Flemish.

In spite of Crommelynck's farcical virulence, a forensic interest in the problems which they embody occasionally keeps his personages weighted down, intellectual symbols, but also didactic ones that become awkward within the huge, unalloyed life of the Farce.

Some of the author's dramatic mannerisms may be due also to the fact that like Ghelderode's, his style was still being shaped at a time when the German expressionists held sway. Although Crommelynck's work appears less influenced by this school than is that of his compatriot, Clouard deems it significant that the brutal, satirical form from beyond the Rhine was an important current during the author's formative years, while noting too the coeval vogue of Synge's *Playboy of the Western World*.

As early as 1924, Ashley Dukes, whose vision enabled him to see the dramatic world that would succeed the naturalists' and who assayed the contemporary plays in that light, had hailed Crommelynck as a new force in the theater and one for whom he demanded wider audiences, correctly epitomizing in *The Youngest Drama* the Belgian's art:

Mr. Crommelynck who abandons the plane of realism and seeks for the ludicrous essentials of his situation, escapes at the same time from the urbanity and the lassitude of these contemporaries. His *reductio ad absurdum* of the sexual motive imparts a new vigor to the theme. His comedy is cruel and grandiloquent but it is elemental. The sap of nature runs in this tree that leans against the wind of Flanders and casts a fantastic shadow on the plain.

Within the broader perspective offered by an additional quarter of a century, it is possible to discern that shadow falling across a whole era in drama and in literature.

Ghelderode

HIS FLEMISH ANCESTRY notwithstanding, Fernand Crommelynck has drawn people whose actions are not necessarily wed to their particular surroundings. *Les Amants puérils, Carine,* and at least Léona in *Chaud et Froid,* suggest a universality that surpasses the physical area of the action. Although Michel de Ghelderode proposes conflicts as fundamental and as unrestricted, his context allows him more frequently to loose on stage the full demonolatry of Flanders. Since *Sortie de l'acteur* (1930) is among the plays of his that have not been fitted to a specifically Flemish cast and since it is also a play about the theater, it might be regarded as a statement by the dramatist himself and examined for whatever theatrical indications, manifest or implied, are expressed.

Actually, Jean-Jacques, the author, has a curiously secondary role in this drama, essentially that of Renatus, the incarnation of the actor, with whose death and resurrection it is concerned. Whereas Jean-Jacques remains at all times a creature of flesh and blood, albeit one occasionally endowed with remarkable intuition, Renatus is able to loose his earthly bonds, releasing the symbolic spirit of the character. The role of the author is more confined within his terrestrial shell through the added contrast of Fagot, the prompter—*le souffleur,* insufflator of life wherever are found scenic machines, on stage, in the church, or at an actor's funeral—hence, the spirit of the dramatic rite, of the Theater.

Jean-Jacques, who has renounced the theater for good, attempts to bridge the gap that has always existed between himself and Mademoiselle Armande, an actress who plays the role of the Saint in the author's unperformed play, and who is in reality the impersonation of Love in its carnal vulgarity and pathos. While the author succumbs to her lure against his own will, Renatus, in his delirium, sums up his own dramatic existence and blends with his external symbols the living drama enacted by the author and Armande—"What anguish! . . . What is it they are playing that is eternal and so very painful?"

Renatus' death is understood only by Fagot. The others feel but the awkward clumsiness of the living before the perplexity of death, and Jean-Jacques, previously described as "inordinately gifted," in whose plays "one dies too much," is dumbfounded: "Is that death? . . . Is that how one dies?" Still, Renatus returns pursued by military angels. The very pure soul of the actor is too saintly for the machinations of paradise. Haunted on earth, hunted in heaven, the ghost longs for nirvana—the ultimate repose of extinction.

But God's policemen always get their man and Renatus' endless calvary is transferred to Elysium. And the theme of the play, "Death, an actor's exit . . ." is unresolved in its timelessness and its mystery. The spirit of the actor lives on with tragic insistence while, in his own search, the author is similarly frustrated. In answer to Jean-Jacques' repeated questions, Fagot speaks these final words: "Sir . . . I do not understand you . . . the key to the mystery? . . . Did you not know that mystery has no door?"

Jean-Jacques' body makes him a figure too frail amidst these spirits to have great significance as such. He has been described in the play as "an impassioned weakling," ineffectual in his enthusiasm, his sorrow, and his quest; he is, furthermore, a participant in the drama, thus subservient to acts not necessarily enlightening as literary confessions. He is, however, a mortal seeking from intercessory phantasms answers whose substance is not of this world. But his own definition of this quest, "Death, an actor's exit . . . ," should be interpreted as a characteristic of personal doubt rather than a metaphysical dilemma. The author attempts to find the meaning of love also, only to conclude: "No. I am alone. And you are alone. . . Even knotted to each other, as we once were, do we cease to be alone?" The vanity of love, of questioning, may illustrate an aspect of Ghelderode's philosophy, but here, these sentiments are important primarily as particularizing characterization. Jean-Jacques is a man: the theory must derive from more than his words.

This play is first of all about the stage. All its characters are actors, or at least performing spirits in the making of the theater. The author, who remains throughout a lay protagonist, is nevertheless on intimate terms with the demiurges. He is able to span the planes between his earthliness and their otherworldly realms by the deep and amicable understanding that he has of their individual personalities. He is Baudelaire's poet walking amidst familiar symbols. "Renatus," says Jean-Jacques, "to each his whimseys. Do not make fun of the one person in the world who understands yours." In the context of this relationship, even Jean-Jacques' less revealing traits become comprehensible. It is the same Renatus who types Jean-Jacques by telling him, "You are, as I am, an impassioned weakling." But spoken by *the* actor, the terms confer far wider significance upon Jean-Jacques. Similarly, the entire personality of the author should be gathered from the spirit of his dialogues with the eternal shades of the stage. His stance, rather than his words, is meaningful.

Jean-Jacques is primarily what Gide would have called a "disquieting" influence, though a strangely reluctant one. It is he who has contaminated Renatus with his plays and instilled in him the persistent theatrical illusion. He has given up writing, he has lost faith in the theater—that is to say, the theater has lost meaning as a convergence of axioms: the theater is the raucous cry of life itself or it is nothing, and Jean-Jacques has given it up because the theater only mimics the most vital impulses.

This concept of the theater as an incantation, as a cry so spontaneous that in even its most formal moments it remains a shred of pulsating reality, is evident not only in the words and attitudes of the protagonists, but in their inversions and contradictions, in their oscillations between the wisdom of oracular shades and the perversions of common souls. Life—a human manifestation after all—is allowed capricious incursions justified only by their very capriciousness, because random and illogical quirks are an attribute of fate. This is a notion to which should be related that of timelessness, in the creation, the performance, and meaning of the drama. Here, the thought is conveyed by the spirit of the actor: "Those great men are concerned about me? It is true that I have served them well... What did you say? Calderon? Oh... And Goldoni? ... And Ben Jonson? They were said to have died so long ago... No? Of course, time does not count in the theater...."

Just as the otherworldly beings endow the clay figures they surround with the eternity of their own meaning, facets of the author—that is to say, concepts of Michel de Ghelderode—must be discovered in them. The theater as an aspect of bitter wisdom, of disenchantment, is represented by Fagot—alias Fagoti, once a famous mime:

JEAN-JACQUES: And you, Fagot? . . . Sexton, prompter, shameful mime, here you are promoted to the rank of waiter? . . .

FAGOT: Mum's the word! You act a part . . . you change because you think that you'll have fun, but you act and there is no fun. . . .

Fagoti, as Pierrot Lunaire, will introduce another of the author's creeds when he bemoans the loss of color, or glitter, and magic upon the stage: "And the moon? . . . She still is shining and I alone love her . . . I have stolen her and hidden her in this theater although they no longer put on fairy scenes here. No, we live in an age that has no fairy scenes. . . ."

Perception of the world as a plaything in the hands of occult forces quite beyond the grasp of rational man, is spoken by the human Renatus who uses words of Ghelderode, an enduring invalid of some years now: "To you, the man of learning, I affirm that one dies of curious ailments about which you know nothing." The passive medium of these supernormal agencies is the woman, here Mademoiselle Armande, saint and sinner, sacred and profane love—an automaton occasionally possessed of voices and a wisdom not her own.

Lastly, there remains the all-important concept of the Farce, the belief that laughter, that an acute awareness of the ridiculousness of people and situations, in no way alters the sincerity of that perception or its pathos. In *Sortie de l'acteur,* only Fagot, and Jean-Jacques, less perfectly, have understood and mourned Renatus. At his burial, the scene enacted by these two begins in the spirit of the Gospel but ends with clownish raucousness. Living, and the concomitant attention to sordid details, so run counter to human dignity as to turn all attempts at dignity into postures even more grotesque than the others. Here, the thought of Ghelderode is rendered by the ever-frustrated expectation of a spadeful of earth upon the coffin and the intrusion of trivial incidents that gradually absorb the entire concentration of the only two genuinely comprehensive mourners.

MICHEL DE GHELDERODE's dramatic writing reveals a number of recurrent attitudes—expressed by thoughts, situations, or motives—that emerge as characteristic marks. Some are conceits and literary affectations; others must be regarded as reactions or experiments. But whether these characteristic marks be analyzed negatively or at face value, all are equally important in yielding an artistic portrait of the author.

Among these, a great number immediately situate the author in his relationship to the theater, its life, and its appurtenances. Clearly, he has lived the dramatic experience intensely and has intimately partaken of its many rites. In a country that still preserves relics of a more fertile past, he has discerned the manifestations of its folklore wherever it comes to life, in villagers' tales, on puppet stages, on the boards of carnivals and fairs. He has loved the travail of prosceniums, wings, flies, greenrooms before the birth of the play and busied himself with its participants: the actors, the prompters, the stage hands. He has endowed them with an existence the depth of whose joy and sorrow stems from the world in which they toil. The clown and the music hall artist were his kin, linked to a common progenitor, and to these he has frequently turned when a myth demanded people to wear the dress of its heroes.

The more a civilization is unsophisticated, the more the dramatic performance is a living reality, a natural food, readily assimilated, free of the intellectual considerations that disfigure the offering on both sides of the modern footlights and which have made the latter increasingly impressive barriers. For him who brings but his naïve being to the theater, its world is a richer one, more mysterious and at the same time infinitely more familiar than can ever be that of the connoisseur.

The warm homogeneity of a more primitive theater may still be experienced in Belgium where the dynamic tempo of more recent centuries has by-passed odd nooks in which an old world still endures. Certain archaic puppet stages, for example, are still imbued with richness of the past. The ten rows of benches, the dolls, the texts, and the language are legacies of a distant past. The sets and clothes stopped keeping pace with the times in the seventeenth century, during the French occupation, and their periwigged Versailles courtiers play with effortless and good-natured anachronism every part demanded of them. They speak the language of their audience, a jargon in which either Flemish or French acts as the corrupting agent according to which other of these two languages is used. They are the performers for whom Ghelderode has written so many of his plays, those that spoof a familiar old devil, like *Duveloor* (1931), or those that tell of the throes of Christ, such as *Le Mystère de la Passion de Notre Seigneur Jésus-Christ* (1924?). Instinctive feeling, dear to the author in all its forms and doubly essential in the theater which is art and ritual, probably account for his predilection. In a puppet program printed in 1952, Ghelderode has said:

[. . .] in the Marolles section, there are strange and ill-begotten creatures, adventurers of the shadows, masquerading under an assumed title and a cardboard crown, and forgetful of their real name—people who are throughout a lifetime, without anyone but children and a few old people ever knowing their real face, the mountebanks of days gone by. They are the ones who have found beneath cellar flagstones, the very springhead of Theater, and who are creating Theater in an untamed state, exemplarily, according to instinctive notions.

The content of the puppet-symbol is important. These dummies and their unpolished performances are a tangible link with the past, a living aspect of Belgian lore, of the great Flemish legacy. They are a spiritual force that can breathe the life that enabled them to survive. Ghelderode, as a Fleming, came naturally to share their Antaean strength. For a number of his plays, he claims that they are "nothing more than a document of folklore" (e.g., *Le Mystère de la Passion de Notre Seigneur Jésus-Christ*).

But the puppets have still another significance: the mystery and the power of the inanimate figure. The marionette is an ideal masque, suprahuman because it brooks no human familiarity and superhuman because it is able to embrace all human percepts as well as the shadows wherein they fade. However, this attribute is not an exclusive one in the author's thought, as it was, for example, with Gordon Craig. Michel de Ghelderode shares with the English theorist only the desire of all who understand anew through art: to find protagonists of sufficient stature to transmute and convey the human quandary. For the Belgian dramatist, the essential human presence—the *instinct*—must sooner or later force upon the suprahuman masque human debilities. And at their weakest, these figurines become merely people. The 1952 edition (Gallimard) of *Les Femmes au Tombeau* is prefaced by the following admonition: "The manuscript of this play written in 1928 bore the subtitle: *Drama for Marionettes*. The author has erased this indication so that the work not be thought of as being reserved merely for actors made of wood."

But more frequently, the Ghelderodian puppet is capable of

greater transmutations. He shares with all inanimate objects in this curious world of the author, the ability to acquire prosaic life and to dispense the full measure of symbolism that comes from such metamorphosis. He then casts on the human thus born the mantle of his magic.

The puppets in *Le Soleil se couche* (1940?) are illustrations of the triple aspect which they assume in this theater. In the somber Spanish retreat where his son Philip wants him to await an edifying death, far from his native and boisterous Ghent, Charles Quint briefly relives his throbbing past through the miracle of his marionettes. These are first for entertainment—the play within the play. They also serve to contrast Charles' residual Flemishness with the grim asceticism of Catholic Spain (Fray Ramon). They are also, because they are plebeian, the mark of his wisdom and of his humanity. But as they near their destiny, the marionettes in their play become accusers and finally, in the mysterious person of their voice, Messer Ignotus, they merge and come to life and their fantastic shape dominates the entire stage.

Puppets, however, are not the sole retainers of sacred mysteries. If their archaic flavor has preserved both the lore and the spontaneity of more ingenuous ages, others have assisted in preserving the tangible world that was once theirs. In fact, all its participants are vital elements in its being and in its deathlessness. An author who found much of his drama where stage drama is born, Michel de Ghelderode has frequently called on the actor to represent himself. For him, the real actor is one marked by the somber powers of the stage and scarcely distinguishable from all who bear its fateful impress. He is an intuitive creature, atuned to the same otherworldly waves actuating the author: both are impelled and inspired by forces apprehensible only to the few elect, the outcasts who toil within this sanctum.

Renatus is the prototype of such creatures, bearing with varying degrees of fortitude the aboriginal curse of his extraordinariness. The actor's agony, like that of the author, stems from his inability to escape, to be other than what he is and will be for all eternity, despite the torturing acuity of his vision. The only consolation that he may countenance is as bitter as the early Camus, whose neo-stoicism it recalls: his awareness of this somber fate gives him dignity. When the aging and penniless Arlequin, Pierrot, and Colombine drift into *Le Ménage de Caroline* (1935), a *tête-de-turc* stall in need of new dummies, Arlequin sighs, "A hard job, very like . . . To have balls thrown at you. . . But if in so suffering, we manage to eat? . . . And what is more, we do not give up our personality, we remain artists."

But whereas for the Sisyphus of Camus, dignity is his sole *raison d'être,* the actor's dignity only serves to stress his art: his is the self-respect of the conscientious artisan, and moral ethics are closely linked in him with professional ethics. In *L'Ecole des bouffons* (1937), a graduating class of misshapen and excommunicated creatures is granted by its master Folial, himself an ennobled jester, the words of redemption: "Your [whole life] owes it to itself to be a ceremonial."

In an eminently visual world, the tragic dichotomy of the actor, the seer who must play the fool, leaves a physical impress upon his features as once did suffering upon the clown Bruno. The spirit of the actor, Renatus, grows old and marked by hard days: he is now Arlequin whose spiritual conflicts are heightened by the material hardships that plague his struggling race. And as he remains ever beyond the comforting pale of convention, he ends in the mask of Folial's horrendous buffoons, creatures of noble birth whose cruel lot has wrenched them physically and spiritually from the warmth of man and God.

It should be noted that even in his least distinguishable form, Ghelderode's actor already shows stigmata. Renatus himself is a clown. The clown is the modern buffoon of earlier days: both are an embodiment of tragic irony, whose grim ambiguity is heightened by their participation in the dramatic ceremonial. It is curious to note that in a drama so consistently shaped by the plastic and spiritual influence of painters, the name of Rouault has never been evoked. The Ghelderodian clown irresistibly calls to mind those poignant figures in circus garb through whom the French artist has expressed some of his own mysticism.

If the buffoon tends to fuse with the other grimacing figures of this drama, the clown preserves a pristine quality hinting at godliness. His pale mask remains an expression of virginity, splendidly pure in contrast to the defiling world into which he has been plunged. Such are the six pathetic figures in *La Transfiguration dans le cirque* (1928?) who, after having in vain attempted a revolution, end in their eternal surroundings —final stage direction: "Upon the bars and trapezes, the six winged, aerial clowns fly about like spirits in a bluish haze."

Not always for immediately apparent reasons, the clown may lend his tragic vision to renew experiences that have a standard form already. Ghelderode's Faust was conceived at first as a character who "must appear to the spectator as a clown to whom a tragedian's part has been given" (*La Mort du Docteur Faust,* 1926 edition). And inverting an identical relationship, his *Don-Juan* was at first (1928 edition) a "Drama-farce for the

music-hall." For Ghelderode, tragedy is an absolute, as meaningful in the world of these proletarian figures as it once was
in the realm of loftier heroes. His tragic clown Faust meets
effortlessly in death the conventional Faust played by an actor
ensnared in the legend and the malevolent parallelisms of his
own life.

Michel de Ghelderode has frequently strayed far afield to
seek the implements of his drama, but no matter how unnatural their experiences, his victims have always remained abjectly human. It is his belief that the most unfathomable and
the weightiest of problems trouble, after all, only men, and his
Flemish eye has never allowed him to see suffering as a physically ennobling experience. Rather, he has scrutinized the pain
and the debasement which it causes. And what redemption is
granted his people comes from the fact that they were human
and acted as humans.

Similarly, because a problem too obtuse soars to levels where
the human thread is snapped, he has kept his loftiest themes
tied down to earthly considerations. Thus, in the microcosm
of the theater, he has come across the humble flesh that informs
the noble but fixed stereotypes performing before the footlights. And in these modest halls—for the pomp of big stages
minimizes the chance of personal tragedy as well as that of
genuine art—he has found universal prototypes whom the
unceasing tyranny of their material circumstances prevents
from ever losing human contact. The clowns, the vaudeville
artists, the second-rate troupers always out of money, unable
to escape drafty stages and unheated boarding houses (*Sortie
de l'acteur*), daily victims of the vicious public ("the public's
evil eye" in *Le Ménage de Caroline*), may be Christ, Faust, or
Thespis, but always they are essentially victims of flesh and

blood. By systematically debasing the great legends, Michel de Ghelderode has ultimately succeeded in transferring a fragment of otherworldliness and of immortality to the humble jesters upon whose shoulders the mantle fell.

WHEN VOLTAIRE advised Diderot that the drama which does not concern itself with noble performers and exalted deeds must fail, he was in fact claiming for the drama sights sufficiently elevated to avoid particularization and sufficiently exact to focus upon what is susceptible of depth. Michel de Ghelderode has not deliberately eschewed princes and dignitaries—there are a number of these in his work—but he has instinctively given far more familiar attributes to those who must bear the brunt of the tragic unfolding: in moments of stress, the prosaic human is revealed beneath the royal purple. Similarly, although his scenes have been laid in nearly every conceivable locale—from the moldy palace of the *Escurial* (1927) to the hold of the ship bearing his *Christophe Colomb* (1927) to the usual dreams and the inevitable frustrations—each is actually set within and upon a stage. The world that has given the playwright so much of its humanity has likewise colored his every horizon: if Ghelderode's victims are frequently actors, his worlds are always a conscious theater, and, more than Anouilh's, a pictorial and primitive one.

In *La Balade du Grand Macabre* (1934), the hero—Death—pauses to recall the lively past of the town he is about to exterminate—a cheerful bourg significantly named Breugellande: "And the sole task of these good people consisted in prohibiting every sort of task, in dancing belly to belly to the tune of bagpipes, in playing bowls, in pole-shooting, in smoking long pipes, in sampling beers and wines, in masticating, in tempted the brush of Breughel for *The Beggars,* or Jacques Callot's burin." *Masques ostendais* (1930) is a pantomime "or rather a plastic projection inspired by the Ostend carnival and suggested especially by certain of Ensor's canvases" (at the time when this play was written Ensor's studio was in Ostend). *La Pie sur le gibet* (1935), which is also the name of one of the elder Breughel's last paintings, takes place "in the sweet land of Brabant, in the days when the man called Breughel the droll roamed through it and painted." However, if the gibbet has been painted pink by the old master, its gilded cord serves nevertheless to hang innocents just as in less cheerful lands.

Individual scenes within a play frequently grow out of the visualization of a painting. The philosopher Videbolle's room in *La Balade du Grand Macabre* is "an interior by Ostade or Teniers." Or again, the vision of one or the other actor finds words that suggest pictures of still other painters. The evocations of Columbus are occasionally those of Jerome Bosch: "chaos, the gymnastic octopodes, hoards of leviathans, underwater craters, an enormous amount of inappropriate poetry."

Or these hallucinations may have a specific pictorial source, such as, in *Le Soleil se couche,* Charles Quint's visions: Melancholia, "such as Dürer graved her," Death, "seen by Holbein," and the like. Even when the specific reference is missing, Ghelderode effects his scenic creations in pictorial terms, making his sets Rembrandt-like contrasts of somber lighting and rich colors, even though the drama frequently develops like a monstrous mushroom within the dank walls of decaying castles. The setting of *Escurial* is a typically drafty and sordid residue of past grandeur: "opaque curtains through which unceasing wafts of air disclose remnants of worn out blazons. In the center of this hall, there are decrepit steps, covered with threadbare carpets, that lead—very high up—to an odd throne poised as if in equilibrium." *L'Ecole des bouffons* is set "in an abandoned convent. It is a hall [. . .] lit in the back and high up by a stained glass rosette wherein the daylight dies."

In *Sire Halewyn,* the castle of Ostrelande is not described, but the mood of its occupants is found to be consonant with the walls after the Hamlet-like prologue that offers a glimpse of the land from the Ostrelande battlements: "There is this heavy bourg where nothing moves, as if I stood guard upon a tomb. There is this immense plain where nothing moves. There is this enormous sky. . . ." *Fastes d'enfer* (1929) will be performed "in a decrepit episcopal palace" for it too is in the usual state of disrepair.

Even in the light of day, decay and chaos maintain a somber note. *Hop Signor!* (1935) takes place in a garden, but it is "a wild garden. Amidst the shrubs and the overgrown weeds, lie sculptured stones, statues of saints, bas-reliefs, capitals, columns, sundials, that give this garden the appearance of an abandoned workyard or yet, that of an old, forgotten cemetery."

Generally, however, what light does filter through is cadaverous and unhealthy: it is the lighting of the late Flemish Middle Ages—of Jerome Bosch's *Prodigal Son* or of Peter Breughel's winter scenes, but seen by an even more somber eye. Just as the Ghelderodian actor may well turn monster, the Ghelderodian scene ends generally by yielding only sufficient phosphorescence to throw a weird outline upon its otherworldly shapes.

The real light, the sole luminosity of this putrid theater, is its color. In the darkest corners glow the most splendid tones. The "vesper shadows" of *L'Ecole des bouffons* are rent by "a traveling show with a loud red façade." The episcopal palace for *Fastes d'enfer* is plunged in the crepuscular darkness of a storm, "But in the foreground stands a heavy table covered with crimson velvet and overlaid with silver and crystals in a sumptuous way." If Charles Quint's retreat in *Le Soleil se couche* has its windowless walls "darkened by Cordova leather," its drapes are nevertheless "crimson" and again, the richly decked table in the foreground is "an *abondance,* in the manner of the Northern painters."

However, these static highlights are unable, by themselves, to pierce the gloom that densely obscures the recesses of these sets. Therefore, the actors, like darting fireflies, streak their own morbid incandescence through the shadows. Hardly a personage in Ghelderode's drama fails to sport rutilant clothes —though they be in tatters. The cast of *Escurial* is typical:

THE KING *(he is a sickly and pallid king, with a vacillating crown and filthy garments. About his neck and fingers, sham jewels. He is a feverish king, given up to black magic and ritual. El Greco, the awkward artist, has painted his portrait.)*

FOLIAL *(the jester, is in his garish livery an athlete on twisted legs, and has the ways of a spider. He comes from Flanders. His head—an expressive ball—is lit with eyes that are like lenses.)*

THE MONK *(black, tubercular.)*

THE MAN IN SCARLET *(with huge and hairy fingers.)*

The people, like the sets themselves, have stepped out of colorful canvases. Here the king has left one of Theotocopuli's frames. In *Mademoiselle Jaïre,* the entire cast is made of variegated characters, "as they can be found here and there in miniatures of the Burgundy period. Some wear turbans or preserve in their dress oriental elements."

The use of masks further facilitates the author's presentation

of pictorial concepts. *La Mort du Docteur Faust* bears the notation, "Copy James Ensor's masks." The latter abound in
Masques ostendais, where they are "various walk-ons in the
Ensor style." In *La Farce des Ténébreux* (1936), they lead a
frenzied bacchanalia; in *Le Ménage de Caroline,* they are the
dummies that come to life and also the already live performers
resembling standard dummies; in *Pantagleize* (1929), they are
the symbolic figures that pass judgment on the hero; in *Don-
Juan* (1928), they denote the double significance of the characters. And so on, throughout nearly every one of these plays.

But the mask of these characters is frequently more subtle,
though it relinquishes none of its color. The black monk in
Escurial is tubercular: his white face establishes a chromatic
contrast, powerful in its stylization. In the same play, as frequently happens on Ghelderode's stage, the man in red—the
executioner—adds his vivid and ominous note. In *Don-Juan,*
the masque of disease is "the little green man."

And conversely, plays where the stylization is that of puppets (*Le Mystère de la Passion, Duveloor, D'un diable qui
prêcha merveilles*), or those whose figures are taken from folk
tales (as in the milk and honey land of *La Balade du Grand
Macabre*), are made up nearly exclusively of monumental caricatures symbolic of the character each means to express.

Harmonizing the colorful mosaic of the people with the pictorial modulations of these sets is Ghelderode's music. Even
before a single word is spoken, these stages give sonorous indications of the intense life that permeates them. Molière's
opening scene in *Le Tartuffe* has been referred to as a dynamic
exposition: the curtain rises on an action already in progress.
In practically every one of Ghelderode's plays, the curtain rises
upon a stage-set already bathed in the atmosphere which will

be that of the play. As in *Le Tartuffe,* the curtain has risen
on a world in action, for here the climate determines the
fauna.

This world, that seeps into the very marrow of its people,
frequently demands dimensions other than those of the
chiaroscuro, too precariously dependent on the capriciousness
of light switches. Therefore, a pedal point set in the selected
key indicates the dominant tone, even before the curtain has
been drawn up, and frequently lasts throughout the action. The
instrument that will furnish the tonic chord is always one
naturally participant in the action. In the somber *Fastes d'enfer,*
it is the rumbling crowd outside. By contrast, in *La Pie sur le
gibet* which has been kept sardonically cheerful, the echoes of
the villagers' merrymaking is the auditory backdrop. The
same accompaniment will come from Brugelmonde after
Capricant's sermon in *D'un diable qui prêcha merveilles*
(1934), though here, the keynote has been used with modulations that conform to the changing mood of the action. More
subtly, the "constant rumbling" parallels the changing fortunes
of *Pantagleize,* while all through *Escurial* "incessantly, in echo
of death, comes the drawn-out wailing of desperate dogs." Carnival music, its laughter and shrieks, are the audible background of *Masques ostendais,* and harbor noises help set the
scene for such plays as *Le Club des menteurs* (1920?) or *Don-
Juan.*

Even if the pedal point is absent, the music establishes at
least an initial tone before the dialogue. Not infrequently, it is
an actual instrument: bagpipe (*D'un diable qui prêcha merveilles*), accordion (*La Balade du Grand Macabre*), tam-
bourines (*L'Ecole des bouffons*). Or it may be the voice of
participants singing, like the watchman in *Le Singulier Trépas*

stages. It bears names as strange, as dissonant, and as expressive as its faces. Here are the women, equivocal, lecherous, spiteful—Sybilla, Luna, Salivaine. And that feminine evocation of Spain and disease, Veneranda. And the sea nymph, Visquosine, "the pretty she-fish/viscous, supple, and quite devilish." Here are the dwarfs, Mèche and Suif; the devils, Diamotoruscant and Capricant. Here are the poets, Gargarismus Begga and Luisekam (lousecomb); the dignitaries of the army —the General Mac-Boum; of State—Aspiquet, Basiliquet; of the Church—Mgr. Breedmaag (large-paunch), the carnivorous Carnibos, the guardian of the holy relics Duvelhond (Devil hound), the Vicaire Kaliphas and the nuncio's secretary, Sodomati. Here are the doctors, Cloribus; drunkards, Porprenaz, Lamprido; philosophers, Videbolle. Here are the cannibalistic negroes, Beni-Bouftout and Bam-Boulah. Here are the Jews in the Church, Simon Laquedeem (reminding us that many of these names are traditional, Isaak Laquedem [sic], e.g., being the name of the wandering Jew in Flanders— see the author's *Choses et gens de chez nous,* 1943), and in high finance, Simon Goldenox. Here are the Flemish masks, the three Mariekes: Marieke Vos, Marieke Pouf, and Marieke Crok. Here are the victims: the wise—Innocenti, Fagoti, Juréal; and the disfigured—Bifrons, Boufranc, Horir, Moscul. Here is Death, Necrozotar. And here, at last, is "the huge mug of the Crowd" (*La Balade du Grand Macabre,* final *personnage*).

If Michel de Ghelderode's characters are essentially actors and if his dramatic center is first of all the area of a stage, one should remember that these are after all very peculiar performers on a peculiar planet. This drama knows no measure. Rather, it is a ceaselessly bubbling and evil cauldron. The actor is a thrice tragic figure, the victim of his vision, his innate

ambiguity, and the perils of his calling. His is a terribly inse-
cure world. Furthermore, in all other respects, he remains a
common mortal—and perhaps one just a little frailer than
average. He is a veritable soundboard for the pathos in every
human. But in the exacerbated world of Ghelderode, plagued
by the evil spirits that add to his already pathetic lot, he
chooses the only temporary alternative to death: he hardens.
The coarse puppet heads and the Ensor masks, the cadaverous
faces of the clowns, are pathological symptoms of his struggle:
he becomes as monumentally contorted as the circumstances
that torture him. Ghelderode may have been speaking through
the voice of Juréal, the gargoyle-maker in *Hop Signor!,* upon
whose work a modern world no longer looks with favor:

Alas, nothing comes from my hand but that which is harsh or
warped! I should make even marble grimace like stone. Oh! I
visualize that new form of Beauty, I see it . . . and cannot render
it. I survive—in truth!—as survive those cathedrals that were
white of yore but have become opaque and sooty, and will be
torn down when they have grown too old.

Such are the dwarfs, in this same play; such is Ben Samuel,
"an ugly head," who desires admittance into *Le Club des menteurs* (1920?); such is Lamprido, "staggering, with purplish
mug and [who] is horribly cross-eyed," in *D'un diable qui
prêcha merveilles;* such are the old folk waiting for *Le Cavalier bizarre,* "human beings who are falling to pieces but who
remain high in color and rich in odor." Ghelderode's is a veritable cult of ugliness such as that bespoken by Pantagleize,
"My girl friend is a she-monkey in the zoo. She is called Cleo-
patra, she has fleas, and eats half of my daily ration every
noontime. In exchange, she makes awful faces at me. And I
love her."

The words call to mind the fact that the women themselves

hardly ever emerge from the prevalent miasma. Even when they are not old hags or outright horrors, even when they are young, their beauty is somehow unpleasant. Pamela, the central figure in *Le Ménage de Caroline,* is a "sordid poodle-like beauty." Even *Don-Juan's* Olympia, the impersonation of Beauty, becomes through overspecialization "tasteless."

The redeemed—there are a limited number of these—fall generally into one of four categories. There are first of all the pristine clowns whose masks, though dolorous, have not yet become grotesque. In the same class are the misshapen in whom a glimmer, usually the eyes, has remained handsome and betokens salvation: Juréal with his "too heavy, wrinkled head, but one lit by admirable pupils," and Folial, the headmaster in *L'Ecole des bouffons,* with "his magnificent look of a blue water that will have at times the metallic glint of superior Volition," both belong to this group.

Another category comprises those whom the legend has safeguarded. When the folktale allows liberties, these figures merely take on the cheerful aspect of harmless carnival masks —not to be confused with an Ensor mask, whose delineation is actually flesh and blood. Such are, for example, the carousers in *La Balade du Grand Macabre.* Others are of course the traditionally holy figures of, or suggested by, the Bible, that appear again and again in the author's medieval Flemish drama from *Les Vieillards* (1919) to *Marie la misérable* (1952). If they escape being marionettes and assume their expected form, as in *Barabbas* (1928), they lose most of their salt and become savorless, conventional types.

Next are found such figures as Madeleintje in *Oude Piet* whom the author's momentary solemnity casts in a somewhat melodramatic light. One of the author's first plays (written in 1920), it sets forth a type too maudlin to endure. But few

Madeleintjes are found later. Such people are by far the least interesting on the Ghelderodian roster. They tend to demand, usually because of their realism, undue attention, and thus hamper the development of a truth conceivable only as an outgrowth of the brooding dramatic mood. They are similar to those types that occasionally weaken Crommelynck's plays for the same reasons.

The fourth group, again reminiscent of a similar one in the work of Crommelynck, is that of the mysterious intercessors between supernatural powers, which they consciously or unconsciously serve, and the protagonists of the drama. In this constantly peremptory idiom, they are easily recognizable: their stature is commensurate with their role and something in them always gleams flamboyantly: their dress or their hair is often red. Whether they speak or remain mute, theirs is a deeply thundering voice. Many of Michel de Ghelderode's plays exhibit such a type. In *Mademoiselle Jaïre,* his name is Le Roux, "a man with an athletic build." He brings the heroine back to life, though neither she nor he desires this to happen and though he is well aware of the consequences entailed.

The same personage will reveal Marguerite to herself in *Hop Signor!* He is Larose, the executioner. And the same "man in scarlet" has already been encountered in *Escurial*. If, in addition to his usually massive proportions, this one is ugly, it is because he plays hardly any role but that of a horrendous presence. Messer Ignotus in *Le Soleil se couche* is the otherworldly master of the marionettes, "A tall and rigid being [. . .]. From beyond the grave must this creature spring that has but the appearance of a man." His mission is to mirror Charles Quint whom he now confronts and whose destiny he has paralleled.

Two such figures collapse in this drama. One of them is the

giant Barabbas, finally entangled in Christ's myth to such an extent as to lose his own personality. The other, more amusingly defeated, is the huge monk Bashuiljus who, notwithstanding the ass's jaw which he redoubtably swings, is finally spirited away by the devil Capricant, the hero of *D'un diable qui prêcha merveilles,* because this is a "morality against the grain."

IN THIS grotesque and evil world which its inhabitants have ended by resembling, life is a hectic struggle, an unending contest with the petty miseries and the great sorrows that lie in wait for men. This travail is abetted by the materializations of perverse fate that elbow their way through the harried herd of mortals, abusive because of their own strength and the helplessness of their victims. As in the Middle Ages of Jerome Bosch, devils of many kinds, Death mounted on a horse (or a human selected for the task), Disease, all manner of monstrous forces, mingle with the crowd, terrifying, torturing, and toughening it. For these people are essentially healthy and therefore resilient; if they are no match for supernatural forces, they can at least harden their own skins.

And so a coarse-grained race grows within the grotesque shadows of this baroque nightmare. It is an essentially sensitive race which, though disfigured through its travail, maintains a healthy trim by preserving its vital sap—the animal man.

On the weird graduation night in *L'Ecole des bouffons,* Folial, the ennobled court jester, must reveal to his disciples the last word, the secret of his art, in fact "of every art that claims greatness!" But led by Galgüt, the monsters stage an uprising. Whip in hand, and with a terrible strength that comes upon

him even as he fights, Folial crushes the rebellion. It is in a
fierce climax worthy of his secret that he impresses the ultimate truth upon his bowed disciples: "Listen to your old Master, listen . . . I tell you, verily . . . The secret of our art, of art,
of the great art, of every art that wishes to endure? . . . (*Silence.
And in a low voice, but distinctly.*) It is cru-el-ty! . . ." The
merciless parody of his wedding night, when the refusal of his
highborn bride opened his eyes forever to truths that his titles
had caused him to forget, explains the metamorphosis of this
man who would have wished only for the bitter peace of his
suffering.

An even more fiendish character is that of *Sire Halewyn,* the
"princely killer of virgins" upon whose gibbets hang seven of
his victims. Yet his "quest for love" is not substantially different from Folial's, and it is he who is fated to die by the hand
of the first woman who would have quenched his longing.
Only the frozen lips of his severed head will know her love.
In the same vein, the cruel king in *Escurial* turns his jester
over to the hangman—but even this supreme convulsion cannot bring back the queen or the love she might have granted
him, and the jester goes to his death richer than the king after
having played a poignant scene with him (among the finer
ones in this theater), wherein, symbolically even as in life,
both change roles to echo the deeper contrast of their respective
fates.

These people have grown the only shell that avails in their
circumstances, and in so doing, they precipitate the vicious
circle of others who must follow suit since they have made
life that much less bearable. This prevalence of coarseness has
enabled Michel de Ghelderode, by contrast, to create two of
his most effective people, Adrian and Jusemina—the eternal

lovers who shield their tenderness in a grave while unbeknown
to them the world explodes and collapses (*La Balade du Grand
Macabre*). Of their voices, for perhaps the only time in his
entire dramatic repertoire, Ghelderode says that they are "harmonious." They are also the only secular promise in this otherwise caustic and barren theater.

Far more often, however, the inhabitants of these worlds
are displaced persons. Jean Francis, quoting references from
the author's *Mes statues* (1943), claims that his characters
might well be reflections of Ghelderode himself (in *Chrysalis*,
1949). Those who scorn the sordid battle harden in their own
way. Pantagleize says: "I don't care a rap for the year, the
month, or the day. For am I not above eras and nations?" And
Faust: "I am tired! To die is not a solution. And to live is to
continue to betray myself, for I am someone superior to myself. . . ." Even the gentle Christophe Colomb has become
scornful: "I see all things from on high. Yes, I come from
another world, I do not belong to yours. . . ."

But these are the lofty and detached figures. The others
battle and toughen at each other's expense, fighting their
neighbors, themselves, and this world into whose image they
have grown but which will ever remain, for them as for us,
strange and alien. Strange, alien land where the spirit grows
numb before the maleficent evocations that mock it, and where
the mind is unavailing, for, in the words of one of the lost
protagonists of *Jeudi-Saint,* "At the end of every thought, there
is emptiness. . . ."

BUT THE tragedy of man is that, try as he may,
he can never be quite an animal. Some residual spark of consciousness always stirs within his being to defeat him. For
Ghelderode's people, whose scale and mode can never be less

than heroic, this modicum is sufficient to engender passions equal to the magnitude of their physical aberrations. Furthermore, these dramatic absolutes brook no accommodation in their conflicting drives: the concomitant suffering of their consuming lusts does not temper their callousness any more than it is tempered by that callousness.

The subjects of the classical Farce—Woman, Greed, Cowardice—are present here, but as in Crommelynck, they lose their particularizing aspects and acquire the metaphysical breadth of anxiety—that of the Flesh, of Possession, of the Unfathomable. As in all great drama, a climate of desire and frustration is established. This is, as Jean Francis has called it, a theater of thirst (see his introduction to a recent edition of *Barabbas,* Brussels: Renouveau, 1949).

As in Crommelynck, and perhaps because both men share a common Flemish ancestry, the carnal force prefigures and colors these scenes. But whereas the elder author's *Carine* remains ambiguous in its resolutions (the uncle's wisdom must be balanced by the heroine's death), Michel de Ghelderode's primitive intuition of the individual leaves no room for doubt: the animal in man—the instinctive being acting consonantly with his inmost nature—grasps at least one form of salvation. Fernand d'Abcaude, the butt of *La Farce des Ténébreux,* is a male Carine—the town's only virgin. He has vowed a chaste cult to the memory of the defunct Azurine whom he had worshipped Platonically during her lifetime. But the inane ridiculousness of his attitude is pointed out to him when he is made to realize that Azurine was in reality Putrégina, the public whore. Yet it is in this latter form that she expresses redemption and the apologue is explicitly deciphered for him by the prostitute Emanuèle—"Let yourself be taught. . . ."

Fernand d'Abcaude will not only be persuaded, he will be

transformed—he is far less brittle than the intransigent Carine. Of Michel de Ghelderode's full-grown dramas, this is the only one that might be placed alongside *La Balade du Grand Macabre* for the relative optimism that it conveys. It is significant that for a final moment, this play, among the very few of the author, can enjoy some genuine sunshine.

The flesh, or better, Desire in the abstract force of the unending paroxysm, finds culminating expression in *Hop Signor!,* one of the author's finest plays. The demon of lust dwells in Marguerite Harstein, Juréal's maiden wife who knows nothing of love. Instinctively, she is drawn to the hangman Larose, to his work, the fascination of which has preserved the virginity of each though their every fiber has gorged on the sterile voluptuousness of public tortures. Both will finally meet on the only bed that can sate them, the headman's block, when at last Larose executes Marguerite Harstein.

The play is a veritable bacchanalia in its carnal might. These two "so terribly chaste virgins" are surrounded by sensual types as powerful and as grimacing as the medieval representations of lechery—the lustful crowd, the pornographic dwarfs, and that remarkable creation, Dom Pilar, the monk in whom the convulsions of ascetic mysticism are closely bound to those of the flesh, and with whom Marguerite plays a scene of bestial grandeur:

PILAR: You are Lust! You are Evil! . . .

MARGUERITE: I am that Evil whose obsession has afforded you such frightful delights. To the very foulest, I give myself . . . *(She embraces Pilar and holds him against her.)*

PILAR: The Devil has taken her shape. . . I shall not sin. . .

MARGUERITE: You shudder, you are slavering. Your face brightens. Do you see angels? . . . *(She releases the monk who slides to the ground.)*

PILAR *(prostrate, hides his face):* Agnus Dei! qui tollis peccata mundi. . .

MARGUERITE *(laughs childishlÿ):* Ah! how weak and limp he is! He has sinned at last!

But by the very definition of her nature, Marguerite is an abnormal creature, and, moreover, that which is exacerbated cannot last indefinitely without losing meaning. The flesh is hardly ever as grueling elsewhere. If it is true that Ghelderode's people are frequently quite lecherous, their carnality is scarcely more than a moral attribute, stigmatic when they are devil's advocates, but not unpleasant when they are comic types.

The outright monsters in this theater, the hypocrites in high places and the women, are, in truth, given to excessive lust, but as they only serve, in general, to contrast the purer types who are deceived or disillusioned by the flesh, one can assume that their pangs remain primarily rhetorical. Again, the great vitality of these people absorbs what might have seemed outrageous in others. It does not seem excessive that the last earthly manifestations of Lazare and Mademoiselle Jaïre should be a sexual impulse, though both are sublime half-spirits. Lust is habitually a harmless, and sometimes even a redeeming aspect of the individual. The carnal urge is not an obsession and is hardly ever conceded the importance and the dignity of tragedy. If the king in *Escurial* or Sire Halewyn kill, the motive should not be sought in the arousal of their senses. They kill out of a feeling of frustration more subtle and less particularized. It is a thirsting for love that has actuated them—but here love must be taken to mean integration. Though far less elegant and scornful, they are nevertheless the same romanticists, the same displaced persons as Pantagleize, Colomb, Faust, or Don-Juan.

A noteworthy trait that reduces to correct proportions the natural sensuousness of these people can be derived from another comparison with Crommelynck. The latter's *Tripes d'or* gives up Azelle to concentrate on the possession of his gold. For Ghelderode's miser, by contrast, possession is possession and all items of property are interesting as such. Hiéronymus, who is characteristically *fat,* has no intention of relinquishing Sybilla, and if he has given her only a dummy infant out of a sense of economy, his greed has in no way inhibited his sexual appetite ("I'll bestride women for you, fat ones, very fat ones, the most flesh possible for my money"). And, significantly, part of the *magie rouge* operated in this play is his endeavor to multiply his wealth by locking male and female coins together in a healthy attempt at procreation.

In spite of its prevalence—or perhaps precisely because of it—the flesh yields no answers, it contains no illusion. The great names—Pantagleize, Juréal, Folial, Don-Juan—will remain chaste. Similarly, cowardice develops less as the failing of individuals than as the expression of a collective or symbolic evil. It is then usually associated with hypocrisy. The plays that most clearly deal with this delinquent aspect of men are *Jeudi-Saint* and *Le Club des menteurs.* The first is a brief sketch of the twelve old men led by the aging Barbara. Their recriminations against life and society come to an abrupt end when Barbara tells them that for obeisance they will be rewarded. *Le Club des menteurs* gathers a series of masks in an imaginary bar whose hostess, Luna, is the symbolic focus of their aspirations. Luna is of course a mere woman, unable even briefly to understand her own allegory. However, with the exception of the poet Saint-Georges, not one of the members will fight to maintain the illusion when they have been

"Just the same, it is always a good thing to have notions . . . you never know what's coming afterwards." In *Le Ménage de Caroline,* a familiar cliché in the mouth of Arlequin, "Ah! death . . ." is promptly cut short by the old Colombine, "Don't twaddle, Arlequin. Deep inside you know very well that death appears less acceptable as you draw nearer to it." The three blind men whom Ghelderode has taken out of Breughel's canvas in *Les Aveugles* think that their next footsteps will bring them into Rome, when in reality they will topple into the waiting grave. Of course, the incident flays vanity, but it also recalls the ubiquitous death's-head of the Middle Ages. Michel de Ghelderode is well aware of that atmosphere but sees no reason for differentiating modern times. He has Pantagleize say: "But, confounded journalist, if you only had my power of observation! And if you had looked at the public instead of pilfering from the encyclopedia, you would write that modern crowds are just as terrorized as those of the Middle Ages."

Death, in this theater, is also the agent of malignant fatality. Renatus' fear of the occult forces that baffle science and reason has already been noted. Many other characters similarly suffer from insidious ills—all equally indefinable, all equally lethal. Such is the mysterious malady consuming Mademoiselle Jaïre: "Sickly, one thought. What sickness? Didn't know, the doctors, something that was at work, invisible. What?" So is Folial sick, sapped by an ailment of which one knows not whether it is physiological, spiritual, or cast upon him by the evil shadows in which he walks. Juréal, who is more specific in his auto-diagnosis, speaks nevertheless of a disease too frightening to have been subdued by medical authorities: "Know that I suffer from a rare malady, that no pilgrimage will cure. I am shriveling! Through the years, my skeleton is getting smaller! Is that not comical?"

Like classical fatality, Death stands in the path of every endeavor. As for Sire Halewyn, as for Marguerite Harstein, it is the final form of lust, of longing, of all thirst. And, a cunning artificer, it prepares its path with the delectation of an adroit playwright. One of Marguerite's suitors, Adorno, has killed another one of these, Helgar. Because Marguerite is discovered in naked expectancy not far from the corpse, she is led to the scaffold, though still innocent. The likewise innocent Borax, who owns *Le Ménage de Caroline,* tries to hide from a policeman by putting on the dresses of his dolls who have fled. But the dolls have perpetrated horrible crimes and Borax cannot escape from the incriminating garments.

In *Magie rouge,* a concatenation of evil circumstances traps the miser. Armador has been making love to Hiéronymus' wife in the latter's cellar while pretending to make gold. He has contrived an elaborate setting of black magic which has enabled him to substitute false coins for his host's gold. Despondent over the prolonged disappearance of his wife and the slowness of Armador, Hiéronymus stabs the toy child which he had given his wife Sybilla. When the counterfeiter at last hands him some token gold, Hiéronymus takes off for the bawdy houses. While he is gone, Armador falls out with the monk and the beggar who had assisted him and kills them before fleeing. Hiéronymus returns pursued by the crowd whom his false coins have roused to fury. When he is cornered in his home, the stabbed doll, with its aura of black magic, as well as the two corpses are imputed to him.

Perhaps most subtle of all the manifestations of these malevolent and irrational forces is that which condemns Pantagleize to death for having started, unknowingly, a revolution by remarking, "What a lovely day!"—an exclamation that happened to be a fatal signal. The absurd situation and especially the somber ending that caps all the other impossible events as naturally as if each were expected, appears to be arranged by the same straight-faced joker who unfolds Kafka plots. But death shows Pantagleize to have been something more than a comic figure.

And the curtain falls. Death is truly the central actor in this drama: all the color, the contortions, the cruelty, and the creeds are unable either to conjure or to propitiate it. It walks its appointed and capricious path and when it has passed, the lights go out. The familiar scythe-wielding skeleton situates this theater in the Middle Ages. But the wake it leaves is that of agents even more venerable—that of the *moerae*.

Confronted by such frightfully harried people and the genuine intensity of their pathos, one might legitimately demur before the epithets "Burlesque Drama," "Tragedy for Music-hall," "Depressing Vaudeville," "Tragedy-buffo," "Drama-farce," "Tragi-farce," "Mystical Farce" and "Farce" which the author first used to designate many of his principal plays. At first glance, such terms would appear to imply qualification of the tragic mold of his heroes. The assumption must be tested through such of Ghelderode's comic concepts as can be gathered from his drama.

In the introduction to the 1935 edition of the marionette play *Le Mystère de la Passion,* the author writes of bygone puppets: "These moments of fleeting beauty did not last. In spite of the austerity of the subject matter, laughter was constantly breaking through. Judas, with his shrill voice, would ruin every effect, or rather, would render each, through contrast, more remarkable still." Thus is set forth once again an essential principle of this orchestration that seeks both its force and its beauty in the contrast of dissonance. The point of view that allows laughter to magnify the most sublime moments is presumably not very different from that which grants tragic relief to characters whose bearing would have appeared to exclude such depth. This conscious apposition of extremes that finds expression in every aspect of Ghelderode's excessive drama, is generally to be accounted for by the dichotomous nature of the Flemish, "race with twin souls" in the words of the author's Charles Quint. One presumes that a violent temperament of race or playwright would tend to emphasize the energy already latent in the opposition of these extremes.

However, for those intensifying contradictions, one element of which is laughter, a fairly plausible reason can be found that dispels the apparent incongruity. Already noted was the burial scene in *Sortie de l'acteur,* which illustrates the author's skepticism as to the possibility of absolute human dignity. In *Les Femmes au Tombeau,* a play which is in fact a religious drama and which has been termed "straightforward" by the author, Jean says, "And so the drama continues, poignant and on occasion laughable." The entire first act, and a number of succeeding scenes, of *Mademoiselle Jaïre* take up anew and amplify that proposition. Jaïre is visited by a strange and terrible curse: one of the Ghelderodian ills has rendered his daughter unconscious for many long days though she is not yet dead. To Jaïre's perplexity and to the torment which the protracted coma causes him, are added the little burlesque incidents that keep mocking the sorrow he feels. A well-intentioned neighbor comes with the news that there is an exceptional sale of black cloth; the carpenter arrives for the coffin, insisting that the corpse is ready; and even worse, life goes on for Jaïre himself:

What a lot of grotesque doings around the most dramatic of events! . . . I myself am grotesque. . . I should be something like the incarnation of exemplary suffering, and there comes to me, oh! irresistibly, oh! the urge, oh! to scratch myself! . . . Ah! . . . with nails of iron. . . I ought to, oh! . . . It has been itching for such a long time. . . Since no one is looking? The Lord take pity on us, pity. . . .

And of course, someone enters at precisely that moment.

Life simply does not pause to respect the solemn efforts of man: stronger than his grief in their insidiousness, are the daily prosaic elements that keep sapping, gnarling, and disfiguring that grief. The vanity of this attempt merges with the other hopeless aspirations of man: all are manifestations of the same thirst that cannot be quenched and that confers upon its ridiculous victims the same pathetically absurd look. The concept is similar to Crommelynck's except that in the latter's drama, the progression from a wholly superficial expression to the final masque of tragedy is more clearly apparent than in that of Ghelderode where a certain simultaneity remains ever present. The younger author assumes that it is entirely possible to laugh while slowly falling victim to the profounder malevolence of the over-all tragedy.

Though it is possible to induce such ambivalence in the public, the critic might still ask why an author should wish to subject his audience to these contrary emotions. The king in *Escurial* provides the substance of the answer when he exclaims: "Laugh again! I love that Flemish laughter in which is heard the gnashing of teeth." For Ghelderode, the minute vision of the elder Breughel is a praiseworthy gift and the bitterness that made it thus is an ancestral legacy. Galgüt has already remarked in *L'Ecole des bouffons:* "That which is bizarre provides a strong source of amusement and of surprise." Laughter thus becomes a threefold Flemish characteristic in that it expresses the realism of the Fleming, his primitive coarseness, and his poignancy. In this respect, it is of course necessary to distinguish between the laughter of the spectator and that of Ghelderode's actor. The spectator's laughter may or may not be genuine—the actor's hardly ever is. The spectator may not always be aware of the actor's dilemma, or if he is, he may refuse to accept it. But on this stage, the performer realizes his own tragedy, no matter how he contorts himself.

Coupled with this Flemish appreciation of laughter is Ghelderode's conception of the stage as a show. If it is a hereditary privilege of his to spot the bottle of gin that keeps up the spirit of the professional mourners in *Mademoiselle Jäire*, he is also well aware that the incongruity is amusing regardless of further implications. Michel de Ghelderode's plays are close enough to the primitive theater to preserve all the elements that make it a place of entertainment. If that theater, in its evolution, has severed the bonds it once had with every segment of the population in such a way as to be replaced for many by the circus and the music-hall, it then behooves the playwright to see what elements have contributed to the success of these new media and to incorporate them if such incorporation is compatible with the essence of the drama envisaged.

Since the actor and his world are susceptible of the profoundest human tribulations and are therefore interesting metaphysically, it is possible for certain dramas like *La Transfiguration dans le cirque* to be enacted entirely by clowns, while for others, like *Don-Juan,* it is possible to transfer the significance of the legend to the music-hall stage. As in the Flemish satirical painters, the form is in no way supposed to invalidate or inhibit the content. One suspects that Michel de Ghelderode subscribed all the more willingly to these arguments because of the humorist and prankster that dwells in him. Occasionally, especially in a play like *D'un diable qui prêcha merveilles,* one encounters strains very reminiscent of college humor—puns that are mostly scatological and facile neo-archaisms. But in the drama as a. whole, the presence of a man who does not always take his heroes too seriously is felt, as in his own asides and his stage directions.

Trois Acteurs, un drame . . . (1926), an amiable parody of *Six Characters in Search of an Author,* is an example of such gratuitous fun on the part of the playwright. Spoofing Pirandello and leading the reader down vaguely familiar alleys— though protesting through his "author,"—"I swear it, I have plagiarized no one! . . ." he abruptly turns the tables on the reader and makes farce types of the actors while killing the author. In a similar frame of mind, Ghelderode will allow an actor to step out of character just for the mischievous fun of so doing. This enjoyment of spoofing for its own sake has led the author to write a number of plays whose sole purpose is to entertain. Such are *Duveloor, D'un diable qui prêcha merveilles,* and even, though it is somewhat more ambitious, *La Balade du Grand Macabre,* which evinces all the exuberant charm of a *fabliau* illustration. This amused discursiveness occasionally causes Ghelderode to stray considerably from the development of the action. Gratuitous scenes such as lengthen the second act of *La Farce des Ténébreux,* the third act of *La Balade du Grand Macabre,* and various parts of *Pantagleize,* etc., tend to show, furthermore, that now and again the author believes laughter for its own sake to be at least as important as the story.

However, for a writer whose theater appears to have grown

consistently out of a straightforward perception of his people and their environment, surprisingly little of his humor is visual. The fun, even that of situations and of characterizations, relies most often on words. Jokes and puns are the most frequent sources of mirth and they flow in a seemingly endless stream.

From puppets, Ghelderode has also taken a form of humor: naïveté. In *Le Mystère de la Passion,* the characters speak their own attributes and the familiar clichés pertinent to them. Christ, for example, says, "Oh! What a terrible way of Calvary! . . . I am going to fall for the first time! . . ." And the device can be transferred, of course, to human beings. However, the cleverness of the author also twists conventional commonplaces into profounder, though equally humorous, paradoxes. Cloribus, the doctor attending Mademoiselle Jaïre, has a glib tongue that types him while providing much of the fun in that grim play:

JAïRE: Doctor!

CLORIBUS: Thrice, my good client! So that with the skin of my diplomas it is possible to reconstruct completely a donkey in parchment. Verily! And our patient goes?

JAïRE: Toward the ground! Touch her once again and it will be finished, the ticktack in the chest!

CLORIBUS: Correction, the sickness will be finished. The aim is to make the sickness stop. It stops through curing or through the death of the one who is ill. Do you follow?

Such figures as Cloribus, completely delineated by their own words (their actions are never of sufficient importance to distinguish them), run through every play of Ghelderode, providing much of the humor and life. In *Pantagleize,* General Mac-Boum, defending high finance against the revolution, is a professional soldier whose fright pierces his military tone and the usual clichés. Porprenaz, the cheerful drunk whose geniality will turn from his appointed rounds even *Le Grand Macabre,* is a bucolic poet whose words are appropriately funny, and who is used on occasion to break a turgid passage by a joke, effecting a change of pace destined to correct scenes that might otherwise appear melodramatic; here, the irreverent drunk ruins one of Death's effects:

NEKROZOTAR *(prophetically):* Beneath the immutable blue, Nature rests in her bliss and men go jogging on serenely. But when the darkness is ripe, there will appear the horrible star that no one expects. Through fire and sword, Creation will collapse and there will remain only clinkers.

PORPRENAZ: Described like a master!

And again, the miser Hiéronymus is typified by even fewer symbols than are to be found in *Tripes d'or.* Hiéronymus' avarice is nearly wholly reflected in the facility with which he inverts common observations and expressions to suit his particular vice and temperament. Even his supreme act of avarice, the mating of his coins, is merely a pun.

Making little use of visual humor, Michel de Ghelderode has naturally neglected most of the classical Farce legacy. Scattered instances are seen in an occasional Molièresque valet such as Fernand d'Abcaude's man Ludion (*La Farce des Ténébreux*), or in the bastinados that enliven that play and *Masques ostendais,* or yet that epic thrashing inflicted by Salivaine upon her long-suffering husband in *La Balade du Grand Macabre.* What visual humor he has used, he has preferred to borrow from the mimicry of clowns, such as head-bumping, acrobatics, and the like. But even such instances quickly give way to words and to the continuity of the action.

This consistent use of speech for comic effect is sooner or later bound to turn into tongue-lashing and, on a broader plane, satire. The latter is especially evident in such plays as *Pantagleize* and that drama reminiscent of Elmer Rice's *Adding Machine, Christophe Colomb,* which mocks the press, governments, civilization, and human stupidity.

And so, even humor reverts to bitterness. Removed from the realm of generalities whose vagueness blunts its sting, it concentrates with acid bite on the individual and it is then as grim as the horizons that have summoned it. Borax does not succeed in cheering the consumptive weight-lifter in *Le Ménage de Caroline:*

BORAX: You will be cured, Hercules, thirteen times a medalist. . . Spit and you will be cured. . . You have a star tattoed on your left arm; it is your star.

JOSEPHIN: But around it there is written: Bosh! . . .

Even Hiéronymus' puns turn to gall in his mouth as he nurses his toy child:

When you grow up, if you grow up, you will be rich, but never inquire whence came this wealth. Enjoy it stupidly! . . . Say to yourself sometimes that your father was tormented and that he did away with his peace of mind for the happiness of his dear ones [. . .]. Do you moan, Hiéronymus! . . . Be like your son! . . . insensible and tearless. That which is accomplished had to be. It is solemn, it is grotesque, it is poignant.

No matter how loud the fun, no matter how outrageous the caricature, it cannot long conceal the suffering flesh. Fate itself may pause awhile, for hypocritical mirth and laughter will appear to have exorcized the evil spell, but all too soon the masquerade is over and its echoing peals have the resonance of death. And the spectator who had not heard the ringing of his own laughter while it was triumphant, suddenly becomes aware of a greater voice whose mockery encompasses even him and makes him a brother of the victim across the footlights.

WHEN PORPRENAZ destroys with anticlimactic prosaism the high-sounding words of Death, he is a comedy character. But when he similarly stifles the lofty speech of the lovers, he becomes sufficiently jarring to raise a literary problem. The laughter that magnifies through contrast what is essentially grim in this theater can be explained as such. But its gratuitousness in moments when it is merely awkward, or its disappearance in others, when it might have been a necessary counterpoise, is less easy to explain.

Porprenaz is not an isolated phenomenon on Ghelderode's stage. From the ambiguous captions of the plays to the sudden *volte-face* of their people, there is manifest, throughout, a steady refusal of pathos, and laughter—the author's—acquires still another meaning. *Oude Piet,* a drama reminiscent of Roger Martin du Gard's peasant Farces, though an apparently more sober and somber one, relates the various attitudes of those grouped about the central figure in expectation of his death. These types are called *physionomies* by the author, and though they are all ugly but for the pristine Madeleintje, they are realistic portraits, not caricatures. The progression of the drama is realistic also. Still, this has been captioned "Burlesque Drama" though the only supporting evidence for such a title is the initial stage direction: "Aside from Piet, Jef, and Madeleintje, all these people must attain the highest expression of ridiculousness," and also, "The roles will be exaggerated toward the end so as to achieve the most grotesque effect possible." Likewise, Faust was originally to have been played by a clown, though the subsequent development of the drama and his part therein failed to justify such typification.

These two plays were among the author's first, and one might of course interpret discrepancies between intent and form as safeguards used by a young author aware that melodramatic writing is one of the hazards incurred by beginners, an awareness that might well have been rendered acute by the literary climate of Belgium in 1920. Later editions revised by a more secure author have removed the captions while maintaining the text. But why then should Ghelderode have at all favored a style of writing which his laughter seemed bent on stifling? A style which, lacking laughter, makes even a relatively late play like *Sire Halewyn* (1934) as unacceptably romantic as any of Rodenbach.

That the author was aware of his romanticism can scarcely be doubted: too many of his characters are undisguised romanticists. The ivory tower from which Colomb ("I shall find the Eden that is deepest within me"), Faust ("One always ends up by meeting oneself"), Don-Juan ("I am bored"), and the others look down upon the world, may be the legitimate vantage point of superior beings. But hardier souls, of whom one might have expected more earthly unconsciousness, suddenly become pallidly moral to justify some ingrown rancor. The blackguard Armador, who carries away Hiéronymus' wife and his gold, feels compelled to account for his actions in terms whose naïveté shocks: "No, I am not an adventurer, and if I followed the armies, if I led the flaming life of Flemish mercenaries, it is because I was without love and without home, the saddest of orphans." Even Jean-Jacques had been moved by a curious urge to apologize for his abnormality (see above). The titular hero of *Barabbas* demands the full re-

sponsibility for his crime, but, pre-Sartrian, is strangely obtuse
about appreciating the validity of acts akin to his. Such short-
comings will make him a confused individual once the threads
of his fate are meshed with those of Christ. One supposedly
illuminated by Christian revelation, he nevertheless takes on
the familiar traits of the avenger, though mercifully stabbed (in
the back) before he has had time to shed blood.

All such overemphasis, when of a merely mechanical nature,
can be mechanically countered, and so Porprenaz, or a gratuitous clown in *Barabbas,* or yet again the recurrent yawn that
interrupts Colomb, Hérode, Laquedeem, Saint-Georges, etc.,
are freely called upon. But the doors through which maudlin
romanticism enters—those of the chambers of horror—are less
easily closed. Michel de Ghelderode's favorite play, *L'Ecole
des bouffons,* is so filled with baroque claptrap and horrendous
doings as to quite remove it from the sympathy of the spectator
upon whom it must impress its underlying truth. Likewise,
the severed head of *Sire Halewyn* is brandished about too often
not to become ridiculous. And no one credits for a moment
the sanguinary threats of Dagüt and Tribord in *La Farce des
Ténébreux*—which their own procrastination in performing
renders even less plausible. There is a limit beyond which even
horror becomes inane. Similarly, excessive vulgarity, though
initially used for laudable ends, becomes inhibiting. The crude
monk in *Magie rouge* and the vile clergy in *Fastes d'enfer* are
occasionally guilty of such excesses.

No one in Ghelderode's plays ever displays any self-consciousness before the overstatement of the sets; yet the action
which these might conjur, or, as noted, mere words, occasion
repeated uneasiness. So, to the danger of a play eluding the onlooker's response because of the inordinate proportions of its

fantastic trappings, is added the peril of an awkwardness that constrains the author to make light of phrases—and hence of feelings—that might have awakened an intimate echo in the spectator.

If the author is thus aware of the danger which neo-romanticism represents orally while neglecting its visual counterpart, one may well wonder whether he is not too consciously living up to a myth, that of the dual nature of the Fleming whose most spiritual visions grow out of coarse images. The crude shell that conceals the mystic outgoing of earlier civilizations is merely the face of the times in which such mysticism may have affected them. The contrast is apparent now only because a comprehensible emotion is expected to entail vestments that can be similarly recognized. The incongruity in such a case springs more from the modern inability to reconcile terms that are consonant than from any innate discrepancy in the terms themselves. It is thus all the more futile to attempt the conscious re-creation of a contrast that exists primarily as the result of an anachronistic judgment, especially when that judgment motivates the desire for that reconstruction. Non-contingent emotions must always outgrow contingent wrappings. The contrived quality of a number of the scenes criticized appears to indicate that Michel de Ghelderode was not always as aware of the incompatibility implicit in the term "neo-primitivism" as he was of a culture from which he undoubtedly springs and of which, in less emphatic moments, he unconsciously proves his profound understanding.

This danger of not remaining unconscious, of being something besides the dramatic artificer, threatens Ghelderode in other ways as well. He becomes particularly vulnerable whenever he departs from an essentially visceral genre to court the mental provinces of another drama. He does so when he sees himself as a moralist, a vision dangerous for even playwrights whose theater does not evolve so consistently out of an atmosphere.

For Ghelderode, whose philosophic beliefs are not always cogent—and which are occasionally quite contradictory—a mental departure is an essentially fatal one. His lack of clarity accounts for the unconvincing evolution of Barabbas and the hazy typification of Simon Laquedeem. The latter also illustrates the ambivalence of Ghelderode towards the Jew, that muddles not a small part of his work. Although he appropriates a number of clichés on the subject of Jews, as in *Fastes d'enfer, Pantagleize, Le Club des menteurs,* etc., he becomes strangely averse to seeing these clichés used by others, in whom they become symbols of ignorance and mob spirit, as bespoken by the repugnant vicar Kaliphas in *Mademoiselle Jaïre,* or the mob—*l'homme-foule*—in *Christophe Colomb:* "In that case, long live Christopher Columbus! (*He dances.*) Long live the Sultan of Turkey! Down with the Jews! Long live France!"

The problem of the Jew is not an isolated one. It is part of an aggregate that comprises evil hunchbacks (Krakenbus, in *Fastes d'enfer*), generally perverted dwarfs (*Hop Signor!, L'Ecole des bouffons*), cannibalistic Negroes (*Pantagleize, Don-Juan, Le Ménage de Caroline*). All these types have in common an original strangeness: the Congo Negro, the ghetto Jew, are still elements sufficiently unassimilated to possess some of the grotesque mystery and terror that set aside the physically disfigured in the Middle Ages.

In making use of these, without attempting to exact moral terms from them, Michel de Ghelderode is using the lore of the land, casting types in the traditional aspect which the legend has given them. He is merely being the true poet of *Christophe Colomb:* "Poets who are neither functionaries nor pimps [. . .] have infinitely more culture [. . .]. They know the world's most ancient fables." Thus, in true medieval spirit, his monks, priests, vicars, and clergymen generally are possessed by all the vices which that profoundly religious age ascribed to them while in the same breath he writes *mystères* that reflect genuine religious transport.

It is the moralist that stirs up contradictions, for the moralist's figures are no longer self-motivated but must bear axioms that could not have originally been theirs and which thus distort their original form. In any number of plays, the author considers people good if they eat, drink, and make merry (this appears to be, for example, the subsidiary moral of *La Balade du Grand Macabre,* whose medieval types are consonant with the author's concept of the instinctive individual). But throughout his other dramas, and indeed in *La Balade* itself, such facile philosophy is scorned, for, as Don-Juan is bitterly advised, "Be a fool, be fat and funny, you will achieve great heights. . . ." The masses are depositaries of common sense when they serve as a threatening counterpoise to corrupt officialdom (*D'un diable qui prêcha merveilles, Fastes d'enfer*), but become a mob of "madmen" and "epileptics" when they attempt a revolution. (These two derogatory epithets are from *Pantagleize.* A similar idea occurs in *La Transfiguration dans le cirque.*)

Goulave concludes *La Balade du Grand Macabre* with the exhortation: "Ring out, ruffians. It is time to drink in Breugellande. Ring out to the sun!" But *La Farce des Ténébreux* ends on a far less arrant note: "Be by day what you will. Our wis-

dom lights up only in the dark. At night, humanize your-
selves! . . ."

"Women, those impure creatures," (*Mes Statues*) are hardly
ever better than hypocrites, "Would a woman allow herself to
be desired beyond the miasmas of deceit?" (*Don-Juan*); or
than cross-grained wives, "[Eve] gave birth not only to humanity but to Stick, Whip, and Broom, all of which had a multiple progeny [and moreover] Eva drank enormously in her
old age" (*La Balade du Grand Macabre*). They are, generally,
the incarnation of all traits unpleasant and evil:

FERNAND D'ABCAUDE: Ugly, thick-headed, swollen, adipose, vulgar,
    starched, vain, authoritarian, underhanded, lustful . . . *(He
    fidgets.)* With what word can I finish her off?
LUDION: Woman!

And yet, it is a woman, the eternal woman, who will be
Fernand d'Abcaude's salvation. The shrewish woman too is an
old survival and an established convention; but such a lay and
proletarian tradition has seldom cast her in the part of the
redeemer.

These people, their moral attributes, and even their own
ethical aura, should they be endowed with one, are acceptable
if they have been handed down as such by the legend; if the
fable is accepted, there is no reason for rejecting any of its
parts. But there is as little reason for granting modern attributes or attaching tangential concerns to static symbols, especially since they usually live not so much as didactic terms, but
as purveyors of a particular flavor. The new moral grafted onto
them generally appears disproportionate, and hence contrived,
and becomes ridiculous when, as often happens, it runs counter to their primitive significance. But the fault is not with the
legend: it is the moralist who has sinned.

FORTUNATELY, a compulsion even more pressing than that of the moralist actuates Michel de Ghelderode: he is before all else the oracle through whom speak the occult voices of the theater. Such plays as *Hop Signor!, Escurial, Magie rouge,* and even *Fastes d'enfer* (because of its very haziness and ambiguity) either shun didactic issues or end up by assimilating them. They are the most successful. That which is first of all power and beauty in them becomes, when uncontrolled, exaggerated violence and excessive horror, making the otherwise fine *Sire Halewyn* or *L'Ecole des bouffons* romantic vehicles whose overstated devices are laughable.

The foreword of *Christophe Colomb* proposes: "Dances, lights, musical parts, some acrobatics, pathos, ridiculousness, tragedy, a thesis for the one who likes them. This play is spectacle and fairy-scene; it is played fast, without emphasis, and seeks the illusion of dreams." This may be taken to be a fair synthesis of Ghelderode's dramatic testament. None of it is new: the words might have prefigured Gozzi or the projected drama of many a romanticist—and the strong romantic surge that indeed shapes Ghelderode's stage has already been noted. The author's innate lyricism and flamboyance would of course confirm such propensities, more readily reconcilable with the simultaneously visionary and realistic temperament of the Flemings than with the measure and abstraction of classicism. Francis (in *Chrysalis,* 1949) lists as the author's favorite playwrights d'Annunzio, Maeterlinck, Strindberg, and Saint-Georges de Bouhéleir. Logically enough, these authors reflect the florid romanticism and the somber realism of the author. Of the Elizabethans with whom the author claims kinship, only their admixture of drama and clownage, and perhaps Marlowe's grandiloquence, seems to justify the comparison. If one's mind

travels back upon reading Ghelderode, one thinks rather of the
cruelty and the frenzy of the immediate post-Elizabethans such
as Tourneur and Jonson. Such influences are, however, hypo-
thetical and too far removed to be probing. Much more immediate forces were at work in the very early twenties when
Michel de Ghelderode first turned to the theater, and his work
bears their distinct imprint.

The period that starts some years before the First World
War and ends shortly after it, saw the heyday of expressionism.
Briefly, this new kind of drama deflated the turgid speech of
the neo-romanticists to terse stylization and replaced the romantic hero with either an ideal symbol or a scenic grouping.
This rejection of realism and the free use of the actor as a
symbol, led of course to a variety of stage tricks, symbolistic
disguises and violent color resulting from the mood of these
plays and the lighting that had replaced the realistic sets. Fantasy had no trouble finding its way into this nonrepresenta-
tional theater, abetted as it was by the necessity which the age
felt to express Freudian subjectivism. These new forces were
giving the stage shapes and dimensions previously unknown.
To these were added the new horizons which the magic of
motion pictures revealed. The age was predisposed to experimentation and excesses. Michel de Ghelderode was to be a
true child of the times.

Of the expressionist movement—on both stage and screen—
he retained a number of tricks, such as the symbolistic characters (*l'homme-foule*, in *Christophe Colomb;* Olympia, or
"the little green man" in *Don-Juan;* the animated loudspeakers
and the phylacteries in the first versions of *La Mort du Docteur
Faust,* etc.). But especially, Michel de Ghelderode acquired the
plasticity which was the great feature of expressionism. Com-

bined with his predilection for puppet stages, this enabled him, in the words of Paul Werrie (in *La Nervie,* 1932), to "dislocate his boards." To this freedom he has added the supple theatrical acrobatics characteristic of clown and music-hall sketches: an indifference to physical and temporal limitations that subordinates external contingencies to those of the action.

This disregard of conventional logic led him from the emancipation of isolated forms and figures to the ultimate creation of a stage world free from the habitual tyranny of space (*Christophe Colomb*), time (*Christophe Colomb, La Mort du Docteur Faust, Trois Acteurs, un drame . . .*), and reason (*La Mort du Docteur Faust, La Balade du Grand Macabre, D'un diable qui prêcha merveilles*). It is a world in which nothing is normal and where familiar borrowings have been made only in order that they might be alive with a fantastic life never theirs hitherto. Ghelderode has said of Cantens' painting: "This work is situated beyond the world" (in *La Nervie,* 1932). In the real meaning that the tangibility of the theater can confer upon such works, the remark certainly applies to Michel de Ghelderode's own work.

This new planet he has peopled with very old types—the ancestral Flemings—and they are no more out of place in this mad setting than they were in the *diableries* of Bosch. The paintings of some late fifteenth and early sixteenth century Dutch masters bear an uncanny resemblance to the fantasy of the Freudian expressionists. Furthermore, the symbolistic actor of the expressionists is nothing more than a renovation of the old morality figures. Here again, any number of traditional Flemish representations—Death, the Devil, etc.—could step into the new current without creating the least stir.

The choral groups that match the scenic configurations on

the expressionist stage become for Ghelderode the musical interludes usually accompanied by archaic instruments. (Of course, if the play demands the accompaniment of a modern idiom, the sirens, the guns, the jazz band are available as in *Pantagleize, Don-Juan, La Mort du Docteur Faust, Le Club des menteurs,* etc.). And the configurations themselves are the weird stage scenes such as the Black Mass celebrated in honor of Putrégina (*La Farce des Ténébreux*), the macabre dance of the ugly old people before the arrival of *Le Cavalier bizarre,* the previously mentioned combat between Simon Laquedeem and the ghost, etc.

In time, as Michel de Ghelderode ceased to rely on specific influences, the jaggedness of the expressionistic rhythm was smoothed and a fluid discursiveness refined his plays, just as he simultaneously turned away from earlier melodrama. After the Pirandellian exercise *Trois Acteurs, un drame . . . ,* plays like *Christophe Colomb, Barabbas, Don-Juan, Pantagleize,* move with greater ease through time and space in quest of their metaphysics. The first atmosphere sketches, those of *Oude Piet* or *Le Cavalier bizarre,* are already fully developed in a satisfactory drama such as *Escurial* which points the way to future evolution. Thereafter, the fluency of the action is allowed to dominate peripheral considerations (with the exception of the intentionally contrived *Sortie de l'acteur*) and the author's sheer fantasy creates *Fastes d'enfer, Magie rouge, La Balade du Grand Macabre,* and especially, *Hop Signor!*

Michel de Ghelderode is a man of the theater. The world that materializes on his stage is created with little transition or analysis. That world is theater as directly as notes themselves are the essence of melody. The only one of his plays that was not conceived in a stage realm is *Sire Halewyn,* an evocation of night-time rides and ghastly sights upon the winter plain of Flanders; yet even it has been performed. If occasionally his vision grows too powerful for the frail instruments of the stage, demanding the aerial acrobatics of *La Transfiguration dans le cirque,* the massive cathedral doors of *Fastes d'enfer,* the flaming Golgotha in *Barabbas,* the final explosion of the world in *La Balade du Grand Macabre,* it will be remembered that this is not a naturalistic stage in the conventional sense, for its realism resides only in the detail. It seeks to evoke its apocalyptic visions solely in the mind of the spectator.

The sorcerer, whose spell so effortlessly conjures up the magic of the stage, also works his necromancy with words, an inseparable part of the magical rite. Michel de Ghelderode is first of all a poet: "One listens to you first of all with one's skin, Michel de Ghelderode, with the skin that receives that drumming of electro-shocks—your words. And your words penetrate, fill the void, draw it in, absorb it. They are before all else a presence. Because they are *your* life." This comment was part of a preface by Jean Francis to a collection of the author's works called *Théâtre d'écoute* (1951), for, as might be expected, a number of Michel de Ghelderode's plays were written for, or first performed on, the air.

But if Ghelderode is a poet, he has given his poetry the plastic dimensions of the stage. Like Cocteau, like Garcia Lorca, his metaphor comes to life and walks the boards of his drama. His worlds, their strange lighting and their intense people, the weird music and the curious dances that are woven into them, are the evocations of a poet even before he has turned to words.

Still, words remain his very special instrument. Their fascination has endowed him with mimetic genius. Fittingly, they are sounds for him before being ideational agents and their ultimate use depends on their particular harmony. According to his own statements, Michel de Ghelderode was introduced to the savor of the French language through Charles de Coster's writing. De Coster, at one time a professor at the Ecole de Guerre in Brussels, was an admirer of Rabelais and a specialist whose interests centered on that period when the language crystallized out of Old French. His *Thyl Ulenspiegel,* written in streamlined sixteenth century French, was ten years in the making. It is a luxuriant work, whose rich vocabulary is enhanced by archaisms, learned orthographies, derivations in their original form, and an occasional Flemish idiom.

Michel de Ghelderode evinces comparable syntactic freedom, and with greater ease than even de Coster, he mingles old words that Belgium has retained, archaic forms, Flemish expressions and, occasionally, a coinage that exists only in the context which it has been given by the author. His verbal enjoyment is reminiscent of Crommelynck. Words may explode in Rabelaisian fashion, echoing the exuberant rhythm of the action, or they may be strung out without any meaning but that of the Flemish chant which they convey, as frequently happens, e.g., in *Mademoiselle Jaïre.*

As indicated previously, Michel de Ghelderode's language is also tempered at times by the anti-romanticist conventions of expressionistic theater. Frequently clipped repartee dovetails with that of puppets whose staccato language his mimetic gift renders admirably, as it does that of clowns and music-hall performers. Nevertheless, lyric passages illuminate nearly all of his work. Their function, like that of all purposeful elements in this drama, is to contribute to the creation of a mood. In *Barabbas,* the poetry renders the significance, the suffering, and the greatness changing the hill where it is enacted into a symbol of pain; in *Sire Halewyn,* it sets the scene on the walls of Ostrelande, and finds echoes as powerful and as somber as the desolate land that gives it resonance; in *Mademoiselle Jaïre,* it attains a liturgical tone for the narration of what lies beyond death; in *La Balade du Grand Macabre,* it shapes the symbol and the eternal words of lovers.

Like the myth itself, the tenacious beliefs that are older than man's wisdom lend the imagery of primitive beliefs that coincide with the imagery of modern physics and psychiatry. In addition to the examples already cited, the sexual significance of the knife should be noted (*La Balade du Grand Macabre, Sire Halewyn*), of blood (*La Balade du Grand Macabre, Sire Halewyn*), of the moon (*Les Femmes au Tombeau, Magie rouge, Mademoiselle Jaïre*), of torture (*Hop Signor!, Les Femmes au Tombeau*), etc.

But words are the all-important leaven in this theater, infusing it with most of its comedy and indeed, with nearly every one of its characterizations. Not content with the idiom of marionettes, of clowns, of poets, nor with borrowing from the Flemish (*Le Mystère de la Passion*) or English (*Don-Juan*) that continues the poetry by translating it into another tongue, Ghelderode has attempted experimental techniques of dialogue to render "certain curious resonances of the soul, a care that situates his play beyond acknowledged eras and at the extremity of silence" (according to the *Lieu et temps* of *Mademoiselle Jaïre*).

Scorning in advance the myopic labors of those who might seek to dissect it, the song, pristine and triumphant, waits, kindling with its life the nights upon which the ritual is appointed and the incantation is heard. That incantation becomes

at times the great voice of death and of man's cruelty. Ghelderode is a poet—the word cancels many of his sins and
not a few of the critic's analyses. If his work is frequently an
experiment, in moments of achievement it is simply an outcry,
that of our generation. Diamotoruscant, the devil in *La Mort
du Docteur Faust,* speaks for the author and for the age: "I am
like everyone else, with a little more despair!" And in the face
of such bitterness, a conviction such as Albert Schweitzer's
settles upon the beholder, a feeling that these are dark days
indeed, drawing their last glimmer from forces now nearly
extinguished. If that persuasion has been achieved, the voice
of these plays will remain as a genuine vestige of our age—
just as in their time, the voice of Molière or of Wycherley.

III

Tomorrow?

of analysis and development in every area and dimension to the limited preoccupations of the author.

In *Victimes du devoir* (1952), a digression by the victim, Mr. Choubert, on the nature of drama, is interrupted by a detective who, like so many people on Ionesco's stage, gradually becomes more brutal until he is killed by a certain Nicolas d'Eu (an apparently gratuitous and meaningless pun). Nicolas d'Eu is a poet who no longer writes because "We have Ionesco and Ionesco is sufficient." The poet continues the interrupted definition of drama and amplifies it: "We shall abandon principles of identity and unity of characters in favor of movement, of a dynamic psychology. . . We are not ourselves. . . Personality does not exist. In us there are only contradictory or noncontradictory forces. . . ." It will be hard to justify this declaration, whether or not the author meant it to be credible.

If the statement is intended to be serious, and certainly the author's theater would seem to indicate that Nicolas, the disciple of Ionesco, is also a spokesman for the author, it must be taken to indicate that the spectator will not be granted characters that resemble him or that are in any way possessed of the assimilable traits that generally define such stage figures. For all their independence, however, these new figures are rationalized to the extent of being projections of "we" who "are not ourselves. . . ." Presumably, they are the expression of impulses that correspond to an essential reality, and these "contradictory and noncontradictory forces" will give the stage a new sort of action, "movement," deriving from this so-called "dynamic psychology." This effort to explain (to render "coherent") the incoherence of the protagonists assumes norms: the characters are susceptible of theoretical analysis even though their presence on stage will deliberately defy apprehension.

If the foregoing is true, the spectator is thought of as an intellectual presence, since he must redefine the incoherence of the formless experiment which he is offered. And yet, intellectual analysis cannot take place in this theater since the avowedly erratic motions of the stage performers are not subject to the spectator's control—the principle of identity is eliminated. The spectator, while he is participant in the dramatic action, must accept that action—the "movement"—as he might accept music, through automatic perception of individual notes, none of which he is allowed to dwell on or to analyze. But contrary to musical development, the development of this action will not allow motives to come into being. There will evolve only a general aura, the loosely termed "movement," which, passively accepted by the spectator in the theater, will become significant for him in retrospect only, upon evaluation. Such an intellectual drama begins *outside* the theater.

The erratic pattern of the performers' action being accepted as a non-analyzable unit, it follows that the play cannot credit topical allusions ("Ionesco is sufficient") nor can it debate the possibilities of a new theater. Thus, if they are to be accepted, the words of the author must be contradicted by the fact of the play—which of course they are not. Ionesco shows little concern about this contradiction: in 1955, *L'Impromptu de l'Alma* berates Ionesco's critics.

If the author is proposing to an intellectual audience a condemnation of contemporary vices, he is not conceiving a new theater, but giving instead to a conventional genre a new form that defeats his purpose. If, on the other hand, he proposes a nonsense pattern that will be suggestive of a particular aura, then he is proposing a theater somewhat in the manner of Jean Cocteau: a poetry of the stage. This is presumably the dream-

like (*onirique*) quality of which Nicolas d'Eu speaks when he
tentatively accepts surrealism as the form of his drama. The
intellectual concerns of Ionesco will show at first glance that he
is failing at least to the extent that Cocteau succeeded. In Cocteau's felicitous moments, his stage people are able to blend in
a harmonious ballet with the remarkably fluid objects around
them. The salvation of the Cocteau object derived, as was seen,
from its human quality. The Ionesco object cannot assume
human grace for the people on Ionesco's stage are as wooden
and as angular as those of Jarry. *Les Chaises* (1951), which is
the confrontation of two annoyingly grotesque old people and
their delusions, is performed with over thirty-five chairs, ten
doors, etc. In *Amédée, ou Comment s'en débarrasser* (1953),
the corpse of the love that once existed between Amédée and
Madeleine grows throughout the play until, as a truly unwieldy
object (and not as Giraudoux's Erinyes) it threatens to collapse
the house in which they live. The expressionistic device is, in
this instance, little more than the non-extensible, physical representation of an idea.

The stubborn, malevolent growth of the mechanical corpse
in *Amédée* is evidence of Ionesco's dynamics and an indication
of why even his surrealistic form cannot develop in the manner
of Henri Pichette into a free lyrical expression that merely
expresses general rejection of the conventional world (*Les Epiphanies, Nucléa*), or into a poetic suggestion such as Audiberti's
(*Le Mal court*) or Schehadé's (*Monsieur Bob'le, La Soirée des
proverbes*) that is able to hint, again without being specific, at
metaphysical concerns. In contradistinction, Ionesco's world is
informed by anger. His is a noisy theater, in which a coffee
mill drowns the voices of the performers (*Amédée*); it is a
meaninglessly frenzied theater, one in which the coffee, as it is

served, becomes a rapidly multiplying number of cups and saucers that soon, like the aforementioned corpse, overwhelm a part of the other stage properties. Like Jean Genet's theater (*Les Bonnes*), this is a cruel theater, one of physical torture and degrading death (in *Victimes du devoir,* Nicolas kills the detective who had been torturing Choubert only to start torturing him in turn; in *La Leçon,* 1950, the professor kills the student who had come to him for tutorial guidance, just as he has killed thirty-nine others and just as he will kill the forty-first that is about to enter as the curtain falls; etc.).

If, as in these instances, the object momentarily acts without expressing an intellectual statement, it is apparent that it is responding, like the meaningless puns and the nonsense repartee, to the perceptible ill temper of the author. Its motion that should have been allowed to develop freely in surrealistic fashion is hampered, as was once the Dada experiment, by a single expression of destructiveness and scorn.

Indeed, the drama of Ionesco is monochromatic. Not only does it reflect too consistently a single one of the author's moods (and drama is poor in proportion to its refusal to exploit its many modulations), but it is poor as well in its subject matter. Choubert tells the spectator that this drama will reject subject matter and plot for they have made detective stories of classical and conventional drama alike. But a completely gratuitous theater is so difficult a notion to conceive that even enlightened readers of Ionesco, such as Saurel ("Ionesco, ou Les Blandices de la culpabilité," 1954), are tempted to see the development of a specific idea in these "anti-plays." Renée Saurel detects in *La Cantatrice chauve* the embryonic tragedy of the married couple, and indeed, the play expresses this idea if it has any claim at all to validity. Moreover, the married couple in its degeneracy establishes convenient limits for a drama that strives to express so little: the living room of the Smiths becomes the focal point for the ridiculous world of petty clichés that mar human existence and elicit the dramatist's disgust. But even within this already narrow sphere, the probing is circumscribed, virtually nonexistent. Anouilh's *Valse des toréadors* proposed a similar topic, but its exploration appears by contrast to suggest an infinitely richer and more complex problem, one that will allow a variety of preceptions. Ionesco uses the image of the couple merely for a statement of his disgust, which his characters will neither motivate satisfactorily nor in any way explain. And long before Ionesco, Roger Martin du Gard had failed in the farcical aspect of his dramatic attempt for having neglected likewise the positive side against which the negative aspect of man contends and without which this simple negation is meaningless.

ARTHUR ADAMOV's plotless theater presents an appearance similar to that of Ionesco. However, his theater is more successful than Ionesco's to the extent that the latter's anger—what Saurel calls his "guilt"—is replaced in Adamov by anxiety. Still, the author's initial motivation is very close to that of Ionesco. Speaking before the performance of *Tous contre tous* in 1953, Adamov opposed categorically the notion of a thesis in his drama—while denying as categorically that this theater is influenced by Kafka or strives for metaphysical allusions. And so, once again, the untenable postulation of a gratuitous theater is advanced, one that will prove even more contradictory in Adamov in that his stage has been allowed more of the conventional aspects and a greater range of moods than has that of Ionesco.

The meaningless puns and nonsense that absurdly reflect the absurd in Ionesco, the systematic debasing of the individual, all this is generally absent from Adamov's plays. These undertake the more difficult task of rendering that absurd through the substance rather than through the form of the play, or, more precisely (for this disciple of Artaud), in rendering the dream that informs an idea of cruelty and of fright.

In the preliminary note to the second volume of his plays (Gallimard, 1955), Adamov has analyzed all his drama up to that date. A glimpse of a street scene was the first insight into what was to be *La Parodie* (1947). From such disconnected bits of drama in pure form, Adamov evolved a "metaphysics": human isolation, the failure of communication between people. "No one hears anyone," says Adamov who, while granting Chekhov this sort of theater, claims to be "disgusted" with psychological plays. He apparently feels that it is possible to create, through people on stage, a drama of specific moods while avoiding a restrictive appropriation by these people alone.

In an otherwise harsh self-appraisal, Adamov singles out as fairly satisfactory *Le Professeur Taranne* (1951). This play is about a man who has copied one "greater" than he was from fear that he might not be able to live up to his own status. Terminology and revolutionary beliefs notwithstanding, this is psychological analysis, and the very last scene wherein Taranne starts undressing after his fraud has been exposed is simply a conclusive visualization of the statement that has been made. If the notion of the man Taranne exists, the notions of a gratuitous "movement," of new "anti-plays," etc., cease. The fact that this play is derived from a dream, an expression of the psyche, does little to remove it from psychological reality.

Adamov accepts necessary parts of the dramatic mechanism

without accepting its totality. An element of brutality, the ever repeated excess of the revolutionary, reinforced here by the theories of Artaud, causes this drama to turn against its chosen forms, as does that of Ionesco. It is hard to understand otherwise why the author should have rejected the example of Kafka. The latter has reduced character analysis to make of a single figure an expression of anxiety, the sole coherent motor in a "movement" such as proposed by Ionesco. A play like Adamov's *L'Invasion* (1949), in which the scarcely legible manuscript of a dead author is scrutinized in vain for coherent significance by anxious legatees, creates a climate similar in scope and purpose to that of Kafka. But Adamov's criticism of *L'Invasion* is that this climate has been swept away by the character of the Hero and his Message to the point of becoming "a romantic play, closer to *Chatterton* than one might think." Inasmuch as anxiety must settle on the figure of human beings if it is to have human significance, the play does revert to Adamov's rejected psychological drama. But this does not imply a necessary Romanticism, and especially not a Romanticism inherent in symbols that must themselves be secondary to the characters on stage.

The violence alluded to is not restricted to the statements of the theorist: it is apparent of course in the subjects of the plays. *La Grande et la petite manœuvre* (1950) and *Tous contre tous* (1952) are both set in police states whose policemen are reminiscent of types already encountered in Ionesco. "I wanted to communicate my fright to others," says Adamov. This fright may again be that of a dream but the "others" are spectators for whom the dream will have the tangible aspect of the actors on stage. To counter this necessity, Adamov has emphasized the expressionistic value of the symbols upon which the blows fall. Nevertheless, these symbols are more than mere objects or intellectual statements for, if they are contrasted with the blow-dealing symbols—the industrialist, the politician, the afore-mentioned policeman—they will be found bleeding. The *mutilé* in *La Grande et la petite manœuvre* who will be progressively more crippled as the play develops, is the image of a man before he is the image of mankind, and his plight is a personal one before being an abstract manifestation of the absurd. This absurd, the idea of which Adamov entertained in the same prefatory speech to his *Tous contre tous,* while opposing the suggestion of a *pièce à thèse* ("the antithesis of the theater"), is less apparent in the police state of *Tous contre tous* than is the thesis. The symbol of those who limp being beset by a majority party connotes topical problems as vividly as it does their spiritual or psychological implications—neither of which can satisfy the theorist Adamov. The author recognizes this. He admits that the play pictures a "social mechanism"—just as he had already been forced to concede a "metaphysics" for *La Parodie.* Though this should give him pause, since the social mechanism is in fact that of people and their interaction, Adamov continues his argument against the so-called Romantic and psychological dramas.

La Parodie, the author's first play, is the best illustration of his arguments. Here, the frightening state was no more than the handless clock, the echoes of terror and the mechanical screams of the age. The play was a remarkable orchestration for rendering absurd the appearance of hollow figures shaped like humans; but in fact, little suggestion of the human presence had been allowed, either directly or positively. It is therefore by a curious argument that Adamov indicts plays that are particularized developments of *La Parodie,* such as *Tous contre*

tous and *La Grande et la petite manœuvre,* for having people
that are insufficiently motivated. Motivation, it would seem,
leads most directly to an apprehension of drama that is conventional, commonly accepted, and little concerned with dynamics of its own (distinct from those of its spectator).

If the modern world provides an image of the absurd, it
first provides specific reminders which are so familiar that they
demand philosophical detachment in order to be interpreted
as merely an expression of the absurd. In *Tous contre tous,* a
note of revolt is sounded by the girl Noémi: "One cannot live
constantly in fear, it isn't possible, it cries out for vengeance in
the end." This crying out for vengeance is also the cry of the
human rising against the dramatic object. And the protagonists
are allowed a further assertion in the lucidity with which they
face death at the end of the play. This is dangerous freedom
indeed for a stage presence that must conform only to patterns
that illustrate an absurd condition.

Against such insinuations of the "sentimental" human, Adamov opposes the obvious machine: although the *mutilé* was
first a dream of the author, Adamov has him lose arms and legs
in sight of the audience without being otherwise affected by the
loss. Thus are asserted the symbol and a surrealistic aura.
Though the *mutilé* is a human of a kind unknown to Ionesco,
he must be discovered within a non-human frame. In a sense,
this is true of every character in every sort of drama, and, as
noted, the drama that demands the greatest measure of reality
finds that reality within the spectator's mind, not on stage.
However, such a drama effects the transfer from stage to mind
as directly as it can, by means of lifelike surfaces (or at least
surfaces that do not go against an essential suggestion of reality). These surfaces extend in every way possible the suasion

of the living actor. The excesses in Adamov provide the key to the true nature of this drama: they stem from an anti-romanticism that has become a mistrust of the human presence itself, though in its metaphysics and its social structure, that human is nevertheless acknowledged.

Adamov claims that *Le Ping-pong* (1955?) marks a turning point in his dramatic evolution. To the uninitiated, the play does not seem very different from his others. The pinball machine around which the participants are grouped becomes a social force (though not an agency of fate, cautions Adamov) and serves as the means by which aspects of the social structure are scanned in attitudes that suggest the dynamics of that structure. Adamov has been careful to emphasize that within the sway of these dynamics, the people are still postulated as being relatively free. Of the principals, he writes: "I have allowed, in particular to Arthur and Victor, a margin of freedom." But ultimately, in his very analysis of the play, Adamov sees even these characters as symbols. As usual, his human is hardly more than a negative quantity, a victim whose capacity to exist is real only to the extent that the physical instruments of his torture are real and will be used on him: it is only by comparison with these instruments that he is found to have significance greater than that of the rudimentary and static object.

Adamov recognizes in his self-criticism that such figures as *le Vieux* (the Boss who manufactures the pinball machines and who will put up a losing battle to maintain his sales volume) are not distinct from the allegory. But even if they should be in the future drama that Adamov promises, will not the stage return to conventional figures that draw their being from an audience's customary emotions and their habitual expression? And if not, does not that stage remain an impersonal place—something even more remote than the dreams that have inspired Adamov?

THE WILLINGNESS OF Samuel Beckett not to relinquish the human presence is apparent in symbolism utterly different from that of Ionesco or Adamov. For a quarter of a century, Charlie Chaplin impersonated the masque of the twentieth century Everyman and gave a silhouette to a contemporary myth. His immortality endures upon the ashes of farcical sketches whose aggregate laughter has evaporated: his is now the substance of the Little Man trapped within the monstrous gears of a young industrial era. In time, the immensity of that machine and of its system made way for worse terrors. Its orderly, if gigantic and impersonal, gears were wrenched free to course at random by those prophets of nonsense whose most respectable voice was that of a chaotic era's existentialists. However, deeper than any transitory beliefs was a valid symbol that lasted.

Charlie Chaplin's boots, toes outward, and a familiar derby, situate the figures of Samuel Beckett attempting to live, *En attendant Godot* (1952). To enlarge Edith Kern's hypothesis ("Drama Stripped for Inaction," 1955), the symbolic name chosen by an Irish author writing in French suggests the divinity, in its first syllable, and that divinity's creation in man's image—the Little Man's, Charl*ot* in the familiar French diminitive form—in the second.

The enduring drama of man attempting to reclaim his incomplete being and the gnawing frustration that is the particular idiom of these times, become in turn the idiom of Beckett's play. Estragon and Vladimir, interchangeable symbols of mankind, are waiting somewhere, anywhere, "on a platform," (called a "Board" in the author's English version). It is a "Country road, with tree"—a functional and isolating desert, out of time and poetry. They are waiting for a particular salvation known to them only as Godot and once vaguely invoked:

ESTRAGON: What exactly did we ask him?
VLADIMIR: Weren't you there?
ESTRAGON: I wasn't paying attention.
VLADIMIR: Well. . . Nothing really definite.
ESTRAGON: A sort of prayer.
VLADIMIR: That's it.
ESTRAGON: A vague supplication.
VLADIMIR: If you wish.
ESTRAGON: And what did he answer?
VLADIMIR: That he would see.

They are not waiting confidently. An older myth and the doubts that have clouded it are early remembered by Vladimir: if only one of the four Evangelists recalls that Christ saved a sinner crucified with him, although all four were present, can secure reliance be placed upon such a crucial event? The hope of salvation, a need of outer assistance, and fear of its failure are drawn into the present by Vladimir's uncertainty.

Their fear is a long-acquired habit: they are tramps, no longer young or healthy, who have walked a great while without finding haven:

VLADIMIR: And where were we yesterday evening, according to you?
ESTRAGON: I don't know. Elsewhere. In another compartment. There is no lack of emptiness.

And hopelessly adrift, they live on the verge of a constant unknown whose vague and various sounds bring them in turn hope or terror—but without ever affecting their lot.

Godot never comes. Occasionally a messenger arrives to explain that Godot's visit has been delayed, but he can offer no consolation beyond a hazy confirmation of the white beard usually ascribed to timeless incarnations.

Estragon and Vladimir remain alone and together, occasionally drawn to each other or apart, but inevitably bound through necessity and inertia. However, their inertia is unfortunately neither that of blindness nor of brutishness:

VLADIMIR: You should have been a poet.
ESTRAGON: I was. *(Points to his tatters.)* Doesn't it show?

And their symbolism reveals a curiously humanitarian compassion in the author who confirms their being ("We are men") and who has Estragon say, in reference to Jesus: "All my life, I have compared myself to him."

Instead of Godot, two other derby-decked specimens briefly cross the stage: the domineering and opulent Pozzo linked to his dumb servant Lucky by a cord with which he leads him. And for awhile, the desolate scene marks the convergence of four isolated, distinct, and yet interchangeable faces of man.

A second act places the static principals in a meaningless new day, a repetitive new season. The tree has sprouted the leaves of an indifferent spring. Pozzo crosses the stage again, blind and led by Lucky to whom he is still bound by the rope. There is no time, only the absolute of misery:

POZZO *(suddenly furious):* Aren't you through plaguing me with your accursed time? It's unheard of! When! When! One day, isn't that sufficient for you, one day just like any other, he became dumb, one day I became blind, one day we will become deaf, one day we are born, one day we die, the same day, the same instant, isn't that sufficient for you? *(More calmly.)* They give birth astride a tomb, the daylight gleams for an instant, and then it is night again. *(He tugs the rope.)* Forward!

The four incomplete characters extend Estragon and Vladimir's initial inability to either communicate or to assist each other. Though such awareness fails to help him, Vladimir understands the recurrent vicissitudes that isolate them: "He begged for our aid. We remained deaf. He insisted. We beat him." And Estragon likewise asserts their cosmic breadth without availing himself of his insight:

VLADIMIR: I tell you he's called Pozzo.
ESTRAGON: That's what we're going to see. Let's see. *(He thinks.)* Abel! Abel!
POZZO: Help!
ESTRAGON: What did I tell you!
VLADIMIR: I'm getting tired of this motive.
ESTRAGON: Maybe the other one is called Cain. *(He calls.)* Cain! Cain!
POZZO: Help!
ESTRAGON: He's all of humanity.

These manacled choruses remain confined between the terms of their quest and the acuity of their vision: "What do we do now?"—"Nothing . . ." Nevertheless, they recurrently attempt to play the game of living:

ESTRAGON: Did you suffer?
VLADIMIR: Suffer! He asks me if I suffered!
ESTRAGON *(points his finger):* It's not a reason not to button yourself.
VLADIMIR *(stooping):* That's right. *(He buttons his fly.)* Never neglect the little things.

But the most spontaneous of such sallies are ultimately objectified, and Estragon pathetically exclaims: "We always find something, don't we Didi, to give us the impression that we exist?" Their paralyzing objectivity thus becomes an intellec-

tual extension of the physical frustration that emprisons them:
"Now . . . (*Happy.*) Here you are again . . . (*Indifferent.*)
Here we are again . . . (*Sad.*) Here I am again." It echoes
Lucky's briefly found voice that attempts the salvation by
thought only to become the broken record of repetitive and
meaningless philosophical jargon. It parallels their futile grasp-
ing at norms and bases upon which to settle a significance for
their being—or at least to confirm the fact of that being:

POZZO: What else happened?
VLADIMIR: My friend hurt himself.
POZZO: And Lucky?
VLADIMIR: So it was he?
POZZO: How's that?
VLADIMIR: It was Lucky?
POZZO: I do not understand.
VLADIMIR: And you, you are Pozzo?
POZZO: Certainly I am Pozzo.
VLADIMIR: The same ones as yesterday?
POZZO: As yesterday?
VLADIMIR: We saw each other yesterday. (*Silence.*) Don't you re-
            member?
POZZO: I don't remember having met anyone yesterday.

This physical ineffectuality dooms even their supreme and
simplest effort toward salvation—suicide. Escape in death becomes simply one more impossible dream. Salvation, if ever it
existed, was anyway in the past: "Hand in hand, we would
have thrown ourselves from the Eiffel Tower, amongst the
first. We were respectable in those days. Now, it's too late.
They wouldn't even let us up." Estragon and Vladimir have
indeed been sentenced for life and the motive that ends each
of its acts indicates that the play proposes to show merely a
segment indefinitely extended of their futile waiting:

ESTRAGON: Well then, shall we go?
VLADIMIR: Let's go. *(They do not move.)*
     Curtain

These are not stylized automata evincing only an expressionistic function. Reference has already been made to the author's humanity: this humanity lowers the symbols occasionally to make them merely very wretched men whose pathos is no longer prototypal statement or theoretical assumption, even though each bears a name whose distinct national origin hints at a specific function beyond that of their immediate symbolism. The recurrent and hopeless attempts at suicide point to their abjectly physical misery:

ESTRAGON: And if we hanged ourselves?
VLADIMIR: With what?
ESTRAGON: Don't you have a bit of rope?
VLADIMIR: No.
ESTRAGON: Then we can't.
VLADIMIR: Let's go.
ESTRAGON: Wait, there's my belt.
VLADIMIR: It's too short.
ESTRAGON: You'll hang on to my legs.
VLADIMIR: Who'll hang on to mine?
ESTRAGON: That's right. . .
VLADIMIR: Let's see all the same. *(Estragon undoes the cord that holds up his pants. These, much too large, fall about his ankles. They look at the cord.)* In a pinch, it might work. But is it strong enough?
ESTRAGON: We'll see. Hold. *(They each take one end of the cord and pull. The cord breaks.)*

But even such sober expression of misery is rare in this nearly wholly stichomythic play whose words are never allowed to inflate the period. The words remain simple, idiomatic, slangy, now and then even vulgar (sex is an illusion like the rest), but with little meaning of their own beyond the dramatic rhythm which they impart to the action. Likewise, there is no poetry in them, though again their aggregate rhythm becomes at length a haunting chant:

VLADIMIR: It's a fact, we're inexhaustible.
ESTRAGON: It's so as not to think.
VLADIMIR: We have excuses.
ESTRAGON: It's so as not to hear.
VLADIMIR: We have our reasons.
ESTRAGON: All the dead voices.
VLADIMIR: Make a noise like wings.
ESTRAGON: Like leaves.
VLADIMIR: Like sand.
ESTRAGON: Like leaves.

And as the common words that have already lost their individual meaning now lose their common significance, individual parts of the prosaic talk become a probing and desperate refrain of "What do we do now?"—"Nothing. . . ." The consummate skill with which this play is written achieves poetry through barrenness: the rough and occasionally awkward form of Ionesco and Adamov does not attain this degree of artistry; their plays remain rudimentary rather than essential.

En attendant Godot sometimes gives evidence of wanting to be rooted in a particular time. Reference has already been made to the specific nationalities which the names imply, as well as to the era which the Eiffel Tower designates. But whatever such intentions Beckett may have had, they are not allowed much scope in this classically naked drama. There is no hero to speak the nonexistent lines. And aside from intermittencies noted during which a wretched highwayman shows through the symbol, there is no suggestion of a restricted or restrictive man on stage, except in the momentary fun of clashing surfaces that become particularizations briefly remembered.

Fin de partie (1956), though in appearance similar to *Godot,* is in fact a much more temporal play. It too has two principal actors, Hamm and Clov, and two subsidiary ones, Nagg and Nell. They too are limited to a single set, a room with a small window high up on each side and no view. They too are waiting, and for them as for the others nothing will happen and they will not act.

The room is the world: "Beyond there is . . . the other hell." Hamm is an invalid in a wheel chair; he is reminiscent of Pozzo, but his Lucky—Clov—shows that this is a different play: he is capable of receiving and of executing certain orders.

Much has been said about the play's setting by critics who have seen it as representing the frightful remainders of a post-atomic age. And yet Hamm says:

I knew a madman who thought that the end of the world had come. He used to paint. I liked him. I used to visit him in the asylum. I would take him by the hand and drag him to the window. Why look! There! All that wheat rising! And there! Look! The sails of the sardine boats! All that beauty! *(A while.)* He'd pull his hand away and go back to his corner. Terrified. He had seen only ashes. *(A while.)* He alone had been spared. *(A while.)* Forgotten. *(A while.)* It seems that such cases are not . . . were not so . . . so rare.

Quite clearly, this is the play of an inner vision.

The way out, suicide, is once again rejected, this time through a fear that boredom renders ridiculous: "It is time for this to end and yet I still hesitate to—*(yawns)*—to end it." Which is echoed in a remarkable line by the more active Clov, one of whose illusions is that he has seen a rat: "If I do not kill that rat, it will die." The futility of their being turns their days and their every gesture to death on the installment plan. A repeated motive echoes this:

HAMM: What's going on?
CLOV: Something's following its course.

In two garbage cans are Nagg and Nell, the "damned progenitors," a reminder of Ionesco's people, who enact the grotesque pantomime of decay. Their stubborn habits and illusions (such as Nell's "elegiacal" comments, "Oh, yesterday!") render them repulsive in their senility. They are the sacrificed flesh, the superficial grimace of life—and perhaps a target of the author's anger. But they too endure a common fate: Clov remarks that Nagg is crying; to which Hamm retorts, "Therefore he lives."

The author's craft is less apparent in *Fin de partie*. He makes use of grosser symbols that are less good receptors for that which is human. Exclamations break what had been a chant in *Godot;* Hamm blurts out on two occasions, "Think, think, you're on earth, it's hopeless!" indicating the compulsiveness of an angered author addressing the spectator directly instead of allowing the latter to address himself to a performing cast. This intrusion by the author breaks up the dramatic weft in several ways. The metaphysical commentary becomes a direct statement and does not grow out of the action as it had in *Godot*. The speeches are longer, more specialized, and less concerned with the dramatic texture. As the stichomythy disappears, so does the incantation.

This less essential speech is that of a less essential play. Although *Fin de partie* has as little action in it as *Godot*, it is less bare and less purposeful. Ambivalent in his dialogue, the author not only assaults the spectator, he also courts him. To this end, he has inserted puns that have no bearing on the dramatic progress. Such is Hamm's boast to Clov that he has been a father to him: "No Hamm [. . .] no home" (a pun especially awkward in French). And there are others.

Mouthpiece for an off-stage presence, these people also pursue on stage an action not directly concerned with their own purpose. Whatever their outlook, they display their metaphysical significance only indirectly in that, to a degree, they are able to interact. Hamm achieves an immediate purpose in being able to have Clov wheel him around the room, and although this purposeless motion is meant to emphasize the oppressiveness of the room (womb-shaped on Roger Blin's stage), the spectator is aware of social synapses before realizing that they are in fact meaningless. In this play, though his statement is part of the over-all lie, Clov is able to say, "I did it on purpose."

These responses to an immediate, if limited and false, normalcy, are enlarged by people who have memories (a link with familiar patterns) which the people of *Godot* had only in relation to a few abstract symbols. But contrary to those of *Godot*, the human beings thus created have been deprived of their author's humanity. The stage has become a pointlessly cruel world in which God ("The rotter! He doesn't exist!") is unavailing and man suffers senselessly: "I sometimes say to myself—Clov, you must manage to suffer better than that if you want them to tire of punishing you one day." The hopelessness too long overstated turns to purposeless masochism.

Because these people are making metaphysical statements at times when they should be enacting a genuine drama, the lament of a terrible waiting fails to awaken in the spectator an

Bibliography

IN THE FIRST PART of this bibliography, only writings for the stage, or in drama form, are included. The lists of secondary sources for individual authors are not exhaustive; they merely refer to works cited and to such others as might be relevant to aspects considered in the text. The playwrights are listed in order of their appearance in the book.

ALFRED-HENRY JARRY
September 8, 1873-November 1, 1907

1894　*Les Minutes de sable mémorial*. Paris: Mercure de France, 1894. The section called *Guignol* (reprinted separately by Guastalla [Paris?], 1948) contains a Part I, "L'Autoclète," and a Part III, "L'Art et la science," in which most of the Ubu cast appears.

1895　*César Antéchrist*. Paris: Mercure de France, 1895. In this the so-called "Acte terrestre" is properly designated as "Ubu roi."

1896　*Ubu roi*. Paris: Mercure de France, 1896. Translated into English by Barbara Wright, *Ubu roi*. London: Gaberbocchus Press, 1951. First performed December 10, 1896, Théâtre de l'Œuvre, Paris.

1896　"Les Paralipomènes d'Ubu," *La Revue Blanche*, XI (1896), 489 f.

1898　*L'Amour en visites*. A writing mostly in dialogue form, Paris: Jean Fort, 1898.

[1898?]   *Par la taille*. Paris: E. Sansot & Cie, 1906. This edition
          lists a *Théâtre Mirlitonesque* (*Ubu sur la Butte; Par la
          taille; Ubu intime; L'Objet aimé; Le Moutardier du
          Pape; Siloques, superloques, soliloques et interloques*).

1899   *Ubu enchaîné*. (Preceded by *Ubu roi*.) Paris: La Revue
          Blanche, 1900. Translated into English by B. Keith and
          G. Legman, *King Turd Enslaved*. New York: Boar's
          Head Books, 1953.

1900   "Les Silènes," *La Revue Blanche*, XXI (1900), 5 f. The
          additional material in *Les Silènes* (Papeete: Les Biblio-
          philes Créoles, 1926) is apocryphal according to René
          Massat.

1901   *Ubu sur la Butte*. Paris: E. Sansot & Cie, 1906. First per-
          formed 1901, Guignol des 4-z' Arts [Lyons?]

[1903?]   *Pantagruel*. Paris: Société d'Editions Musicales, 1911.
          First performed January, 1911, Théâtre des Célestins,
          Lyons.

1903   *L'Objet aimé* [Paris: E. Sansot & Cie, 1906?] The first
          edition usually given is Paris: Arcanes, 1953.

[1905?]   *Le Moutardier du Pape* [Paris: E. Sansot & Cie, 1906?]
          The first edition usually given is Paris: Mercure de
          France, 1907.

          Ubu cocu. Paris-Geneva: Trois Collines, 1944. A com-
          posite of scenes (possibly apocryphal) linking "L'Auto-
          clète," "L'Art et la science," and parts of "Les Paralipo-
          mènes d'Ubu." Translated into English by B. Keith and
          G. Legman, *Turd Cuckolded*. New York: Boar's Head
          Books, 1953.

Note also an *Almanach du Père Ubu, illustré* (1899), an *Almanach
illustré du Père Ubu* (Paris: A. Vollard, 1901), and a *Nouvel Almanach du Père Ubu* (1902). André Lebois (*Alfred Jarry l'irrem-
plaçable*. Paris: Le Cercle du Livre, 1950) mentions an undated
Léda, called "opéra bouffe." Jacques-Henry Lévesque (see below)

alludes to a *Théâtre de marionnettes*. Paris: E. Sansot & Cie, n.d.
In [1953?] the Collège de Pataphysique [Paris?] published *L'Ou-verture de la pêche* and [in 1954?], a so-called "œuvre lycéenne de Jarry," *Le Futur malgré lui*.

About the Author

Chassé, Charles, *Dans les coulisses de la gloire: D'Ubu roi au Dou-anier Rousseau*. Paris: Edit. de la Nouvelle Revue Critique, 1947.

Chauvenu, Paul, *Alfred Jarry, ou La Naissance, la vie et la mort du Père Ubu*. Paris: Mercure de France, 1932.

Lévesque, Jacques-Henry, *Alfred Jarry*. Paris: Pierre Seghers, 1951.

Rachilde (Mme Marguerite Vallette), *Alfred Jarry, ou Le Surmâle de lettres*. Paris: Grasset, 1928.

GUILLAUME APOLLINAIRE
(GUILLAUME-ALBERT-WLADIMIR-ALEXANDRE-APOLLI-
NAIRE DE KOSTROWITZKY)
August 26, 1880-November 9, 1918.

1898   *A la cloche de bois*. Unpublished.

1916   *La Bréhatine* (with André Billy). A motion picture scenario, unpublished.

1916   *L'Homme sans yeux, sans nez et sans oreilles*. A ballet scenario based on his poem "Le Musicien de Saint-Merry," unpublished.

1917   *Les Mamelles de Tirésias*, "Drame surréaliste en 2 actes et 1 prologue." Paris: Edit. Sic, 1918. First performed June 21, 1917, Conservatoire Maubel, Montmartre.

1917   *Couleur du temps*, "Drame en 3 actes et en Vers." (In *NRF*, LXXXVI [1920], 694 f.) Paris: Edit. du Bélier, 1949. First performed November 24, 1918, Théâtre Lara, Paris.

1918   *Casanova,* "Comédie parodique." Paris: Gallimard, 1952.

Marcel Adéma (see below) mentions also the unpublished *Le Mar-chand d'anchois, La Température,* as well as certain other name-less *piécettes.*

About the Author

Adéma, Marcel, *Guillaume Apollinaire le mal-aimé.* Paris: Plon, 1952.

Billy, André, *Apollinaire vivant.* Paris: La Sirène, 1923.

—— *Guillaume Apollinaire.* Paris: Pierre Seghers, 1947.

Moulin, Jeanine, *Guillaume Apollinaire: Textes inédits.* Geneva: Droz; Lille: Giard, 1952.

Pia, Pascal, *Apollinaire par lui-même.* Paris: Edit. du Seuil, 1954.

JEAN-MAURICE COCTEAU
July 5, 1889

1916   *Parade,* "Ballet réaliste." Paris: Rouard Lerolle, 1919. First performed [1916?] in Rome.

1920   *Le Bœuf sur le toit* (a ballet). Paris: La Sirène Musicale, 1920. First performed February 21, 1920, Comédie des Champs-Elysées, Paris.

1921   *Le Gendarme incompris,* "Critique bouffe" (with Ray-mond Radiguet). Paris: Edit. de la Galerie Simon, 1921.

1921   *Les Mariés de la Tour Eiffel.* Paris: NRF, 1924. First performed June 18, 1921, Théâtre des Champs-Elysées, Paris.

1922   *Antigone.* Paris: Gallimard, 1928. First performed De-cember 20, 1922, Théâtre de l'Atelier, Paris.

1924   *Les Biches* (a ballet). Paris: Edit. des Quatre Chemins, 1924. First performed January 6, 1924, Théâtre de Monte-Carlo.

1924   *Les Fâcheux* (a ballet). Paris: Edit. des Quatre Chemins,

1924. First performed January 19, 1924, Théâtre de
Monte-Carlo.

1924   *Roméo et Juliette,* "Prétexte à mise-en-scène." Paris: Au
Sans Pareil, 1926. First performed June 2, 1924, Théâtre
de la Cigale, Paris.

1925   *Œdipe-roi.* Paris: Plon, 1928. First performed June
1937, Nouveau Théâtre Antoine, Paris.

1926   *Orphée.* Paris: Stock, 1927. Translated into English by
Carl Wildman, *Orphée.* London: Oxford U. Press, 1933.
First performed June 17, 1926, Théâtre des Arts, Paris.

1927   *Le Pauvre Matelot,* "Complainte en 3 actes." Paris: Heu-
gel, 1927.

1927   *Oedipus-rex,* "Opéra-oratorio." First performed May 30,
1927, Théâtre Sarah-Bernhardt, Paris.

1930   *La Voix humaine.* Paris: Stock, 1930. Translated into
English by Carl Wildman, *The Human Voice.* London:
Vision, 1951. First performed February 17, 1930, Comé-
die Française, Paris.

1932   *La Machine infernale.* Paris: Grasset, 1934. English ver-
sion by Carl Wildman, *The Infernal Machine.* London:
Oxford U. Press, 1936. First performed April 10, 1934,
Comédie des Champs-Elysées, Paris.

1936   *L'Ecole des veuves.* Paris: Morihien, 1949. First performed 1936, Théâtre de l'A.B.C., Paris.

1937   *Les Chevaliers de la Table Ronde.* Paris: Gallimard, 1937.
First performed October 14, 1937, Théâtre de l'Œuvre,
Paris.

1938   *Les Parents terribles.* Paris: Gallimard, 1938. English
version by C. Frank, *Intimate Relations.* (In Eric Bentley's *From the Modern Repertoire,* Series III, Blooming-
ton: Indiana U. Press, 1956.) First performed November
14, 1938, Théâtre des Ambassadeurs, Paris.

1940   *Les Monstres sacrés.* Paris: Gallimard, 1940. First performed February 17, 1940, Théâtre Michel, Paris.

1940   *Le Bel Indifférent.* Paris: Morihien, 1949. First per-
        formed 1940, Théâtre des Bouffes-Parisiens, Paris.

1941   *La Machine à écrire.* Paris: Gallimard, 1941. Translated
        into English by Ronald Duncan, *The Typewriter.* Lon-
        don: Dennis Dobson, 1947. First performed April 29,
        1941, Théâtre Hébertot, Paris.

1941   *Renaud et Armide.* Paris: Gallimard, 1943. First per-
        formed April 1943, Comédie Française, Paris.

1946   *L'Aigle à deux têtes.* Paris: Gallimard, 1946. Adapted
        in English by Ronald Duncan, *The Eagle Has Two
        Heads.* London: Vision, 1948. First performed Novem-
        ber 1946, Théâtre Hébertot, Paris.

1946   *Le Jeune Homme et la mort.* A ballet, first performed
        [1946?], Opéra de Paris.

1949   *Théâtre de poche.* Paris: Morihien, 1949. (*Parade; Le
        Bœuf sur le toit; Le Pauvre Matelot; L'Ecole des veuves;
        Le Bel Indifférent; Le Fantôme de Marseille; Anna la
        bonne; La Dame de Monte-Carlo; Le Fils de l'air; Le
        Menteur; Par la fenêtre; Je l'ai perdue; Lis ton journal;
        La Farce du château.*)

1949   *Un Tramway nommé Désir.* Paris: Bordas, 1949. An
        adaptation of *A Streetcar Named Desire* by Tennessee
        Williams, based on Paule de Beaumont's translation.
        First performed October 17, 1949, Théâtre Edouard VII,
        Paris.

1950   *Phèdre.* "Tragédie choréographique." First performed
        [1950?], Opéra de Paris.

1951   *Bacchus.* Paris: Gallimard, 1952. First performed De-
        cember 20, 1951, Théâtre Marigny, Paris.

1953   *La Dame à la licorne.* A ballet, first performed May 9,
        1953, Gärtner Theater, Munich.

Note also the following motion pictures: *Le Sang d'un poète*
(1932), *Le Baron fantôme* (1943, only the dialogue is Cocteau's),
L'Eternel Retour (1944, scenario and dialogue), *La Belle et la Bête*

(1945), *Ruy Blas* (1947, with Pierre Billon), *La Voix humaine* (1947, with Roberto Rossellini), *Les Parents terribles* (1948), *L'Aigle à deux têtes* (1948), *Orphée* (1949), *Les Enfants terribles* (1950).

About the Author

Crosland, Margaret, *Jean Cocteau*. London: Peter Nevill, 1955.

Dubourg, Pierre, *Dramaturgie de Jean Cocteau*. Paris: Grasset, 1954.

Lannes, Roger, *Jean Cocteau*. Paris: Pierre Seghers, 1948.

Mauriac, Claude, *Jean Cocteau, ou La Vérité du mensonge*. Paris: Odette Lieutier, 1945.

Millecam, Jean-Pierre, *L'Etoile de Jean Cocteau*. Monaco: Edit. du Rocher, 1952.

HIPPOLYTE-JEAN GIRAUDOUX
October 29, 1882-January 31, 1944

1928   *Siegfried*. Paris: Grasset, 1928. English version by Philip Carr, *Siegfried*. New York: Dial Press, 1930. First performed May 3, 1928, Comédie des Champs-Elysées, Paris.

1929   *Amphitryon 38*. Paris: Grasset, 1929. Adapted in English by S. N. Behrman, *Amphitryon 38*. New York: Random House, 1938. First performed November 8, 1929, Comédie des Champs-Elysées, Paris.

1931   *Judith*. Paris: Emile-Paul, 1931. First performed November 4, 1931, Théâtre Pigalle, Paris.

1933   *Intermezzo*. Paris: Grasset, 1933. Adapted in English by Maurice Valency, *The Enchanted*. New York: Random House, 1950. First performed February 27, 1933, Comédie des Champs-Elysées, Paris.

1934   *Tessa*. Paris: Grasset, 1934. First performed November 14, 1934, Théâtre de l'Athénée, Paris.

1935   *La Guerre de Troie n'aura pas lieu*. Paris: Grasset, 1935.

Translated into English by Christopher Fry, *Tiger at the Gates*. New York: French, 1956. First performed November 21, 1935, Théâtre de l'Athénée, Paris.

1935   *Supplément au Voyage de Cook*. Paris: Grasset, 1937. Adapted in English by Maurice Valency, *The Virtuous Island*. New York: French, 1956. First performed November 21, 1935, Théâtre de l'Athénée, Paris.

1937   *Electre*. Paris: Grasset, 1937. Translated into English by W. Smith, *Electra*. (In Eric Bentley's *From the Modern Repertoire,* Series II, Denver: U. of Denver Press, 1952.) First performed May 13, 1937, Théâtre de l'Athénée, Paris.

1937   *L'Impromptu de Paris*. Paris: Grasset, 1937. First performed December 3, 1937, Théâtre de l'Athénée, Paris.

1938   *Cantique des cantiques*. Paris: Grasset, 1938. First performed October 12, 1938, Comédie Française, Paris.

1939   *Ondine*. Paris: Grasset, 1939. Adapted in English by Maurice Valency, *Ondine*. New York: Random House, 1954. First performed May 3, 1939, Théâtre de l'Athénée, Paris.

1942   *L'Apollon de Bellac*. Neuchâtel: Ides et Calendes, 1946. Adapted in English by Maurice Valency, *The Apollo of Bellac*. New York: French, 1954. First performed as *L'Apollon de Marsac,* June 16, 1942, Municipal Theater, Rio de Janeiro.

1943   *Sodome et Gomorrhe*. Paris: Grasset, 1943. First performed October 11, 1943, Théâtre Hébertot, Paris.

1943   *La Folle de Chaillot*. Neuchâtel: Ides et Calendes, 1945. English adaptation by Maurice Valency, *The Madwoman of Chaillot*. New York: Random House, 1949. First performed December 22, 1945, Théâtre de l'Athénée, Paris.

1944   *Pour Lucrèce*. Paris: Grasset, 1953. First performed November 4, 1953, Théâtre Marigny, Paris.

Note that Giraudoux has also written two motion picture scripts, *Le Film de la duchesse de Langeais* (Paris: Grasset, 1942) and *Le Film de Béthanie* (Paris: Gallimard, 1944).

About the Author

Bourdet, Maurice, *Jean Giraudoux, son œuvre*. Paris: Edit. de la Nouvelle Revue Critique, 1928.

Debidour, Victor-Henry, *Jean Giraudoux*. Paris: Edit. Universitaires, 1955.

Houlet, Jacques, *Le Théâtre de Jean Giraudoux*. Paris: Pierre Ardent, 1945.

Magny, Claude-Edmonde, *Précieux Giraudoux*. Paris: Edit. du Seuil, 1945.

Leefmans, Bert M-P., "Giraudoux's Other Muse," *The Kenyon Review*, XVI (1954), 611 f.

Lefèvre, Frédéric, "Une Heure avec Jean Giraudoux," *Les Nouvelles Littéraires*, February 20, 1926.

Marker, Christian, *Giraudoux par lui-même*. Paris: Edit. du Seuil, 1952.

Mercier-Campiche, Marianne, *Le Théâtre de Giraudoux et la condition humaine*. Paris: Domat, 1954.

Sørensen, Hans, *Le Théâtre de Jean Giraudoux*. Copenhagen: University of Aarhus, 1950.

PAUL-LOUIS-CHARLES-MARIE CLAUDEL
August 6, 1868-February 23, 1955

1882 or 1883 *L'Endormie*. Paris: Champion, 1925.

1888 *Une Mort prématurée*. Destroyed; there remains "Morceau d'un drame," in *La Revue Indépendante*, May 1892.

1889 *Tête d'or* I. Paris: Librairie de l'Art Indépendant, 1890. (Anonymously.) *Tête d'or* II. [1894-95] Paris: Mercure de France, 1901. Translated into English by John Strong

Newberry, *Tête d'or*. New Haven: Yale U. Press, 1919.
First performed April 25, 1924, Théâtre Art et Action,
Paris.

Tête d'or III. [1951] Stage version for Jean-Louis Bar-
rault, unpublished.

1890   *La Ville* I. Paris: Librairie de l'Art Indépendant, 1893.
(Anonymously.)

La Ville II. [1897] Paris: Mercure de France, 1901.
Translated into English by John Strong Newberry, *The
City*. New Haven: Yale U. Press, 1920. First performed
February 24, 1926, Salle Patria, Brussels (in Dutch).

1892   *La Jeune Fille Violaine* I. Paris: Excelsior, 1926.

La Jeune Fille Violaine II. [1898] Paris: Mercure de
France, 1901. First performed March 14, 1944, Salle
d'Iéna, Paris.

L'Annonce faite à Marie. [1910] Paris: NRF, 1912. With
an Act IV variant, Paris: Gallimard, 1939. Definitive stage
edition, Paris: Gallimard, 1948. Translated into English
by Louise Morgan Sill, *The Tidings Brought to Mary*.
New Haven: Yale U. Press, 1916. First performed December 20, 1912, Théâtre de l'Œuvre, Paris.

1893-94 *L'Echange* I. Paris: Mercure de France, 1901. First performed January 22, 1914, Théâtre du Vieux-Colombier,
Paris.

L'Echange II. [1950-51] Paris: Mercure de France, 1954.
First performed December 13, 1951, Théâtre Marigny,
Paris.

1893-94 *L'Agamemnon d'Eschyle*. Foochow: Chez la veuve Ro-
zario, 1896. Corrected, Paris: Pléiade, 1951.

1894-95 *Tête d'or* II. *See* 1889.

1896   *Le Repos du septième jour*. Paris: Mercure de France,
1901. First performed [1929?], Poland.

1897   *La Ville* II. *See* 1890.

1898   *La Jeune Fille Violaine* II. *See* 1892.

1905   *Partage de midi*. Paris: Bibliothèque de l'Occident, 1906.
        First performed December 16, 1948, Théâtre Marigny,
        Paris.

1909   *L'Otage*. Paris: NRF, 1911. Translated into English by
        John Heard, *The Hostage*. Boston: John W. Luce, 1945.
        First performed June 5, 1914, Théâtre de l'Œuvre,
        Paris.

1910   *L'Annonce faite à Marie*. See 1892.

1913   *Protée* I. Paris: NRF, 1914.
        Protée II. [1926] Paris: Gallimard, 1927. First per-
        formed February, 1955, Comédie de Paris.

1913-14 *Le Pain dur*. Paris: NRF, 1918. Translated into English
        by John Heard, *Crusts*. Boston: John W. Luce, 1945.
        First performed March 12, 1949, Théâtre de l'Atelier,
        Paris.

1915   *La Nuit de Noël de 1914*. Paris: Librairie de l'Art Catho-
        lique, 1915.

1916   *Le Père humilié*. (In *NRF*, LXXII [1919], 533 f., and
        LXXIII [1919], 674 f.) Paris: NRF, 1920. Translated
        into English by John Heard, *The Humiliation of the
        Father*. Boston: John W. Luce, 1945. First performed
        1953, Théâtre de l'Apollo, Paris.

1916   *Les Choéphores; Les Euménides d'Eschyle*. Paris: NRF,
        1920. Corrected, Paris: Pléiade, 1951. *Les Euménides*
        first performed March 27, 1935, Théâtre de la Monnaie,
        Brussels.

1917   *L'Ours et la lune*. Paris: NRF, 1919.

1917   *L'Homme et son désir* (a ballet). Paris: NRF, 1917.

1919-24 *Le Soulier de satin, ou Le Pire n'est pas toujours sûr*.
        4 vols., Paris: NRF, 1928-29. Stage edition, Paris: NRF,
        1944. Translated into English by the Rev. Fr. John
        O'Connor, *The Satin Slipper*. London: Sheed & Ward,
        1931. First performed November 27, 1943, Comédie
        Française, Paris.

1922   *La Femme et son ombre* I. Sketch for a ballet, in *Poèmes de guerre*. Paris: NRF, 1922.

1923   *La Femme et son ombre* II. Paris: Pléiade, 1956. First performed March, 1923, Imperial Theater, Tokyo.

1926   *La Parabole du festin* I. Paris: Ronald Davis, 1926.
        La Sagesse, ou La Parabole du festin [1933-35]. Paris: NRF, 1939.

1926   *Protée* II. See 1913.

1927   *Le Livre de Christophe Colomb.* Paris: Gallimard, 1933. Noted as libretto for Milhaud's opera, Vienna-Leipzig, Edit. Universelle, 1929. Translated into English as *The Book of Christopher Columbus.* New Haven: Yale U. Press, 1930. First performed 1930, Staatsopera, Berlin.

1927   *Sous le rempart d'Athènes.* Paris: NRF, 1927. First performed in 1927, Palais de l'Elysée, Paris.

1933-35 *Jeanne d'Arc au bûcher.* Paris: NRF, 1939. First performed May 6, 1939, Théâtre Municipal, Orléans.

1933-35 *La Sagesse, ou La Parabale du festin. See* 1926.

1938   *L'Histoire de Tobie et de Sara.* Paris: NRF, 1942.

1938   *Le Jet de pierre,* "Suite plastique en XII mouvements." Paris: Pléiade, 1956.

1949   *Le Ravissement de Scapin.* In *Opéra,* LV (January, 1952), 5 f.

1951   *Tête d'or* III. See 1889.

Note also in the *Théâtre complet* (2 vols., Paris: Pléiade, 1951, 1956), *Pan et Syrinx* (1933-35) and *La Lune à la recherche d'elle-même.*

About the Author

Bentley, Eric, "Theater, Religion and Politics," *Theater Arts,* XXXIV (1950), 30 f.

Cornell, Kenneth, "Claudel's Plays on the Stage," *Yale French Studies,* V (1950), 82 f.

Jeanrenard, Arthur, "L'Esthétique de Paul Claudel," *Trivium,* II (1944), 66 f.

Madaule, Jacques, *Claudel.* Paris: L'Arche, 1956.

—— *Le Drame de Paul Claudel.* Paris: Desclée De Brouwer et Cie, 1936.

—— *Le Génie de Paul Claudel.* Paris: Desclée De Brouwer et Cie, 1933.

Samson, Joseph, *Paul Claudel poète-musicien.* Geneva: Milieu du Monde, 1947.

Tonquédec, Joseph de, *L'Œuvre de Paul Claudel.* Paris: G. Beauchesne, 1917.

JEAN-PAUL SARTRE
June 21, 1905

1943 *Les Mouches.* Paris: Gallimard, 1943. English version by Stuart Gilbert, *The Flies.* New York: A. A. Knopf, 1952. First performed 1942, Théâtre de la Cité (Sarah-Bernhardt), Paris.

1944 *Huis clos.* Paris: Gallimard, 1945. English version by Stuart Gilbert, *No Exit.* New York: A. A. Knopf, 1952. First performed May, 1944, Théâtre du Vieux-Colombier, Paris.

1946 *Morts sans sépulture.* Lausanne: Marguerat, 1946. Translated into English by Lionel Abel, *The Victors.* New York: A. A. Knopf, 1949. First performed November 8, 1946, Théâtre Antoine, Paris.

1946 *La Putain respectueuse.* Paris: Nagel, 1946. Translated into English by Lionel Abel, *The Respectful Prostitute.* New York: A. A. Knopf, 1949. First performed November 8, 1946, Théâtre Antoine, Paris.

1948 *Les Mains sales.* Paris: Gallimard, 1948. Translated into English by Lionel Abel, *Dirty Hands.* New York: A. A. Knopf, 1949. First performed April 2, 1948, Théâtre Antoine, Paris.

1951   *Le Diable et le Bon Dieu.* Paris: Gallimard, 1952. Trans-
        lated into English by Kitty Black, *Lucifer and the Lord.*
        London: H. Hamilton, 1953. First performed June 7,
        1951, Théâtre Antoine, Paris.

1953   *Kean.* Paris: Gallimard, 1954. Translated into English
        by Kitty Black, *Kean.* London: H. Hamilton, 1954. First
        performed November 17, 1953, Théâtre Sarah-Bernhardt,
        Paris.

1955   *Nekrassov.* Paris: Gallimard, 1956. Translated into Eng-
        lish by Sylvia and George Leeson, *Nekrassov.* London:
        H. Hamilton, 1956. First performed June 8, 1955, Théâ-
        tre Antoine, Paris.

Sartre has also written two motion picture scenarios: *Les Jeux
sont faits* (Paris: Nagel, 1947; translated by Louise Varèse, *The
Chips are Down.* New York: Lear, 1948), and *L'Engrenage*
(Paris: Nagel, 1948; translated by M. Savill, *In the Mesh.* London: A. Dakers, 1954).

About the Author

Albérès, R.-M., *Jean-Paul Sartre.* Paris-Brussels: Edit. Universi-
    taires, 1953.
Fergusson, Francis, "Sartre as Playwright," *Partisan Review,* XVI
    (1949), 407 f.
Grene, Marjorie, *Dreadful Freedom: A Critique of Existentialism.*
    Chicago: U. of Chicago Press, 1948.
Jeanson, Francis, *Le Problème moral et la pensée de Sartre.* Paris:
    Edit. du Myrte, 1947.
—— *Sartre par lui-même.* Paris: Edit. du Seuil, 1955.
Rabi, "Les Thèmes majeurs du théâtre de Sartre," *Esprit,* X
    (1950), 433 f.
Sartre, Jean-Paul, "Forgers of Myths—The Young Playwrights of
    France," *Theatre Arts,* XXX (1946), 324 f.

Van Hecke, Roger, "Sartre? Un bon écrivain mais pas un philosophe," *Le Figaro Littéraire,* November 4, 1950.

JEAN ANOUILH
June 23, 1910

1929   *Humulus le muet.* Unpublished.
1929   *Mandarine.* First performed 1933, Théâtre de l'Athénée, Paris.
1930   *Attila le magnifique.* Unpublished.
1931   *L'Hermine.* In *Les Œuvres Libres,* Vol. 151 (1934), 159 f. Translated into English by M. John, *The Ermine.* (In *Plays of the Year,* Vol. 13, 1955.) First performed April 26, 1932, Théâtre de l'Œuvre, Paris.
1932   *Le Bal des voleurs.* In *Les Œuvres Libres,* Vol. 209 (1938), 179 f. Translated into English by L. Hill, *Thieves' Carnival.* London: Methuen, 1952. First performed September 17, 1938, Théâtre des Arts, Paris.
1932   *Jézabel.* In *Nouvelles Pièces Noires,* 1946 (see below).
1934   *La Sauvage.* In *Les Œuvres Libres,* Vol. 201 (1938), 5 f. First performed 1938, Théâtre des Mathurins, Paris.
1934   *Y'avait un prisonnier.* In *La Petite Illustration,* No. 724 (1935). First performed March 21, 1935, Théâtre des Ambassadeurs, Paris.
1935   *Le Petit Bonheur.* Unpublished.
1936   *Le Voyageur sans bagage.* In *La Petite Illustration,* No. 817 (1937). First performed February 16, 1937, Théâtre des Mathurins, Paris.
1937   *Le Rendez-vous de Senlis.* In *Pièces Roses,* 1942 (see below). First performed 1940, Théâtre de l'Atelier, Paris.
1939   *Léocadia.* In *Pièces Roses,* 1942 (see below). English version by Patricia Moyes, *Time Remembered.* London: Methuen, 1955. First performed November, 1939, Théâtre de la Michodière, Paris.

1941   *Eurydice.* In *Pièces Noires,* 1942 (see below). Trans-
         lated into English by Kitty Black, *Legend of Lovers.*
         New York: Coward-McCann, 1952. First performed
         December 18, 1941, Théâtre de l'Atelier, Paris.

[1942?] "Oreste." *La Table Ronde,* III (1945), 55 f. A fragment
         of a play, possibly an anticipation of *Antigone.*

1942   *Antigone.* In *Nouvelles Pièces Noires,* 1946 (see below).
         Adapted in English by Lewis Galantière, *Antigone.*
         New York: Random House, 1946. First performed Feb-
         ruary 4, 1944, Théâtre de l'Atelier, Paris.

1945   *Roméo et Jeannette.* In *Nouvelles Pièces Noires,* 1946
         (see below). First performed December 3, 1946, Théâtre
         de l'Atelier, Paris.

1946   *Médée.* In *Nouvelles Pièces Noires,* 1946 (see below).
         Translated into English by Luce and Arthur Klein, *Me-
         dea.* (In Eric Bentley's *The Modern Theater,* Series V,
         New York: Doubleday & Co., 1957.) First performed
         March 26, 1953, Théâtre de l'Atelier, Paris.

1947   *L'Invitation au château.* In *Pièces Brillantes,* 1953 (see
         below). Translated into English by Christopher Fry,
         Ring Round the Moon. London: Methuen, 1950. First
         performed November 4, 1947, Théâtre de l'Atelier, Paris.

[1948?] *Episode de la vie d'un auteur.* First performed November
         3, 1948, Comédie des Champs-Elysées, Paris.

1948   *Ardèle, ou La Marguerite.* Paris: La Table Ronde, 1949.
         Translated into English by Lucienne Hill, *Ardèle.* Lon-
         don: Methuen, 1951. First performed November 3, 1948,
         Comédie des Champs-Elysées, Paris.

1949   *Cécile, ou L'Ecole des pères.* Paris: La Table Ronde,
         1954. English version by L. and A. Klein, *Cecile, or The
         School for Fathers.* (In Eric Bentley's *From the Modern
         Repertoire,* Series III, Bloomington: Indiana U. Press,
         1956). First performed October 28, 1954, Comédie des
         Champs-Elysées, Paris.

La Répétition, ou L'Amour puni. Geneva: La Palatine, 1950. First performed October 25, 1950, Théâtre Marigny, Paris.

1950   Colombe. In *Pièces Brillantes,* 1953 (see below). Adapted in English by Louis Kronenberger, *Mademoiselle Colombe.* New York: Coward-McCann, 1954. First performed February 11, 1951, Théâtre de l'Atelier, Paris.

1951   La Valse des toréadors. Paris: La Table Ronde, 1952. Adapted in English by Lucienne Hill, *The Waltz of the Toreadors.* (In *Plays of the Year,* Vol. 8, 1953.) First performed January 9, 1952, Comédie des Champs-Elysées, Paris.

1953   L'Alouette. Paris: La Table Ronde, 1953. Translated into English by Christopher Fry, *The Lark.* London: Methuen, 1955. First performed October 14, 1953, Théâtre Montparnasse, Paris.

1955   Ornifle, ou Le Courant d'air. Paris: La Table Ronde, 1956. First performed November 4, 1955, Comédie des Champs-Elysées, Paris.

1956   Pauvre Bitos, ou Le Dîner de têtes. In *Pièces Grinçantes,* 1956 (see below). First performed October 11, 1956, Théâtre Montparnasse, Paris.

The following collections of Anouilh's plays have been published: *Pièces Noires* (*L'Hermine; La Sauvage; Le Voyageur sans bagage; Eurydice*), Paris: Edit. Balzac, 1942; Paris: Calmann-Lévy, 1945. *Pièces Roses* (*Le Bal des voleurs; Le Rendez-vous de Senlis; Léocadia*), Paris: Edit. Balzac, 1942; Paris: Calmann-Lévy, 1945. *Nouvelles Pièces Noires* (*Jézabel; Antigone; Roméo et Jeannette; Médée*), Paris: La Table Ronde, 1947. *Pièces Brillantes* (*L'Invitation au château; Colombe; La Répétition, ou L'Amour puni; Cécile, ou L'Ecole des pères*), Paris: La Table Ronde, 1951. *Pièces Grinçantes* (*Ardèle, ou La Marguerite; La Valse des toréadors; Ornifle, ou Le Courant d'air; Pauvre Bitos, ou Le Dîner de têtes*), Paris:

La Table Ronde, 1956. Anouilh has also written unpublished scripts for the following motion pictures: *Anna Karénine, Caroline chérie, Cavalcade d'amour, Deux sous de violettes, Monsieur Vincent, Pattes blanches.* And a ballet scenario, *Les Demoiselles de la nuit.*

About the Author

Blanchart, Paul, "Jean Anouilh, ou Le Sauvage," *Théâtre,* III (1945), 151 f.

Champigny, Robert, "Theatre in a Mirror: Anouilh," *YFS,* XIV (1954-55), 57 f.

Gignoux, Hubert, *Jean Anouilh.* Paris: Edit. du Temps Présent, 1946.

Marsh, Edward Owen, *Jean Anouilh, Poet of Pierrot and Pantaloon.* London: W. H. Allen & Co., 1953.

Radine, Serge, *Anouilh, Lenormand, Salacrou: Trois dramaturges à la recherche de leur vérité.* Paris: Trois Collines, 1951.

FERNAND CROMMELYNCK
November 19, 1885

1905   *Le Sculpteur de masques* I. Brussels: Deman, 1908.
        Le Sculpteur de masques II. [1911] Brussels: Lamertin, 1918. First performed February 1, 1911, Théâtre du Gymnase, Paris.

1906   *Nous n'irons plus au bois.* Brussels: Le Thyrse, 1906. First performed April 28, 1906, Théâtre du Parc, Brussels.

[1907?] *Chacun pour soi.* Brussels: Revue Générale, 1907.

1911   *Le Sculpteur de masques* II. *See* 1905.

1913   *Le Marchand de regrets.* Brussels: Alde, [1913?]. First performed 1913, Théâtre du Parc, Brussels.

1920   *Le Cocu magnifique.* Paris: La Sirène, 1921. First performed December 20, 1920, Théâtre de l'Œuvre, Paris.

1921   *Les Amants puérils*. Paris: La Sirène, 1921. First performed March 14, 1921, Comédie Montaigne, Paris.

1925   *Tripes d'or*. Paris: Emile-Paul, 1930. First performed April 29, 1925, Comédie des Champs-Elysées, Paris.

1929   *Carine, ou La Jeune Fille folle de son âme*. Paris: Emile-Paul, 1930. First performed December 19, 1929, Théâtre de l'Œuvre, Paris.

1934   *Une Femme qu'a le cœur trop petit*. Paris: Emile-Paul, 1934. First performed January 11, 1934, Palais des Beaux-Arts, Brussels.

1934   *Chaud et Froid, ou L'Idée de Monsieur Dom*. Paris: Fayard, 1936. First performed November 24, 1934, Comédie des Champs-Elysées, Paris.

1954   *Le Chevalier à la lune, ou Sir John Falstaff*, "Comédie en cinq actes (de Shakespeare) restituée en sa forme originale." Brussels: Edit. des Artistes, 1954.

Chroniclers of Crommelynck mention the following unpublished plays: *L'Ange qui pleure, Le Chemin des conquêtes, Le Cœur volant, Maison fondée en 1550, Le Matin du troisième jour, Le Cimetière des belles amours, La Gourgandine, Va mon cœur.*

About the Author

Arland, Marcel, "Carine, ou La Jeune Fille folle de son âme," *NRF*, CXCVIII (1930), 433 f.

Berger, André, *A la rencontre de Fernand Crommelynck*. Liège: La Sixaine, 1947.

Houville, Gérard d', "Carine," *Le Figaro*, December 23, 1929.

Mauriac, François, " 'Tripes d'or' de Crommelynck," *NRF*, CXLI (1925), 1051 f.

Rivière, Jacques, "Les Amants puérils," *NRF*, XCII (1921), 622 f.

Rouveyre, André, "Carine," *Mercure de France*, CCXVII (1930), 671 f.

—— "Le Cocu magnifique," *Mercure de France,* CCI (1928), 693.

Ruth, Léon, "Fernand Crommelynck," *Choses de Théâtre,* May, 1922.

MICHEL DE GHELDERODE
April 3, 1898

1919   *Les Vieillards.* Brussels: La Vache Rose, 1924. Rewritten as *Jeudi-saint.* Brussels: La Renaissance du Livre, 1943.

1920   *Le Cavalier bizarre.* Antwerp: Ça Ira, 1938.

[1920?] *Le Club des menteurs.* Brussels: La Renaissance du Livre, 1943.

1920   *Oude Piet.* Brussels: La Renaissance d'Occident, 1925. First performed 1925, Œuvriers de la Renaissance d'Occident, Antwerp.

1921   *Un Soir de pitié.* In *La Revue Mosane,* VII, VIII (1929), 5 f.

[1924?] *La Farce de la Mort qui faillit trépasser.* Brussels: La Sirène, 1952. Originally in Flemish translation by J. Vervaeke, *Van den Dood die bijna stierf.* Brussels: Gudrun, 1925. First performed November 19, 1925, Vlaamsche Volkstooneel, [Antwerp?]

[1924?] *Le Mystère de la Passion de Notre Seigneur Jésus-Christ.* Brussels: La Renaissance d'Occident, 1925. First performed March 30, 1934, Théâtre des Marionnettes de Toone, Brussels.

[1926?] *La Mort du Docteur Faust.* Ostend-Bruges: Edit. de la Flandre Littéraire, 1926. First performed January 27, 1928, Théâtre Art et Action, Paris.

1926   *Trois Acteurs, un drame.* . . . Brussels: La Renaissance d'Occident, 1929. First performed April 2, 1931, Théâtre du Parc, Brussels.

1927   *Beeldekens uit het leven van Sint Fransiskus.* In *Vlaam-*

sche Volkstooneel, IV (1928). Flemish translation by Willem Doevenspeck. First performed February 2, 1927, Vlaamsche Volkstooneel, [Antwerp?]

1927   *Christophe Colomb.* Brussels: La Renaissance d'Occident, 1928. First performed October 25, 1929, Théâtre Art et Action, Paris.

1927   *Escurial.* Brussels: La Renaissance d'Occident, 1928. Translated into English by Lionel Abel, *Escurial.* (In Eric Bentley's *The Modern Theater,* Series V. New York: Doubleday & Co., 1957.) First performed January 12, 1929, Théâtre Flamand, [Brussels?] (in Flemish).

[1927?]   *Vénus.* Ostend-Bruges: Edit. de la Flandre Littéraire, 1927.

1928   *Barabbas.* Brussels: Labor, 1932. Originally in Flemish translation by Jan Boon, *Barabas.* Brussels: Standaard, 1931. First performed March 21, 1929, Vlaamsche Volkstooneel, [Antwerp?]

1928   *Don-Juan.* Brussels: La Renaissance d'Occident, 1928.

1928   *Les Femmes au Tombeau.* Brussels: Tréteaux, 1934.

[1928?]   *La Transfiguration dans le cirque.* Brussels: La Renaissance d'Occident, 1928.

[1929?]   (With Jean Barleig) *Het Meisje met de Houten Handen.* Wenduyne: Putnam, 1929. Flemish translation by Joris Dewaele.

[1929?]   *Le Massacre des Innocents.* Brussels: La Scène, 1929.

1929   *Pantagleize.* Brussels: Le Vrai, 1934. First performed April 24, 1930, Palais des Beaux-Arts, Brussels (in Flemish).

[1929?]   *La Tentation de Saint Antoine.* Brussels: La Scène, 1929.

1929   *Fastes d'enfer.* Brussels: Houblon, 1943.

1930   *Masques ostendais.* Antwerp: Ça Ira, 1935.

1930   *Sortie de l'acteur.* Brussels: Houblon, 1942.

1931   *Duveloor, ou La Farce du diable vieux.* In *Le Rouge et le Noir,* March 27, 1931.

1931   *Magie rouge.* Brussels: Tréteaux, 1935. First performed April 30, 1934, Estaminet "Barcelone," Brussels.

1931   *De Sterrendief.* Courtrai: Vermaut, 1931. Flemish translation by Jozef Contrijn. First performed April 7, 1932, Vlaamsche Volkstooneel, [Antwerp?]

1931   *De Zeven Hoofzonden.* Courtrai: Vermaut, 1931. Flemish translation by Jozef Contrijn. First performed December 23, 1934, Audenaerde.

1932   *Godelieve.* Antwerp: De Oogst, 1934. Flemish translation by Jozef Contrijn. First performed September 4, 1932, Ostend.

1933   *Les Aveugles.* In *L'Avant-Poste,* VI (1936), 5 f. Originally in Flemish translation by Jozef Contrijn, *De Blinden.* In *Volk,* V (1936), 150 f.

[1933?] *Adrian et Jusemina.* Brussels: Tréteaux, 1935.

1934   *La Balade du Grand Macabre.* Brussels: Tréteaux, 1935.

1934   *D'un diable qui prêcha merveilles.* Brussels: Houblon, 1942.

1934   *Mademoiselle Jaïre.* Brussels: Houblon, 1942.

1934   *Sire Halewyn.* Brussels: La Renaissance du Livre, 1943. Originally in Flemish translation by Albert van Hoogenbemt, *Sire Halewijn.* In *Volk,* IX (1936), 268 f. First performed January 21, 1938, Théâtre Communal, Brussels.

1935   *Le Ménage de Caroline.* Brussels: Tréteaux, 1935. First performed October 26, 1935, Théâtre du Commissariat de l'Exposition de 1935, [Brussels?]

1935   *Hop Signor!.* Brussels: Les Cahiers du Journal des Poètes, 1938.

1935   *La Pie sur le gibet.* In *L'Avant-Poste,* III (1938).

1935   *Le Singulier Trépas de Messire Ulenspiegel.* Malines: C. E. L. F., 1951. Originally in Flemish translation by Jozef Contrijn, *De Dood van Ulenspiegel.* In *Volk,* III (1937), 60 f.; IV (1938), 125 f.; V (1938), 154 f.

1936   *La Farce des Ténébreux.* Brussels: Houblon, 1942.

1937   *L'Ecole des bouffons.* Brussels: Houblon, 1942.
[1940?]   *Le Soleil se couche.* Brussels: Houblon, 1942.
1952   *Marie la misérable.* In *Théâtre IV,* 1955 (see below).
        First performed June 14, 1952, in front of the Eglise
        Saint-Lambert, Brussels.

In addition to these plays, there exists a *Théâtre d'écoute* (*Le
Singulier Trépas de Messire Ulenspiegel; Le Perroquet de Charles-
Quint; La Folie d'Hugo van der Goes*), Harlem-Mechlin-Paris:
C.E.L.F., 1951. Ghelderode's *Théâtre* comprises thus far *Théâtre
I* (*Hop Signor; Escurial; Sire Halewyn; Magie rouge; Mademoi-
selle Jäire; Fastes d'enfer*), Paris: Gallimard, 1950; *Théâtre II* (*Le
Cavalier bizarre; La Balade du Grand Macabre; Trois Acteurs, un
drame . . . ; Christophe Colomb; Les Femmes au Tombeau; La
Farce des Ténébreux*), Paris: Gallimard, 1952; *Théâtre III* (*La
Pie sur le gibet; Pantagleize; D'un diable qui prêcha merveilles;
Sortie de l'acteur; L'Ecole des bouffons*), Paris: Gallimard, 1953;
Théâtre IV (*Un Soir de pitié; Don-Juan; Le Club des menteurs;
Les Vieillards; Marie la misérable; Masques ostendais*), Paris: Gal-
limard, 1955. This last volume announces three more containing
"in addition to the bibliography, the *Théâtre pour marionnettes*
and the *Théâtre érotique,*" the following plays: *Barabbas; Les
Bourgeois de Gand; Ars Moriendi; Un Caprice de Goya; Comte
sans tête; Les Tribulations métaphysiques de Pantagleize; Le Geste
d'Onan; Le Siège d'Ostende; La Folia; Le Sommeil de la raison;
Le Voleur d'étoiles; Le Soleil se couche; Images de la vie de Saint
François; La Mort du Docteur Faust.* Chroniclers of Ghelderode
mention the following unpublished plays: *La Mort regarde à la
fenêtre; Le Repas des fauves; La Nuit tombe sur la Flandre; L'An-
née de la peste.*

About the Author

Francis, Jean, *Michel de Ghelderode, dramaturge des pays de par-
    deça.* Brussels: Labor, 1949.

Francis, Jean, and Roger Iglesis, "Michel de Ghelderode," *Chry-salis*, III, IV (1949), 5 f.

Guth, Paul, "A la recherche de Michel de Ghelderode, l'auteur dramatique sulfureux," *Le Figaro Littéraire*, April 1, 1950.

Iglesis, R., and A. Trutat, *Michel de Ghelderode: Les Entretiens d'Ostende*. Paris: L'Arche, 1956.

Mauduit, Jean, "Michel de Ghelderode, ou L'Ange du bizarre," *Etudes*, Vol. 265 (1950), 82 f.

La Nervie, VII, VIII (1932). A special issue devoted to Michel de Ghelderode.

L'Avant-Poste, III (1938). A special issue devoted to Michel de Ghelderode.

EUGENE IONESCO
November 13, 1912

1948 *La Cantatrice chauve*. In *Théâtre*, 1953 (see below). First performed May 11, 1950, Théâtre des Noctambules, Paris.

1950 *La Leçon*. In *Théâtre*, 1953 (see below). First performed February 20, 1951, Théâtre de Poche, Paris.

1950 *Jacques, ou La Soumission*. In *Théâtre*, 1953 (see below). First performed October 1955, Théâtre de la Huchette, Paris.

1951 *Les Chaises*. In *Théâtre I*, 1954 (see below). First performed April 22, 1952, Théâtre Lancry, Paris.

1952 *Victimes du devoir*. In *Théâtre I*, 1954 (see below). First performed February, 1953, Théâtre du Quartier Latin, Paris.

1953 *Amédée, ou Comment s'en débarrasser*. In *Théâtre I*, 1954 (see below). First performed April 14, 1954, Théâtre de Babylone, Paris.

1955 *Le Tableau*. Unpublished. First performed October, 1955, Théâtre de la Huchette, Paris.

1955   *L'Impromptu de l'Alma.* Unpublished. First performed
       February, 1956, Studio des Champs-Elysées, Paris.

Note also: *L'Avenir est dans les œufs* (1951), *Le Nouveau Loca-taire* (1953), as well as various short sketches, a number of which
have been performed on the air. The following collections of
Ionesco's plays have been published thus far: *Théâtre* (*La Canta-trice chauve; La Leçon; Jacques, ou La Soumission; Le Salon de
l'automobile*), Paris: Arcanes, 1953. *Théâtre I* (*La Cantatrice
chauve; La Leçon; Jacques, ou La Soumission; Les Chaises; Vic-times du devoir; Amédée, ou Comment s'en débarrasser*), Paris:
Gallimard, 1954.

About the Author

Saurel, Renée, "Ionesco, ou Les Blandices de la culpabilité," *Les
Temps Modernes,* CIII (1954), 2286 f.

ARTHUR ADAMOV
August 23, 1908

1947   *La Parodie.* Paris: Charlot, 1950. First performed June
       5, 1952, Théâtre Lancry, Paris.
1949   *L'Invasion.* Paris: Charlot, 1950. First performed No-vember 14, 1950, Studio des Champs-Elysées, Paris.
1950   *La Grande et la petite manœuvre.* In *Théâtre I,* 1953
       (see below). First performed November 11, 1950, Théâ-tre des Noctambules, Paris.
1951   *Le Professeur Taranne.* In *Théâtre I,* 1953 (see below).
       First performed March 18, 1953, Théâtre de la Comédie,
       Lyons.
[1951?] *Le Sens de la marche.* In *Théâtre II,* 1955 (see below).
       First performed March 18, 1953, Théâtre de la Comédie,
       Lyons.
[1952?] *Comme nous avons été.* Unpublished.

1952   *Tous contre tous.* In *Théâtre I,* 1953 (see below). First
performed April 13, 1953, Théâtre de l'Œuvre, Paris.
[1953?] *Les Retrouvailles.* In *Théâtre II,* 1955 (see below).
[1955?] *Le Ping-pong.* In *Théâtre II,* 1955 (see below). First
performed March 2, 1955, Théâtre des Noctambules,
Paris.

Adamov's collected *Théâtre* includes thus far: *Théâtre I* (*La
Parodie; L'Invasion; La Grande et la petite manœuvre; Le Profes-
seur Taranne; Tous contre tous*), Paris: Gallimard, 1953. *Théâtre
II* (*Le Sens de la marche; Les Retrouvailles; Le Ping-pong*), Paris:
Gallimard, 1955.

About the Author

Lynes, Carlos, Jr., "Adamov or 'le sens littéral' in the Theatre,"
YFS, XIV (1954-55), 48 f.
Saurel, Renée, " 'Tous contre tous' d'Arthur Adamov," *Les Temps
Modernes,* XCI (1953), 2031 f.

SAMUEL BECKETT
1906

1952   *En attendant 'Godot.* Paris: Edit. de Minuit, 1952. Translated into English by the author, *Waiting for Godot.*
New York: Grove Press, 1954. First performed January
5, 1953, Théâtre de Babylone, Paris.
1956   *Fin de partie.* Paris: Edit. de Minuit, 1957. First performed April 3, 1957, Royal Court Theatre, London.
1957   *Acte sans paroles.* Paris: Edit. de Minuit, 1957. First
perfomed April 3, 1957, Royal Court Theatre, London.

About the Author

Kern, Edith, "Drama Stripped for Inaction: Beckett's *Godot,*"
YFS, XIV (1954-55), 41 f.

GENERAL BIBLIOGRAPHY

Antonini, Giacomo, *Il Teatro contemporaneo in Francia.* Milano: Corbaccio, 1930.

Apollinaire, Guillaume, *L'Esprit nouveau et les poètes.* Paris: Jacques Haumont, 1946.

—— *Il y a.* Paris: Albert Messein, 1925.

—— *Ombre de mon amour.* Vesenaz près Genève: Pierre Cailler, 1947.

—— *Les Peintres cubistes.* Paris: Figuière, 1913.

—— *Le Poète assassiné.* Paris: L'Edition, 1916.

—— *Le Théâtre italien.* Paris: Louis Michaud, [1910].

—— *Vitam impendere amori.* Paris: Mercure de France, 1917.

Artaud, Antonin, *Le Théâtre et son double.* Paris: Gallimard, c. 1938.

Audiberti, Jacques, *Théâtre.* Paris: Gallimard, 1948-.

Bellessort, André, *Le Plaisir du théâtre.* Paris: Perrin, 1938.

Bergson, Henri, *Le Rire.* Paris: F. Alcan, 1900.

Bloch, Jean-Richard, *Destin du théâtre.* Paris: Gallimard, 1930.

Breton, André, *Anthologie de l'humour noir.* Paris: Edit. du Sagittaire, 1940.

Camus, Albert, *Le Mythe de Sisyphe.* Paris: Gallimard, 1942.

Claudel, Paul, *Œuvres complètes.* Paris: Gallimard, 1952-.

Closson, Herman, *Sous-sol* (1925). Unpublished.

—— *Spectacle, ou La Comédie du public* (1928). Out of print.

—— *Godefroid de Bouillon.* Marseilles: Les Cahiers du Sud, 1933.

—— *La Farce des deux nues.* Brussels: Sablon, 1945.

—— *Shakespeare, ou La Comédie de l'aventure.* Brussels: Edit. Universitaires, 1945.

—— *Le Jeu des quatre fils Aymon.* Brussels: Toison d'Or, 1943.

—— *Hélène, ou La Dissemblance.* Brussels: Sablon, 1945.

—— *La Passante illuminée.* Brussels: Sablon, 1945.

—— *Borgia.* Brussels: Houblon, 1944.

—— *L'Epreuve du feu.* Brussels: Houblon, 1944.

—— *Le Jeu de Han* (1949). Unpublished.

—— *Yolande de Beersel* (1949). Unpublished.

Clouard, Henri, *Histoire de la littérature française du symbolisme à nos jours.* 2 vols., Paris: Albin Michel, 1947-49.

Cocteau, Jean, *Œuvres complètes.* 11 vols., Lausanne: Marguerat, 1946-51.

Coindreau, Maurice, *La Farce est jouée.* New York: Edit. de la Maison Française, 1942.

Duché, Jean, "Jean-Paul Sartre répond à la critique dramatique," *Le Figaro Littéraire,* June 30, 1951.

Dukes, Ashley, *The Youngest Drama.* London: E. Benn, 1924.

Fergusson, Francis, *The Idea of a Theater.* Princeton: Princeton U. Press, 1949.

—— "Sartre as Playwright," *Partisan Review,* XVI (1949), 368 f.

Freud, Sigmund, *Wit and its Relation to the Unconscious.* New York: Moffat, Yard and Co., 1916.

Genet, Jean, *Œuvres complètes.* Paris: Gallimard, 1951-.

Ghelderode, Michel de, *Choses et gens de chez nous.* Liège-Paris: Maréchal, 1943.

—— *Mes Statues.* Brussels: Carrefour, 1943.

—— *Prosper de Troyer.* Courtrai: Steenlandt, 1931.

Ghéon, Henri, *L'Art du théâtre.* Montréal: Edit. Serge, 1944.

Gide, André, "Le Groupement littéraire qu'abritait le 'Mercure de France'," *Mercure de France,* CCXCVIII (1940-46), 169 f.

—— *Journal.* Paris: Gallimard, 1948.

—— *Le Journal des Faux-monnayeurs.* Paris: Gallimard, 1927.

Giraudoux, Jean, *Bella.* Paris: Grasset, 1926.

—— *Eglantine.* Paris: Grasset, 1927.

—— *Juliette au pays des hommes.* Paris: Emile-Paul, 1924.

—— *Littérature.* Paris: Grasset, 1941.

—— *Siegfried et le Limousin.* Paris: Grasset, 1922.

—— *Suzanne et le Pacifique.* Paris: Emile-Paul, 1921.

—— *Visitations.* Neuchâtel: Ides et Calendes, 1947.

Goris, Jan-Albert, *Du Génie flamand.* Brussels: Raymond Dupriez, 1945.

Gouhier, Henri, *L'Essence du théâtre*. Paris: Plon, 1943.

Greig, John Young Thomson, *The Psychology of Laughter and Comedy*. New York: Dodd, Mead and Co., 1923.

Hobbes, Thomas, *The English Works of Thomas Hobbes*. 11 vols., London: J. Bohn, 1839-45.

Jarry, Alfred, *Œuvres complètes*. 8 vols., Monte-Carlo: Edit. du Livre, 1945-48.

Kant, Immanuel, *Critique of Judgement*. London: Macmillan and Co., 1931.

Krishna Menon, V. K., *A Theory of Laughter*. London: G. Allen & Unwin Ltd., 1931.

Lemonnier, Camille, *Le Mort*. Brussels: Typ.-Lithographie Populaire, 1894.

Lerberghe, Charles van, *Pan*. Paris: Mercure de France, 1906.

Lilar, Suzanne, *The Belgian Theater since 1890*. New York: Belgian Government Information Center, 1950.

McClaren, James C., *The Theatre of André Gide*. Baltimore: The Johns Hopkins U. Press, 1953.

Martin du Gard, Roger, *La Gonfle*. Paris: Gallimard, 1928.

—— *Le Testament du père Leleu*. Paris: Gallimard, 1938.

Obey, André, *Théâtre*. Paris: Gallimard, 1948-.

Pichette, Henri, *Les Epiphanies*. [Paris?]: K Editeur, 1948.

—— *Nucléa*. Paris: L'Arche, 1952.

Sartre, Jean-Paul, *L'Etre et le Néant*. Paris: Gallimard, 1943.

Schehadé, Georges, *Monsieur Bob'le*. Paris: Gallimard, 1951.

—— *La Soirée des proverbes*. Paris: Gallimard, 1954.

Schopenhauer, Arthur, *The World as Will and Idea*. 3 vols., London: K. Paul, Trench, Trübner & Co., 1896.

Solvay, Lucien, *Le Théâtre belge .d'expression française depuis 1830*. Brussels: Goemaere, 1936.

Soumagne, Henry, *Les Epaves*. (1919). Out of print.

—— *L'Autre Messie*. Paris: Les Masques, 1923.

—— *Bas-Noyard*. Brussels: La Renaissance du Livre, 1925.

—— *Les Danseurs de gigue*. Paris: Les Feuillets Bleus, 1926.

—— *Terminus*. Brussels: Larcier, 1932.

—— *Madame Marie*. Paris: Maison de l'Œuvre, 1928.

—— *Hiérarchie*. Brussels: Bolyn, 1935.

Spencer, Herbert, *Essays: Scientific, Political and Speculative.* 3 vols., London: Longman, Brown, Green, Longmans and Roberts, 1858-74.

Sully, James, *An Essay on Laughter*. London: Longmans, Green & Co., 1902.

Touchard, Pierre-Aimé, *Dionysos: Apologie pour le théâtre*. Paris: Edit. du Seuil, 1949.

Copyright Acknowledgments

THE AUTHOR WISHES to thank the following publishing houses:

Gallimard, for permission to quote from the works of Jean-Paul Sartre and Michel de Ghelderode;

Bernard Grasset and the legal heirs of Jean Giraudoux, for permission to quote from the works of Jean Giraudoux;

Les Editions de Minuit, for permission to quote from the works of Samuel Beckett;

La Table Ronde, for permission to quote from the works of Jean Anouilh.

Index